Law, Culture, and Ritual

Law, Culture, and Ritual

*Disputing Systems in
Cross-Cultural Context*

Oscar G. Chase

Foreword by Jerome S. Bruner

NEW YORK UNIVERSITY PRESS
New York and London

NEW YORK UNIVERSITY PRESS
New York and London
www.nyupress.org

Library of Congress Cataloging-in-Publication Data
Chase, Oscar G.
Law, culture, and ritual : disputing systems in cross-cultural context /
Oscar G. Chase ; foreword by Jerome S. Bruner.
p. cm.
Includes bibliographical references and index.
ISBN–13: 978–0–8147–1651–9 (cloth : alk. paper)
ISBN–10: 0–8147–1651–2 (cloth : alk. paper)
1. Dispute resolution (Law)   2. Culture and law.   I. Title.
K2390.C443   2005
303.6'9—dc22   2005013716

New York University Press books are printed on acid-free paper,
and their binding materials are chosen for strength and durability.

Manufactured in the United States of America

10 9 8 7 6 5 4 3 2 1

To
OLIVER GOTTFRIED CHASE
and
ARLO MONELL CHASE
lawyers for a better world

Contents

Foreword by Jerome S. Bruner   ix

Preface   xiii

1   Introduction   1

2   The Lesson of the Azande   15

3   "Modern" Dispute-Ways   30

4   American "Exceptionalism" in Civil Litigation   47

5   The Discretionary Power
     of the Judge in Cultural Context   72

6   The Rise of ADR in Cultural Context   94

7   The Role of Ritual   114

8   How Disputing Influences Culture   125

9   Conclusion   138

     Afterword:
     The Classroom and the Terror of Relativism   141

     Notes   145

     Bibliography   185

     Index   197

     About the Author   207

Foreword

Jerome S. Bruner

Disputing is, of course, inevitable. No culture ever achieves the utopian harmony necessary to rise above it. To survive, every culture everywhere requires an acceptable means for settling disputes so as to forestall losers' revenge, or their alienation. To achieve this necessary acceptance, "Justice must satisfy the appearance of justice," to cite one of Felix Frankurter's famous dicta.

To resolve disputes in this even-handed way requires not just a *spirit* of justice but also agreed-upon *procedures* for judging the claims of contending parties—what we grandly call in Western society a "legal system." But the means by which disputes are resolved take many forms in different societies, and their comparative study makes one acutely aware that the "appearance of justice" is not the same everywhere.

We've now become accustomed to saying that ways of resolving disputes *reflect* the cultures in which they arose. But Professor Chase also argues that the ways in which disputes are managed also play an important role in *shaping* the cultures in which they operate. Yet, how can ways of resolving disputes both reflect a culture *and* shape it?

In his effort to resolve this puzzling dilemma, Professor Chase follows two related paths, one speculative and the other empirical, the broader picture and the fine detail. It soon becomes clear in his account that to understand any particular procedural detail, one must understand both the dispute-resolving *system* in which it operates and also, at the same time, understand how that system sustains and even amplifies the culture as a whole. Why do the African Azande use a *benge* oracle for resolving disputes—a system in which a small dose of poison is fed to a young chicken, the chicken's death or survival signaling which is the guilty and which the innocent party to the dispute? One cannot understand such seemingly bizarre ritualization unless one understands the pervasive ritualization of witchcraft as a whole in this fascinating society. Ritualism pervades Azande society, its different forms affecting each other in some mutually interconnected way.

One can usually find a more or less convincing explanation of how procedural differences in adjudication "fit" the cultures in which they hold sway—thanks to the searching monographs of gifted anthropologists, however varied their explanations may be. What is more difficult, however, is to discern how particular dispute resolution systems, once in play, both "fit" the culture and work their way back into it to accentuate or modify its way of life.

Oscar Chase explores this back-and-flow issue not only among the African Azande but also in our own American culture. What makes the account gripping is its richness of procedural detail, combined with its broader insights about a culture's way. His exploration of the Azande is supported by the rich resources provided by E. E. Evans-Pritchard's famous work on these people, "EP" (as he is known among his students) being among the most gifted anthropologists of our era. But it is in examining our own legal system that Professor Chase brings his own enormous expertise to bear. His discussion, for example, of why Alternative Dispute Resolution has come so to the fore in America examines a stunning range of possibilities—political factors, practical ones, and (with great originality) such cultural-psychological factors as the increasing privatization of American life and our loss of certainty about our culture's general values.

What I want to celebrate particularly about this book is not only its broadly cultural perspective but also its scrupulous sensitivity to the nature and limits of legal *procedure* wherever practiced. For wherever law is practiced and however formalized it may become, it cannot be understood without reference to its procedures. It is by their appositeness and subtleties that law succeeds or fails. Our author brings to his task the refined discipline of a highly trained legal scholar as well as a fresh sensitivity to the ways of our own culture. He helps us see the underlying rationale not only of such exotica as the Azande *benge* but also of our own familiar legal system, which we too easily take for granted—like our puzzling affinity both for procedural adversariality and, more latterly, for Alternative Dispute Resolution! He is a great hand at making cultural conflicts more comprehensible!

A final word about my experience in watching the growth of this book. I have had the good fortune of teaching the New York University Law

School seminar on "Culture and Law" jointly with Professor Chase. Our students read parts of the manuscript while the book was in early drafts. Their reactions were revealing, reminiscent of the old proverb that "the fish will be the last to discover water." Reading and discussing this book-in-progress seemed to waken our students anew to the water they had come to take for granted: the way dispute resolution systems not only resolve disputes but also alter the options and expectancies of those who live under their sway—not only among the Azande in distant Africa but also here at home in our contemporary America. "Elsewhere" helped them to recognize better our own familiar here and now.

The study of law has gone through many changes in the last decades. It has become less hermetic, more open to other ways of understanding the social worlds in which we live. I can think of few books on law's ways that reflect those changes more discerningly than this one.

Preface

After years of studying, teaching, and writing about the law of
civil litigation in the United States, my curiosity caused me to investigate
in ever more exotic places the question "how do others do it?"—with the
"it" being "deal with disputes." This took me first to the study of comparative law, in which the "others" are various modern states with Western-
style legal systems, and then to anthropology, in which discipline the "others" may be peoples who organize themselves very differently from the
peoples of modern states. It is only somewhat surprising that the further I
moved from my original boundary, the better I understood the place that I
had left. It was not so much that I gained sophistication about the details
of this or that rule of practice. Rather, through exposure to the variety of
strikingly different means that have been developed to deal with disputes,
I came to better appreciate the deep connections between social order and
disputing systems. As Clifford Geertz puts it, "We need, in the end, something more than local knowledge. We need a way of turning its varieties
into commentaries one upon another, the one lighting what the other
darkens."[1]

This book is in part an attempt to do just that—to lighten our understanding of disputing practices in one corner of the world by examining
"how others do it," and why. It is easier to see the deep and reciprocal connection between a people's disputing institutions and their culture when
we are shocked not only by their difference from us but also by their own
commitment to what appears to us as bizarre. Such is the purpose of my
effort in chapter 2 to understand why oracle consultation made perfect
sense to the Azande of central Africa. Once this study frees us even somewhat of the preconception that there is only one right way to find truth
and justice, which just happens to be ours, we can better uncover the cultural underpinnings of our own dispute resolution practices. Chapters 3
through 6 are the products of such archeological digging into modern dis-

puting. I stand firmly against that school of thought that still sees procedural techniques as the product of mandarin technicians alone. I will argue as well for reflexivity, by which I mean that the dispute processes used, ritualized, and usually celebrated in every society play an important part in the transmission of its metaphysics, its morality, and its sense of propriety about hierarchical and other personal relations.

Since this book grows out of my teaching at NYU School of Law, I have benefited much from the colleagues with whom I have cotaught. Their insights and observations have helped shape this work, and I am grateful to them. Jerome Bruner, Paul Chevigny, David Garland, and Fred Myers have taught one or another iteration of the Culture and Disputing seminar with me and have helped steer me through the joys and mysteries of interdisciplinary scholarship. Andreas Lowenfeld, Linda Silberman, and Vincenzo Varano, with whom I have cotaught Comparative Civil Procedure, offered new and helpful perspectives on the legal systems of the world. Our students brought multiple disciplinary orientations to the conversation and represented a variety of nations and cultures. I learned much from their questions and comments.

Neil Andrews of Clare College, Cambridge, Paul Carrington of Duke Law School, Arthur Rosenthal, and my NYU colleagues Jerome Bruner, David Garland, and James B. Jacobs have been critical and sensitive readers of drafts and, far more important, valued sources of support and encouragement. Thanks are due as well to my excellent research assistants Michael Bolotin, Seth Gassman, Laura Kilian, Sagit Mor, Francisco Ramos Romeu, Benyamin Ross, and Bryant Smith.

I gratefully acknowledge the Filomen D'Agostino and Max E. Greenberg Research Fund of New York University Law School for its financial support; the Rockefeller Foundation for the fellowship that provided an uninterrupted month of work at its Bellagio Center; and the Institute of Comparative Law at the University of Florence for the hospitality that was an early and important stimulation to my interest in comparative law. An earlier version of chapter 5 was published in *Discretionary Power of the Judge: Limits and Control*, edited by M. Storme and B. Hess. I am grateful to the editors and to Kluwer, the publisher, for permission to reproduce portions of it. I am similarly grateful to the *Cardozo Journal of International and Comparative Law* for permission to use portions of my article, "Legal Processes and National Culture"; to the *American Journal of Comparative Law* for permission to use portions of my articles "American 'Exceptionalism' and Comparative Procedure" and "Some Observations on the Cultural Dimension in Civil Procedure Reform"; and to the *Tulane Journal of International and Comparative Law* for permission to use portions of my article "Culture and Disputing."

Above all, thanks to my family. Arlo M. Chase and his bride, Susanna L. Kohn, read an entire early draft and made thoughtful comments and suggestions. Oliver G. Chase and Rashmi Luthra helpfully challenged many of my preconceptions from the perspective of their wide range of multicultural experience and interdisciplinary study. Jane Monell Chase has been a source of wonderful intellectual stimulation and much needed encouragement. Thanks for your boundless love, patience, and support.

1

Introduction

No human society is free of disputes. But how will the disputes be addressed? Here we encounter myriad manifestations of human ingenuity and imagination. "Institutionalized responses to interpersonal conflict, for instance, stretch from song duels and witchcraft to moots and mediation to self-conscious therapy and hierarchical, professionalized courts."[1] We find all these "dispute-ways" and more.[2] Even apart from what it is they dispute about, and what kinds of claims will be validated by their society, a people must decide how to process those claims and grievances. Will (or must) the parties allow a third person to resolve their quarrel (so-called triadic disputing)? Or will the disputing remain one on one ("dyadic"), to be fought out, negotiated out, or left to fester? If triadic, will the third party be a go-between, a mediator, or an umpire? If the latter, will the umpire's decision be final, or will it be subject to review? And will the umpire have some kind of official status (including state power to enforce decisions) or will she be more like an arbitrator—a neutral whose power is derived from the consent of the parties? Where will the relevant norms be found? How will the decision maker resolve disputes over facts and decide what "really" happened? A task repeated in societies around the world is to separate truth from falsehood. How? Any society's approved way of handling disputes is the result of conscious and unconscious choices that are made within the constraints of the knowledge, beliefs, and social structure available to it.

Among the Central African Azande, the *benge* oracle would be consulted. A small portion of poison would be fed to a baby chick as the question was put to the oracle: "If the plaintiff tells the truth, let the chicken die, let the chicken die, let the chicken die . . ." The chick lived (or died). The oracle had spoken.[3] In another time and place (the United States) a judge orders that a jury be consulted. A group of strangers is summoned to a special hall, used only for airing disputes. They hear from the plaintiff, the defendant, and the conflicting witnesses. The strangers retire to a private room and caucus. They return with a verdict.[4] In yet another time and place (most of Continental Europe and Latin America), the facts are determined by a specially trained judge whose decision is based primarily on documents and who may not even allow contesting parties to testify.[5] Every one of these methods is defended in the place it is (or was) used as the best way of getting at the truth about an ultimately unknowable past.[6] Each of the peoples described possess the same innate capacity to reason and observe the world around them. Why have they reached such different conclusions? How do their preferred methods of disputing reflect their worlds? Do their "dispute-ways" in turn affect their beliefs about the world they inhabit?

That so many different societies have found different solutions to the common human goal of handling disputes while maintaining a cohesive collective life argues for the study of disputing in cultural and social context.[7] In this book I explore the deep and reflexive connection between culture and disputing processes, a connection that is found even in modern states characterized by technical and elaborate rules of process. The recognition and understanding of this relationship will enrich our capacity to evaluate recommendations for change—particularly when they involve borrowing from other societies. After sketching out my core argument in a bit more detail, I will discuss some unavoidable issues of definition and theory. This introduction will close with a road map of subsequent chapters.

Dispute processes are in large part a reflection of the culture in which they are embedded; they are not an autonomous system that is predominantly the product of insulated specialists and experts. More, they are institutions through which social and cultural life is maintained, challenged, and altered, or as the same idea has been expressed, "constituted" or "constructed." These institutional practices importantly influence a society and its culture—its values, metaphysics, social hierarchies, and symbols—even as those practices themselves reflect the society around them. In adopting the phrase "importantly influence," I follow Melford Spiro, who uses the same term, opposing it to the stronger claim that some idea or practice is "determined" by cultural heritage.[8] Culture is so complex that it would be extravagant to hold that any one set of institutional practices can "determine" it. I thus address the old question of how the social conventions and rules that make social life possible are developed and sustained. My enlistment of dispute processes in the service of answering that question fits comfortably, if not perfectly, within the modern "enterprise of actually tracing the uneasy relationship of law to culture [that] has begun in earnest."[9] As I explain later in this chapter, however, my concerns are both broader and narrower than "law": broader, because there are many societies whose dispute processes do not involve law as we understand it; narrower, precisely because my obsession with process allows me to neglect the substantive norms affecting the dispute. I apply the "constitutive perspective," so valuable in understanding how "law" is embedded in social life, to the broader range of practices of disputing.[10]

Clifford Geertz's famous metaphor helps us to understand the constitutive perspective. "Man," he observes, creates governance "by enclosing himself in a set of meaningful forms, 'webs of signification he himself has spun.' . . ."[11] Because we inhabit a universe devoid of meaning and lacking intrinsic social structure, we must create both. They are a product of mental processes that include observation, calculation, and imagination. The web is spun with our social arrangements, our symbolic systems, our epistemology, our psychology, and our practices. Moreover, each of these informs the others. The web that holds us is composed partly of those institutions that make social life possible and partly of the internally held system of ideas and beliefs that makes the universe tolerable. Each of us must engage this task. But because we are social animals we are neither free to, nor must we, spin each web entirely anew. We are socialized into a web that at least in part has been spun for us and is communicated by parental instruction, by education, by the functioning of institutions, and by drama and ritual. The procedures we use to resolve disputes are both strands of the web and are among the means by which we transmit its outlines to other members of our society.

An understanding of the *meaning* of particular dispute processes for its participants is essential. To get at these meanings we need an interpretive approach. We must use the related tools of thick description and "cultural contextualization of incident."[12] That is, we must observe the relevant practices closely and must place them within the culture in which they operate. The task of contextualization is dependent on comparison and contrast; we see what is particular to a society by placing it next to those that differ. In developing my arguments I will therefore employ comparative studies of modern legal regimes as well as anthropological descriptions of small-scale societies.

An interpretive approach to disputing practices is both suggested and aided by the rituals they so often employ in the service of legitimacy, ceremonials that express in lovely (or terrifying) metaphor the longings and passions that are central to the cultures that produce them. Sometimes they bring into sharp relief the psychic needs shared by all humans but expressed in muted, or at least different, ways in other cultures. Because, perhaps, it is so important and yet so difficult, the creation of disputing institutions has often invoked visual artistry. A wonderful example is the mask worn by Benin diviners when announcing a verdict. A photograph appears on the book jacket. The closed eyes suggest dispassion, much like the blindfold traditionally worn by the figure of Justice,[13] while the beautifully composed face also suggests a sense of the calm confidence that the justice giver wishes to communicate (or that the society wishes to experience).

But interpretive explanation is not sufficient. Disputing is hardly about meaning making alone. Because disputes are found in every society, finding an effective means of handling them is an essential task of social life. We must also explore the way function and cultural representations interpenetrate. A disputing practice will be better understood when we see how it works symbolically *and* functionally. We can understand the American jury, for example, interpretively, as a representation through action of the societal ideal of populist, egalitarian decision making. And we can understand it functionally as a generally accepted way of choosing between contested versions of fact. Either understanding alone would be inadequate.

Power, too, is always at issue when dispute processes are developed, employed, challenged, and reformed. Dispute-ways are never neutral as between competing social groups, even if they are in fact neutral as between the individual disputants. Who gets to decide disputes, and the means they use to decide, will privilege and handicap different sectors of society. We will see when we turn to the Azande of Central Africa how the ritual control of the oracle underpins their critical social distinctions. And is this same dynamic not illustrated as well by ongoing struggles in the American legal system over the ambit of jury power? As Laura Nader argues, elites will endeavor to restrict court access when the courtroom becomes an arena for effective social change.[14]

Since culture is nonetheless my main interest, readers familiar with socio-legal studies may locate my claim that disputing processes "reflect" culture in the continuing debate about whether law "mirrors" society. The notion that law roughly but invariably reflects the culture in which it is found, while virtually axiomatic for some observers, does not command unanimity.[15] An extended meaty challenge to the mirror thesis has recently been offered by Brian Z. Tamanaha,[16] who points to the globalization of commerce and the transplantation of legal practices and concepts as reasons to doubt the persuasiveness of the thesis. It is only partly accurate to locate my book smack within this debate. As I have noted, "law" is relevant here only because it is a product of and a source of dispute. My claim is not limited to law; it is about official systems of disputing, whether or not they could be identified as "legal." Nonetheless, as disputing processes often take the form of legal institutions, and as I argue for a close cultural connection, I must take seriously the objections to the mirror thesis. If I am successful, this book will undermine a particular claim of the anti–mirror theorists, i.e., that official institutions for handling disputes are in large part shaped by professional elites acting within a virtually untrammeled range of technicians' power. While no one argues that these institutions are wholly the product of a professional priesthood totally insulated from the society they inhabit, and while I do not claim that these priests are putty in the hands of "culture," I do emphasize the cultural side. The metaphysics, values, symbols, and social hierarchy of any collectivity will set the bounds within which it organizes its dispute-handling institutions.

This analysis has implications for the various current projects of procedural reform, especially those emphasizing the harmonization of rules across national boundaries. It is no exaggeration to claim that "[t]he debate on law and culture might seem to hold the key to comparative law's nature as a scholarly field and also to its potential as a source of practical guidance for legal policy—as, for example, in regard to legal transplants . . . and harmonization of law between legal systems."[17] As globalization has led to homogenization of substantive law, it is no surprise that a move toward uniformity in dispute processing has followed.[18] My approach shows why the latter move has encountered more difficulties than substantive harmonization—all the more surprising because it has involved "only" process. Finally, the power of dispute-ways to reciprocally influence the culture in which they are embedded raises a concern that must be considered by those engaged in such harmonization efforts. It may argue for conserving a practice like the American civil jury, because of its role in the maintenance of important values, but it may argue as well for breaking new ground. For example, the introduction of the jury in a society in transition from totalitarianism would be profoundly expressive of a new era of popular participation in government. It would symbolize the relocation of authority and could even change the way individuals conceptualize their relationship to authority.

Even those who are not persuaded by my arguments will, I hope, be enriched by the detailed exploration of the connections that are at its heart.

The Issue of "Culture"

My use of culture as an explanatory variable (dispute-ways reflect culture and in turn affect culture) invokes a term that needs defining and some defending as well. "Constructing a definition for anthropology's core concept has always been difficult, but at no time more so than the present."[19] The main difficulties spring from the inherent vagueness of the concept, its potentially misleading message of immutability of practice and belief, and its failure to acknowledge individual departures from, and even opposition to, a social orthodoxy.[20] These problems must be acknowledged and care taken to avoid their pitfalls, but they do not trump the utility of the concept. I agree with Amsterdam and Bruner: "We seem to need a notion of culture that appreciates its integrity as a composite—as a system in tension unique to a people not in perpetuity but at a time and place."[21]

For what purpose do we "need" this notion of culture? I suggest that we need it in part because it serves as a short-hand way of referring to commonalities in practices, values, symbols, and beliefs of particularized groups of people. We need "culture" too, for its power to explain why remarkably different institutions arise in different societies to deal with problems that are essentially the same. I embrace a concept of culture that entails commonalities that persist over time but are hardly eternal and that are widely, but not uniformly, shared by a definable collectivity.[22] To quote Kroeber and Kluckhohn, "the essential core of culture consists of traditional (i.e., historically derived and selected) ideas and especially their attached values; culture systems may, on the one hand, be considered as products of action, on the other as conditioning elements of further action."[23]

More specifically, the definition of culture used here includes the "traditional ideas, values and norms" that are widely shared in a social group.[24] Culture includes propositions of belief that are both normative ("killing is wrong except when authorized by the state") and cognitive ("the earth is round").[25] Culture also includes the symbols that represent those mentalities for its people (the figure of Justice with her scales; a desktop globe). Does culture properly defined also include the institutions and social arrangements that are particular to a society (law courts; astronomy faculties)? The answer must depend on the purposes of the definition. In the context of this work, disputing practices and institutions are one variable. It is argued that this variable both explains and is explained in part by culture (ideas, values, norms, and symbols). The two therefore cannot be entirely conflated in this enterprise. Disputing institutions are at once a product of, a contributor to, and an aspect of culture. Their form can be evidence of some pervasive quality of a society, but to avoid the trap of tautology, I will support any such claims with other evidence of the same quality elsewhere in the beliefs and practices of the society in question. It is then coherent to argue that dispute-ways are reflexively intertwined with both ideation and practice: "[C]ulture thus consists of meanings, conceptions, and interpretive schemes that are activated, constructed, or brought online through participation in normative social institutions and routine practices. . . ."[26] Disputing is one of those "routine practices."

Anyone who would contrast one culture with another faces the difficult problem of finding boundaries, of identifying the social unit to characterize as a separate culture. With respect to a geographically isolated small-scale society such as the Azande, described in chapter 2, this presents only modest difficulties, especially if the time frame is circumscribed, though even then there may be differences in "culture" among subgroups. Far more troublesome is the ascription of culture to modern peoples whose principal common identity is citizenship in a nation state of many millions of people. At this point I mean only to surface the issue. I will return to it in chapter 4 when I discuss the special case of American "exceptionalism." As we will see, both interpretive and empirical forms of inquiry support the claim that even this most heterogeneous of nations, the United States, has a particular culture, and that it is deeply connected to its official disputing practices.

The Explanatory Power of Culture

Not only is the invocation of "culture" defensible as a tool for understanding dispute processes; it is also necessary. It fills gaps left open by other studies of the relationship between disputing and society. Simon Roberts, for example, has explored the puzzling variation in the acceptability of violent self-help in different small-scale societies.[27] Violent disputing will be found, it is said, where existing social arrangements do not permit or facilitate the emergence of third parties who might mediate or otherwise direct the quarrel away from violence. This may be because living arrangements, kinship groups, and the like do not permit anyone in the group to be neutral when a dispute breaks out. Roberts acknowledges the limited utility of these explanations in explaining the practices of all the societies observed, and he ultimately attributes the degree of violent disputing (or, alternatively, settlement-directed talking) to "the values and beliefs held in the societies concerned."[28]

Economic life, i.e., the way a people survives in the world, whether as small bands of hunter-gatherers or as a complex modern state, surely affects disputing, but again cannot explain all of the differences observed.[29] Dispersal is a common method of dealing with ongoing disagreements within small bands, but it is less likely to be found where harsh local ecology means that each member's survival depends on continuing cooperation.[30] Yet there are also often differences in dispute-ways among societies with similar economic and social systems. Interesting is Roberts's report that "[o]ne respect in which societies of hunters and gatherers differ a great deal from each other is in the extent to which fear of supernatural agencies is seen to be important in the prevention and handling of conflict."[31] It is these cases that display the deep connection between the symbolic tools of a people and its preferred means of dealing with dispute. I pursue this theme in detail in the next chapter, using the Azande as a case study.

A detailed argument for a relationship between economic organization and forms of disputing is provided by Katherine S. Newman.[32] She presents a typology of preindustrial societies based on eight kinds of "legal systems" that she ranks in accordance with their level of "complexity."[33] The latter is determined by whether one or more of five characteristics of dispute-resolution systems (such as use of a third-party decision maker) is found in the society.[34] Newman examined a sample of societies that she constructed from anthropological texts to test her hypotheses.[35] She concludes that in precapitalist societies a "materialist approach" is useful "for explaining the distribution of legal institutions. . . ."[36] But despite her investment in materialism, Newman recognizes that a full understanding of the disputing processes in a society requires more than an economic dimension: "Indeed, the 'idiom' of law, the language in which its concepts and conflicts are expressed, is surely a matter of cultural determination. . . . Many ritual taboos, religious practices, and normative values embodied in legal codes appear to have little connection to economic relations."[37] My interest includes the matters that economic approaches obscure, matters nicely summed up, in Newman's phrase, as the "idiom" of dispute-ways. This necessarily enlists the concept of culture and demonstrates its enduring utility.

The Boundaries of "Dispute"

My second core concept, dispute, also poses a definitional challenge. Its elasticity stretches across a range of human disagreements, from spousal spats to world wars.[38] Disputes can arise from perceived or real acts of wrongdoing or from conflicting claims to desired goods.[39] And, of course, the method of disputing can take many forms, from reasoned discourse to armed and fatal combat. Some prescription of scope is desirable in the interest of manageability. Since my goal is to examine the relationship between socially countenanced dispute-ways and the culture in which they are found, I will focus on intragroup disputing. Although the conduct of warfare is itself subject to the regulation of each culture, such rules reflect considerations very different from those applied to disputes within the group. I will try to stick primarily to disputes that are serious enough to occasion the use of what can loosely be called an institutionalized form of disputing. Such self-imposed limitations cannot, however, be absolute because the categories are themselves so porous. The capacity of the official and the informal to bleed into each other is illustrated by the American judiciary's enthusiastic embrace of forms of dispute resolution still called "alternative." This is taken up in chapter 6, "The Rise of ADR in Cultural Context."

In most societies there is more than one approved way to deal with disputes. And some persons may carry on their disputes in socially disapproved but not uncommon means, such as domestic violence in the United States. The method used in a particular situation will depend on the relationship between the parties, the nature of the dispute, and the costs of various possibilities. One may therefore ask how I choose a particular process for comment. Why focus on official processes such as the *benge* oracle or jury trial? I do not contend that study of informal or illegal means of disputing would not provide much of interest to the student of culture, but I argue that the study of the most prominent, public, and official forms of disputing will also express cultural and social themes. And, because of their privileged, not to say sanctified status, they will have the greatest impact on the broader society. Those practices are not only a means of resolving disputes; they are a means of signaling values, beliefs, and social roles.

To be sure, the risk of focusing on officially constituted institutions and practices is that, as the anti–mirror theorists mentioned above would hold, they are the captives of the political, professional, or economic elites of their societies and for that reason are a poor vehicle for the study of the relation between culture and process. In part, this book is itself an extended effort to refute that approach. In my view, any analysis that totally separates professional elites from the culture in which they are embedded is unrealistic. Even Pierre Bourdieu, who argues that it is in part the ritualized monopolization of tools of language and practice that gives the domain, or "field," of law and its practitioners the power and privilege that they enjoy, argues as well for the interconnectedness of law (a particular form of dispute practice) and "the social order itself."[40]

There are two ways in which professionalized dispute-process elites will interconnect with the society in which they operate: in most cases, they will themselves be products of that culture, and will in general share its metaphysics and values. These will inevitably affect their view of what is right and good in choosing among competing methods of identifying true facts and just norms. Second, even if elite organizers of dispute-ways do not themselves actually believe in the validity of broadly held norms and beliefs, there is an incentive to create procedures that resonate effectively with those subject to them, as those are more likely to win acceptance.[41] This requires a cultural connection.

The disputing-culture link is at its most robust in cultures that do not strongly differentiate between dispute practices and everyday life, such as small-scale, technologically simple societies. In technologically complex modern societies, disputing practices are more likely to mirror the broader culture to the degree that the state is a stable democracy. In that case, the ruling elite is likely to emerge from the general public, and therefore to share its values. Its legitimacy, moreover, will be dependent on general satisfaction with the dispute practices it constructs. It is not surprising, contrariwise, that the institutions imposed by colonial governments may differ sharply from the folk practices previously employed. British rule over the Azande was a good example—force of arms enabled the imposition of British-style courts for important matters, though it did not enable internalization by the subjects. Postcolonial elites may, for reasons of their own, maintain imported dispute institutions. Here again, the failure of those institutions to mirror still-pervasive cultural values does not present a strong challenge to my overall thesis of connectedness. Given enough time, the imposed order and the local culture may reach an accommodation that involves some mutual interpenetration.[42]

Norms of Behavior or Norms of Process?

In examining dispute-ways transculturally we find variety in norms (rules of proper conduct) as well as in processes (rules for dealing with violations of norms and other disputes). The link between norms of behavior and cultural values has been often noted. I want, as much as possible, to explore instead the processes side. Thus, it is of relatively little importance to my enterprise that the Azande, an African people discussed at length in chapter 2, consider adultery a serious wrong. It is much more interesting and important for this project that they consult oracles to determine whether it has occurred.

The distinction between the two dimensions—norms and processes—is not easy to maintain, in part because the distinction is itself a product of social construction.[43] In some small-scale societies there is no explicit category of lawlike norms; they seem rather to be imbedded in custom and invoked implicitly in the way disputes are resolved and life is lived.[44] Even in technologically sophisticated societies, processes and norms are sometimes inseparable. The elusive nature of the boundary between procedure and substance is thus, to take a close-to-home example, a chestnut of civil procedure in the United States.

The U.S. Supreme Court has occasionally had to explore this boundary because the Court has the statutory power "to prescribe general rules of practice and procedure" for cases in the U.S. courts but cannot promulgate rules or statutes governing substantive law.[45] Keeping the two separate has proven troublesome.[46] The Supreme Court acknowledges that a rule that affects important normative rights can still be procedural in nature.[47] One might have thought, for example, that the power of a court to compel a litigant to undergo an involuntary medical examination would be "substantive," or a matter of norms, in the sense used here. Notwithstanding the importance of bodily privacy in America, the Court held that the issue could be considered procedural within the context of litigation and thus a legitimate matter for judicial rule making.[48]

The cultural aspect of the norms/processes construct is highlighted by Christopher Stone's essay, "Should Trees Have Standing? Toward Legal

Rights for Natural Objects."[49] "Standing" is one of the doctrines of American law that regulates access to court. An action brought by a party that does not have standing will be dismissed, even if the underlying claim has merit. Since the rules of standing do not purport to turn on the legality of the defendant's conduct, it is in that sense a rule of process. Stone's essay, as its provocative title suggests, reconsiders law's approach to nature. Do natural objects have legal claims apart from their "owners"? To put the issue in terms of standing is intriguing and very helpful to my present point. Even if trees were accorded standing, the question whether they have substantive rights would still be open. Stone notes that "to say that the natural environment should have rights is not to say anything as silly as that no one should be allowed to cut down a tree."[50] However, he also recognizes that the procedural decision would signal a profound shift in the relationship between humans and the environment and would have many ramifications for primary conduct, "because until the rightless thing receives its rights, we cannot see it as anything but a *thing* for the use of 'us'—those who are holding rights at the time."[51] Thus, a procedural change may have a profound effect on cultural assumptions and even on an understanding of the nature of reality.[52] The issue of standing for trees at once illustrates the difficulty of keeping a strict divide between norms and processes and suggests something of the deep connection between ideas about process and cultural assumptions.[53]

This attempt to draw some boundaries between norms and processes invites exploration of how the concept of "law" fits into my argument. Of course, for much of the twenty-first-century world, dispute institutions are embedded in a system usually referred to as the rule of law. But while "law" cannot exist without such formal institutions, dispute-ways are found even where law, as usually defined, is absent.[54] This distinction is important. Focusing on the practices of disputing, rather than on legal systems created by some societies to handle disputes, expands the space of the inquiry. Whether the disputing methods of technologically simple societies constitute legal systems is not so easy to say. The answer turns as much on one's definition of law as on careful observation of the people in question. So, with Roberts,[55] I think it better not to limit the discussion to practices and beliefs properly considered "legal." I ask, rather, how people dispute, and what their dispute-ways say about them and their constructed world.

Ironically, a catholic approach to disputing means that I cannot avoid the concept of law entirely. Law is too important a concept for the dispute systems of too many people. Legal systems, too, are socially constructed dispute-ways and in that vein, attention must be paid. To tip my hand a bit, one might say that "law" and "oracles" serve similar functions for different peoples. Law is considered as a cultural construct in chapter 3.

Looking Forward

In this introduction I have given the reader a sense of the purpose and importance of my project. I have sketched the utility—indeed, necessity—of a cultural understanding of dispute processes. And I have dealt with knotty problems of scope and definition. In chapter 2 I use an ethnography of the Azande to show in detail how dispute institutions are culturally imbedded and socially constructed and how dispute institutions themselves play a role in the construction and transmission of social arrangements, belief systems, and values. Far from being an irrelevant piece of exoticism, I think that by plainly revealing the place of dispute procedures in their social life, a study of these people helps us better understand the culture-disputing connection. Attention to the Azande therefore suggests a way of looking at disputing "culturally" in modern societies.

Chapter 3 applies the lesson of the Azande—that dispute practices are both reflective and constructive of culture. I take the difficult step back needed to see the dispute practices that prevail in the developed nations in broader context. For them, as for the Azande, dispute practices are cultural constructs. Processes have been devised that are in part rituals that validate the social transformations that follow their application. These dispute-ways communicate something of what people believe about the universe and about a proper social order. To sharpen the point, I engage in an extended metaphoric analysis of the ways in which law and evidence function like oracles.

Chapter 4 moves from the general features of disputing regimes used in modern states to a comparative and cultural account of the institutionalized disputing practices used in the United States. I focus on the formal rules of American civil procedure and show that they are reflective of deeply held values and beliefs.

Chapter 5 addresses a peculiar aspect of American dispute-ways, the rise of the doctrine of "discretion" in American court procedures, and shows how an interpretive understanding of this doctrine sheds light on its growth as well as on the nature of the system that employs it. This chapter also considers the interrelationship of the goals and needs of the elites that operate the legal system, and social and cultural developments exogenous to it.

In chapter 6 I examine another puzzling phenomenon, the turn to Alternative Dispute Processing (ADR) in late-twentieth-century America. I present the evidence of the shift away from adjudication as such to alternate forms as arbitration and mediation and sketch out the doctrinal judicial and legislative acts that facilitated it. A review of the history of disputing in the United States shows that the search for alternatives to the courtroom has long been a backdrop to the dominance of litigation, though often within particular subcultures. The vigor with which the search has been pursued of late is traceable to a combination of institutional, political, and cultural forces that are explicated there. Some proponents of mediation have urged that its emphasis on mutuality and relationship building (in place of adversarial litigation) will nurture such angels of being and will improve society as a whole. This intriguing notion implicitly recognizes the constitutive nature of dispute institutions, so I use this chapter to begin an examination of that process.

Chapter 7 explores the role of ritual in disputing. I argue that rituals that evoke other social practices are used to legitimate dispute-ways and are therefore another connection with culture. I also claim that over time disputing practices themselves take on a ritual-like quality that enables them to effect the social transformations that are the end result of the dispute process.

In chapter 8 I turn directly to the constitutive or constructivist claim: the contention that dispute processes are important to the maintenance and creation of culture, broadly understood. I therefore look closely at the psychological and social processes through which belief is collectively and individually internalized.

The conclusion suggests the utility of my cross-cultural observations. I argue that policymakers considering changes in disputing practices should not disregard the capacity of officialized dispute-ways to resonate throughout the broader system of values, symbols, beliefs, and institutions. This is not an argument against reform, but a plea for wisdom in its development.

A brief afterword shares the extraordinary experience I have gained from teaching material that challenges the settled and familiar understandings of students and teacher.

We are now ready to spend some moments with the Azande.

2

The Lesson of the Azande

For the people who are the subject of this chapter, the Azande of Central Africa,[1] common sense dictates that the best way to determine the truth of contested facts is to consult *benge*, the poison oracle. Because this practice makes no sense to observers from a technologically advanced society, it challenges us to understand it in the context of Zande culture. Observing their society in some detail allows us to see the interpenetration of officially countenanced disputing practices and the culture in which they operate—a gaze we can later direct elsewhere. That is the lesson that I take from the Azande.

Consider the Zande trial of an adultery accusation, preserved in a 1982 video recording.[2] Under Zande law, adultery is a crime, so when a man and a woman were brought before their village chief and accused of an illicit relationship by their respective spouses, it was no small matter. The aggrieved spouses claimed that the alleged adulterers were seen in a compromising situation. The chief, who held court in a large thatched roof structure, sat behind a desk and wore a European-style military hat. He was attended by various court functionaries, who came to attention and saluted, Western-style, when they addressed him. At the first court hearing we see the accusers and the accused questioned by the chief. All stood and addressed him respectfully. The accusers repeated their allegations. The accused denied them categorically. The chief did not himself seek to determine the truth except by pressing the parties to repeat their denials. After asking the accused if they would accept the judgment of the oracle, to which they readily assented, the chief ordered the issue referred to *benge* and the court adjourned.

The consultation of *benge* proceeded out of doors some days later. An operator held a small chick in place with his foot and forced it to swallow a small amount of fluid containing the mystical *benge*, a ritually prepared toxic substance. A questioner then addressed the oracle, roughly as follows: "Oracle, if [so-and-so] slept with [so-and-so], if he knew her as a man, [etc.], let the chicken die."[3] The question was repeated several times in a ritualistic form of speech. The chicken expired, thus proving to the satisfaction of the operator that the adultery took place. The oracle was consulted again, this time about the conduct of the female defendant, with the same result.

The scene then shifted back to the chief's court with the accused and accusers again in attendance. The chief's assistant reported the verdict of the oracle for all to hear. The chief addressed the accused, asking them, in essence, what they had to say for themselves. They answered sheepishly, with the male defendant murmuring, "It [the oracle] must refer to a time several years ago." Neither defendant asserted his or her innocence or otherwise tried to impugn the verdict. Both, when pressed, admitted to having had sex with the other. Following the admission, the chief testily chastised the couple for taking up the court's time with their earlier false denials. The adulterous couple was sentenced to labor on the chief's behalf, to pay the costs of the *benge* consultation, and to pay compensation to the wronged husband.

It may be that the couple was actually guilty as charged. Or perhaps they felt unable to defy the combined power of the chief and the oracle, even if innocent. Or perhaps, despite actual innocence, they themselves came to believe in their guilt, trusting the oracle more than their own memories.[4]

However uneasily this practice may sit in our worldview, it makes perfect sense to the traditional Azande. In their understanding of the universe, supernatural forces are powerfully active in everyday life and oracles are the best way to divine and deal with them. This profoundly affects their socially countenanced ways of disputing. It is as natural for a Zande court to consult an oracle about a disputed issue of fact as it is for an American to consult a jury. In this chapter I first describe the complex involvement of the Azande with the supernatural. I then return to the use of divination in processing disputes. With that background I show how Zande disputing processes contribute to the maintenance of their social structure and help to constitute Zande mental life. In that context I then consider the social impact of British-imposed changes in the Zande system of justice. I will close this chapter with a brief conclusion, summarizing the relation between Zande dispute processes and their culture.

The Belief System of the Azande: Witchcraft, Oracles, and Magic

Our knowledge of traditional Zande life and its dependence on oracles to deal with social relations, illness, and even death is due to the English anthropologist E. E. Evans-Pritchard. His 1937 book, *Witchcraft, Oracles, and Magic among the Azande*, is a "masterful study"[5] of their society.[6] Although he professes only a modest interest in legal matters as opposed to "mystical beliefs and rites,"[7] the Zande dispute-ways were so closely tied to the supernatural that Evans-Pritchard's text allows a close examination of the relationship. Whether the Azande still hold their traditional beliefs and act on them accordingly is largely irrelevant to my present purpose. Invoking the concept of the "ethnographic present,"[8] it is enough that they once did so. It is noteworthy nonetheless that oracular consultation apparently continues today.[9] The previously described 1982 film[10] documents use of the traditional oracles, despite many years of colonial and postcolonial rule and the coexistence of Christian practices.[11]

Evans-Pritchard was not contemptuous of the Azande, despite what to many would seem their bizarre view of the world. Indeed, he admired many of their qualities: he states that they are "unusually intelligent, sophisticated, and progressive, offering little opposition to foreign administration, and displaying little scorn for foreigners."[12] At the same time, Evans-Pritchard tells us, "As we watch him carrying out the many economic and social tasks of day-to-day existence we are amazed at the extensive part of [Zande] life which is given over to oracles and magic and other ritual performances."[13] In reconciling the apparent contradiction between intelligence and belief in a system based on the supernatural, Evans-Pritchard is, first, incredulous at their reliance on oracles: "And yet Azande do not see that their oracles tell them nothing!"[14] But he then explains,

> Their blindness is not due to stupidity, for they display great ingenuity in explaining away the failures and inequalities of the poison oracle and experimental keenness in testing it. It is due rather to the fact that their intellectual ingenuity and experimental keenness are conditioned by patterns of ritual behavior and mystical belief. Within the limits set by these patterns they show great intelligence, but it cannot operate beyond these limits. Or, to put it another way: they reason excellently in the idiom of their beliefs. . . .[15]

It was as hard for the Azande to understand how Europeans failed to see the witchcraft that is all around as for the Europeans to comprehend their belief in it. As one informant told Evans-Pritchard, "'Perhaps in their country [England] people are not murdered by witches, but here they are.'"[16] Witchcraft supplies an essential ingredient in the chain of causality:[17] "[It] explains *why* events are harmful to man and not *how* they happen."[18] For example, if a granary collapses and injures or kills people sitting under it, the Azande understood that the collapse may have been caused by termite damage to the beams. It is witchcraft, however, that answers the question why the collapse took place at the particular time when these particular people were sitting under it.[19]

Witchcraft for the Azande was a very different phenomenon from that understood by Westerners. For them it was not an exotic practice like that which "haunted and disgusted our credulous forefathers."[20] It was a normal part of everyday life: "It is so intertwined with everyday happenings that it is part of a Zande's ordinary world. There is nothing remarkable about a witch—you may be one yourself, and certainly many of your closest neighbors are witches."[21]

Because it was so pervasive, and yet not observable with the ordinary senses, witchcraft and the fear of it were major reasons for consulting oracles. Consultation was advisable as an aid in making decisions, so that witchcraft could be avoided or counteracted.

> The poison oracle, *benge*, is by far the most important of the Zande oracles. Zande rely completely on its decisions, which have the force of law when obtained on the orders of a prince. . . . No important venture is undertaken without authorization of the poison oracle. In important collective undertakings, in all crises of life, in all serious legal disputes, in all matters strongly affecting individual welfare, in short, on all occasions regarded by the Azande as dangerous or socially important, the activity is preceded by consultation of the poison oracle.[22]

The process by which the oracle was consulted followed the lines we saw in the adultery trial: the oracle gave the answer by killing or sparing the chick, as determined by the form of the question. Usually the directions were alternated, with the oracle asked to kill the bird if the answer was affirmative and the next time asked to spare it if the answer was negative.[23] A proper consultation involved two tests. The second had to confirm the answer given in the first questioning. If the chick survived the first test, a different one had to die in the second test (or vice-versa) for the judgment to be valid.[24] The consultation was replete with ritual. In part for this reason, "great experience is necessary" to have a proper consultation.[25] Only men or older boys could be present, and then only if they observed temporary taboos against sex and some foods. It was the questioner's responsibility to make sure that the oracle understood the questions and that it had all the facts necessary to answer it. The oracle was addressed with special forms of speech, using "analogies and circumlocution."[26] Moreover, the men present had to dress, speak, and generally comport themselves as if in the presence of a prince or other superior.

Even the gathering of the poison was closely governed by ritual. The substance is an extract of a particular vine or creeper.[27] As it did not grow anywhere close to their own lands, the Azande had to travel for several days to retrieve it. For mystical reasons, they did not wish to plant it in their own area. Prior to a gathering trip, oracles were consulted to determine the success of the venture. Taboos were observed by all in the party. Mystical processes were observed in harvesting and preparing the substance actually to be used.

Most consultations concerned matters of health, as the Azande believed that virtually all serious illness was caused by witchcraft or other sorcery. If someone became ill, consultation was necessary to determine whose witchcraft was causing the disease. The patient, in addition to using indicated folk medicine,[28] usually consulted an oracle, with *benge* considered the most authoritative. What if *benge* confirmed the identity of the person doing witchcraft and causing an illness? Ritual action to protect the victim by ceremonially neutralizing sources of witchcraft quickly followed. This was not exclusive of medicinal approaches but in addition to them.[29] If the victim recovered after a few days, the poison oracle was praised for its help. If not, the process was repeated to identify other witches that might be contributing to the problem.

If the sick person died despite the ritual activities described, the agenda shifted from prevention to vengeance. In precolonial times, if the verdict was confirmed by the *benge* oracle of the prince, the witch would have to pay compensation, or be killed.[30] After the imposition of colonial rule, vengeance was sought only by magic.[31] The bereaved kin asked the poison oracle to select a person to act ritualistically as avenger and to choose a magician to assist him.[32] The avenger's duty was "to dispatch magic on the tracks of the witch under the direction of the magician who owns it, and to observe the onerous taboos that enable it to achieve its purpose."[33] The magician loosed magic that hunted out the witch responsible for the death and killed him. "Azande say of [the magic] that 'it decides cases' and that it 'settles cases as judiciously as princes.'"[34] When someone in the vicinity died after the magic has had time to work, the bereaved consulted *benge* to determine if this person was the witch who caused the death of their kin. If the answer was positive, they informed their prince, who then consulted his own oracle. "When the oracle of the prince agrees with the oracle of the kinsmen vengeance is accomplished."[35] The period of mourning was over and the kin could live normal lives.[36] Here we see the mutually supportive role of witchcraft, magic, and oracles: belief that the original death was caused by magic was proved when a second death occurred after the vengeance magic had been loosed.[37] That the magic caused the second death could be proven only by the *benge* oracle. Continued belief in the reliability of the oracle was therefore critical in helping the Azande deal with death and mourning.

Oracles in Zande Disputing

Reliance on the *benge* oracle to confirm the success of vengeance magic demonstrates its role in what is certainly a kind of dispute resolution, albeit a dispute about mystical forces: the oracle was the judge that pronounced that murder by witchcraft had been avenged. The powers of the oracle also resolved disputes about less mystical matters, notably accusations of adultery. Witchcraft and adultery were in fact the principal occasions for using the oracle in what Evans-Pritchard calls "Zande legal procedure."[38] He tells us that "in the old days [the poison oracle] was in itself the greater part of what we know as rules of evidence, judge, jury and witnesses."[39] Adultery was an issue of great concern to the polyganous Azande men. It was even thought that a man might suffer misfortune because of it, i.e., "a man may be killed in warfare or in a hunting accident as a result of his wife's infidelities."[40] Given the seriousness of the matter and the consequent desire to prevent and punish it, it is not surprising that procedures for making and resolving accusations were well established. Nor is it surprising that, like witchcraft accusations, proof depended in large part on the oracle. As Evans-Pritchard observes, the Azande would not see a bright line between the kind of facts at issue in each of these spheres; witchcraft and adultery are both done clandestinely and, for the Azande, mystical forces are the best source of reliable knowledge.[41] Thus, a suspicious husband would first arrange a private consultation with an oracle. If it reported his suspicion well founded, he would then bring a formal accusation before his prince. This charge could be based solely on the evidence of the oracle, although other evidence might also play a role. Unless the defendant was able to prove that he was elsewhere at the time of the alleged adultery, the issue would be referred to the oracle.[42] "The accused man would defend himself less by urging the absence of circumstantial evidence than by offering to give *ngbu* or test."[43] He was permitted to select a man "of substance" to consult an oracle on behalf of the prince, and "the declaration of the oracle settled the case."

I will shortly turn to the social and intellectual messages of this form of fact finding, but first I should deal with the questions of how the Azande regarded incorrect verdicts, and whether and how they prevented cheating. If we are to believe Evans-Pritchard, the Azande did not regard these as debilitating problems. They did not believe that cheating occurred in the administration of *benge* (an opinion also reached by Evans-Pritchard),[44] but they did allow that the oracle could reach an inaccurate result.[45] "Even an innocent man does not cite objective evidence or the futility of the oracle in his defense, but counters the mystical machinery that has delivered the judgement against him by appeal to other mystical entities and urges that the oracle was corrupted by witchcraft or sorcery, or a breach of a taboo."[46]

> No one believes that the oracle is nonsense, but every one thinks that for some particular reason in this particular case the particular poison used is in error in respect to himself. Azande are only skeptical of particular oracles and not of oracles in general, and their skepticism is always expressed in a mystical idiom that vouches for the validity of the poison oracle as an institution.[47]

Zande disputing therefore allowed a kind of right to appeal. The oracles of a prince (who were needed to "review" the findings of the commoners' oracles) were occasionally challenged by a further appeal to that of the king, whose oracle was considered final and, generally, infallible. During the reign of Gbudwe, which ended in 1905, the king was more likely to quash the verdicts of some of his sons than others, apparently having different degrees of confidence in their oracles.[48] A disappointed litigant could, however, claim that the verdict of the king's consulter was inaccurate, and might beseech the king to have the oracle consulted in his presence. If this oracle agreed with the previous test, "the appellant would be lucky if he escaped with a heavy fine and was not executed for having given Gbudwe a pledge without justification."[49] If the previous verdict was shown to have been improperly obtained, the challenger would be made whole and, it was said, the official who yielded it would be dismissed from the king's service.[50] "A king's consulter of oracles was a man of public importance and would often be entrusted later with the administration of a province or district."[51] For all of these reasons the oracular system of justice seems to have enjoyed a great deal of confidence.

The Zande trial and accompanying procedures graphically demonstrate the social and psychological power of belief in the oracle. These processes also show how the dispute resolution system provided an occasion for a public affirmation of the Zande metaphysical world. Although the actual consultation was done in relative privacy, with only the operators and representatives of the accused present, the announcement of the verdict in reliance on the oracle was very much a public matter.

Zande Dispute-Ways and Their Influence on Social Relations

I now turn to a more detailed examination of the relationship between the *benge* consultation judgment and the main features of Zande society. Disputing institutions were vital in maintaining Zande social relations. This is seen prominently in relations of class and of gender.

Class

The Zande empire was a hierarchical society ruled by a royal member of a hereditary aristocracy.[52] The kingdom was divided into subunits presided over by the younger brothers and sons of the king. There was a sharp differentiation between "commoners" and "nobility." The manner and physical appearance of the latter showed that "they are men whose superiority is never challenged and whose commands receive immediate obedience . . . and rely for the necessities of life on the labour and tribute of commoners."[53] This class structure manifested itself in the mystical idiom in many ways. The princely class shared the belief system of their subjects, but acted upon it in accordance with their status.[54] The nobles were never accused of witchcraft. "There is an established fiction that Avongara [the noble lineage] are not witches and it is maintained by the overwhelming power and prestige of the ruling princes."[55] In general, "lesser people" did not consult oracles about more powerful members of the community.[56] Nor would a witch doctor accuse a prince of witchcraft,[57] though princes consulted witch doctors at their own private seances.[58] "Princes, however jealous of each other they may be, always maintain class solidarity in opposition to their subjects and do not allow commoners to bring contempt on any of their relatives."[59]

One of the only situations in which a death would not be attributed to witchcraft or sorcery was when a man had been executed by royal mandate. To claim that witchcraft operated in this situation would be treasonous and could lead to the execution of the accuser.[60] In this and other respects we see the intertwining of the mystical and legal systems. We have already seen that a death could not be considered avenged until the demise of the witch responsible for the original death was confirmed by the prince's oracle. It was also true that (prior to British rule) "a man could not act on a charge involving punishment or compensation without the king's oracle approving his case, though in other matters he might act on the advice of his private oracle."[61] As Evans-Pritchard summarized the relationship between status and dispute-ways,

> Control of the poison oracle in all legal cases gave the princes enormous power. No death or adultery could be legally avenged without a verdict from their oracles, so that the court was the sole medium of legal action and the king or his representative the sole source of law.[62]

The superior power of the oracle of the king and other nobles was overtly traced not to their status but to mystical forces. When asked why the king's oracle was the best in the land, the Azande explained that this was the case because the greatest care was taken to see that "the poison was not polluted during gathering, storage, and in operation."[63] The supreme legal and mystical authority of the king's oracle, each of which derived from the other, may be seen as the linchpin of the society. "Had there been any appeal from the king's oracle to private oracles there would have been general confusion, since everybody would have been able to produce oracular verdicts to support his own point of view and there would have been no way of deciding between them."[64]

Gender

The connection between the Azande dispute system and their social arrangements is also clear when we look at gender relations. Family life was characterized by inferiority of women and the authority of elder males. Women could be married contrary to their wishes and were frequently paid in compensation for murder by witchcraft or for adultery. They were sometimes cruelly treated by their husbands and had little means of protection or redress. They played no part in public life and were looked upon as child bearers and servants rather than as companions and equals. Only the daughters of the royal class enjoyed moderate freedom from male control. Hence women did not take a prominent part in magical and oracular processes.[65] Most magic was unknown to women, partly because many magical medicines were used in connection with male activities, such as hunting. Women traditionally were expected to use magic only with regard to purely feminine pursuits and concerns, like childbirth.

The restriction on female use of magic had strong political overtones: "Magic gives power which is best in the hands of men. In so far as women need magical protection against witchcraft and sorcery they may rely on their husbands to perform rites for the welfare of the family as a whole."[66] While any man of a certain age might consult *benge*, the most important oracle, "Women are debarred not only from operating the poison oracle but from having anything to do with it. They are not expected even to speak of it, and a man who mentions the oracle in the presence of women uses some circumlocutory expression."[67] Women (and children) were permitted to consult only the termite oracle, which is less prestigious; its answers could be challenged by resort to *benge*.[68] The exclusion of women from the use of the *benge* oracle was a powerful expression of the subordinate position of women in Zande society.

> When we consider to what extent social life is regulated by the poison oracle we shall at once appreciate how great an advantage men have over women in their ability to use it, and how being cut off from the main means of establishing contact with the mystical forces that so deeply affect human welfare degrades woman's position in Zande society. I have little hesitation in affirming that the customary exclusion of women from any dealings with the poison oracle is the most evident symptom of their inferior social position and means of maintaining it.[69]

Evans-Pritchard's sense of the exclusion of women as both symptom of their social position and a way of maintaining it accords with my general view of dispute-ways. They serve important social and symbolic purposes beyond providing an acceptable means of resolving disputes. The Azande recognized that their *benge* prerogative is one of the ways women are controlled, "For men say that women are capable of any deceit to defy a husband and please a lover, but men at least have the advantage that their oracle poison will reveal secret embraces."[70] The prohibition against female use of *benge* was not, however, justified by Zande men as a way of underscoring women's inferiority. The exclusion was instead explained by mystical necessity. Use by females would have corrupted the oracle. This gave the exclusion more power as a labeling device than if it were done for that purpose. In the latter case it would be frankly political and would lose the power of connection with the mystical. Social construction works best when the effect is unstated and seems part of the natural order of things. It is fascinating in this context that "the oracle is the main guardian of a wife's fidelity since wives and lovers believe in its powers as firmly as husbands."[71] The adultery trial described earlier certainly bears out this claim. To emphasize, it was the *process* of disputing that helped subordinate women.

Zande Dispute-Ways and Metaphysics

The oracular justice of the Azande was as important to their metaphysics as to their social arrangements. The whole of the Zande belief system was made up of separate but related parts. "Witchcraft, oracles and magic form an intellectually coherent system. Each explains and proves the others. Death is proof of witchcraft. It is avenged by magic. The achievement of vengeance magic is proved by the poison oracle. The accuracy of the poison oracle is determined by the king's oracle, which is above suspicion."[72] Beliefs in the supernatural world of magic and witchcraft were for the Azande the "unquestioned basic assumptions upon which . . . all other reasoning must perforce be based. These are beliefs and assumptions collectively held, which every individual unconsciously accepts as a result of the pervasive influences exercised by society. . . ."[73]

Evans-Pritchard's English countrymen were, "in the main, incredulous or contemptuous. . . . They ask what happens when the result of one test contradicts the other which it ought to confirm if the verdict be valid;

what happens when the findings of oracles are belied by experience; and what happens when two oracles give contrary answers to the same question."[74] Those kinds of questions were either irrelevant to the Azande or easily handled within their system of thought.[75] For the most part the oracles were consulted on mystical matters, such as whether so-and-so was doing witchcraft against the person consulting the oracle. These findings can never be tested empirically by the ordinary senses, but only by other mystical agents. Therefore, the very act of the test was a confirmation of the validity of the underlying concept. Second, the oracles were most often consulted as advisors. In this capacity, their predictions were rarely tested because the advice was followed: if an oracle advised against making a long journey because of the possibility of harm, and the person therefore remained safely at home, the oracle would be seen to have saved his life. Rarely would one who received such a warning make the journey and test the oracle. If he did go, it would be after taking steps to neutralize the threatening witchcraft. If the trip then proceeded without incident, the oracle would be appreciated for having advised him to counteract the threatening agents. Conflicting verdicts were also dealt with in mystical terms, for sorcery, witchcraft, taboo violation, or spoiled *benge* could explain occasional errors or inconsistencies.

Nor was there evidence of cheating in the use of *benge*, by manipulation of the doses or the like. This is not surprising since a person consulting it as a way of avoiding future harm would hardly want to cheat. On the other hand, the Azande were likely to accept without corroboration a verdict that accorded with their desires but to seek further confirmation of a finding that was inconvenient or unpleasant. Or, they could and apparently did sometimes interpret the response creatively, to accord with actual wishes.

In a world in which divination is seen as a path to knowledge of everyday kinds, and in which a supernatural belief system with explanatory and predictive power is essential to one's understanding of social and metaphysical existence, resort to oracles to determine the truth of litigated facts seems entirely sensible. But it is also true that the Zande trial was in turn crucial to the ongoing construction of their belief system.

Synthesis: The Influence of Disputing, Zande-Style

Consider the effect on the community of the adultery trial that I described. A trial has been aptly described as a ceremony of social transformation.[76] When properly performed, the ritual transforms the relations between the parties (as from claimant to creditor or from accused to adulterer). It also transforms the relations between the judge and other members of the society (from person to authority). Like all rituals, the Zande trial gained power with repetition and with acceptance of the resulting transformation. Each time the oracular judgment was announced, relied upon by social elites to legitimate the exercise of power, and assented to by those subject to them, the process was legitimated but so too was the belief system that underlay it. Far from a matter of metaphysics in the abstract, these beliefs took on a tangible reality that made them all the more powerful. The circle from belief to process back into belief was thus complete.

It may be argued that among the Azande the dispute resolution practices were not necessary to the maintenance of the social structure and metaphysics, as these were the product of far more widespread practices and deep beliefs. This position could be maintained even as one concedes that the dispute system is a product of the wider culture and the beliefs inherent in it. To be clear, I do not argue that the dispute-ways of the culture are alone responsible for its maintenance. As Evans-Pritchard put it, "In this web of belief every strand depends upon every other strand, and a Zande cannot get out of its meshes because this is the only world he knows."[77] I do maintain that the regular and prominent invocation of mystical forces in Zande disputing made them a particularly important "strand." In chapters 7 and 8 I will expand upon the reasons why disputing rituals are so influential in many societies. Here we can observe the dynamics particular to the Azande.

Evans-Pritchard concludes that the "legal" uses of the oracle were the most important ingredient in sustaining belief. In a critical passage, he notes,

> In Zandeland its verdicts were backed by the full authority of the king and the decisions of his oracles were final. . . . A man could not act on a charge involving punishment or compensation without the king's oracle approving his case, though in other matters he might act on the advice of his private oracle. In legal disputes, therefore, the authority of the poison oracle

was the authority of the king, and *this alone prevented any serious challenge to its veracity.*[78]

Under British rule, which began around the turn of the nineteenth century, the oracular justice was disapproved, and Zande kings lost most of their authority over legal disputes.[79] The Azande did not welcome the new dispute-resolution system imposed by the British, for the judgment of the oracle was no longer accepted: "[T]hey do not approve of European methods, for in their opinion the only sure evidence of guilt or innocence is not allowed." Even the accused preferred the traditional fact finding because under the European procedures they could be condemned on the testimony of the woman alone. "To-day, all that a husband has to do is consult the oracle, and if it says that his wife is unfaithful, to beat her until she produces some evidence which the government courts will recognize as such. An innocent man has no means of proving his innocence."[80] Evans-Pritchard observes some profound effects of the British legal system: "The new legal codes, which refuse to admit witchcraft as a reality, will not accept evidence of oracles, and will not permit vengeance, have also considerably altered social behaviour."[81] Among the effects of British rule, he mentions the "undermining of the power of the royal class and of the authority of men over women."[82] These changes led to the rise of new associations for the practice of magic.[83] Unlike traditional Zande magic, which involved only loose affiliations between individuals, these organizations were formal and somewhat rule bound. Their rites and hierarchy did not respect the traditional nobility. Women as well as men could and did join, could be leaders, and could sponsor new male or female members: "The inclusion of women is a revolutionary breakaway from custom in a society where segregation of the sexes is rigidly enforced. . . . It is a function of the new order of things."[84]

It would seem that by the time Evans-Pritchard did his fieldwork, the British antipathy to magic and the prohibition of its use in formal legal settings had caused changes in society but had not destroyed faith in all oracles and magic. Vengeance for death by witchcraft, for example, was not abandoned even though claims for compensation could no longer be pursued and the witch could not be speared.[85] Rather, the death of the witch was accomplished by magic. And, as the 1982 video described earlier indicates, faith in the oracle survived British rule sufficiently that its practice had been revived. Interestingly, the participants enlisted the symbols of the former rulers to reenhance its validity, as when the chief/judge wears European-style military head gear and requires his subordinates to salute. The impact of the colonial changes to the disputing system was profound, but limited by the very fact that it was imposed from without and accordingly seen as foreign. The Azande were well aware of change and loss. "Although Gbudwe died only twenty-one years before I commenced my work in his kingdom, his reign was already looked back to with regrets by those who had experienced his rule. To them it was the Golden Age of law and custom."[86]

What does Zande disputing tell us about the "mirror" theory of law? It is clear enough that prior to British conquest there was no differentiation between the beliefs and practices of ordinary Zande and those charged with addressing important disputes. Disputing institutions and practices *did* mirror culture. That the British, and following them, Western or Marxist-oriented national governments, imposed disputing systems based on an entirely different worldview hardly disproves this. Indeed, the survival of oracular consultation as a kind of underground justice system shows the depth of the connection. At the same time, changes in Zande society following the coming of British justice exemplifies its reflexive nature.

The processes the Azande used for resolving their disputes were a link in a circular chain from belief to authority to action and back to belief: the central role of the oracle as a fact finder supported their system of social stratification, their ideas about appropriate gender relations, and their metaphysics. This is the "lesson" of the Azande.

3

"Modern" Dispute-Ways

We have seen how the formal disputing institutions and processes used by the Azande reflect and influence such disparate aspects of their society as political hierarchy, relations between the sexes, the nature of reality, and the means of finding truth. Can these processes of reflection and influence be seen in modern societies as well?

In this chapter and the next I explore the relation between culture and disputing in my own society, the United States. I will divide the analysis into two levels. On the first, presented in this chapter, I look at American disputing as more or less congruent with modern legal regimes that have their primary origin in Europe and have spread, by borrowing or conquest, throughout the developed world. For simplicity I will refer to this as "modern" dispute resolution, reflecting its broad-brush uniformity in technologically sophisticated states, and differentiating it from traditional, less formal processes typically found in small-scale, technologically simple societies. In the next chapter I turn to U.S. disputing more specifically, distinguish it from the other modern legal systems, and look more carefully at its distinctive features in relation to its distinct culture.

The formal processes of all modern dispute systems share several important features. The most fundamental is that they appraise the conflict in its "objectively obtainable aspects (the evidence)" and then resolve it in accordance with norms formally encapsulated in legislation and case law, "rules of law."[1] As Lawrence Friedman has observed, the "law of modern states" is both dense and ubiquitous.[2] It consists of "an enormous mass of rules and regulations, statutes, ordinances, decisions, on every conceivable subject of modern life. . . ."[3] It is complex and impenetrable to all but highly skilled practitioners. This system relies on formal, logic-based reasoning as a way of identifying the correct rule out of the great mass that might apply. It is an article of faith that right answers are possible.

To be sure, most disputes in modern states are resolved without resort to expensive and time-consuming "official" institutions. Even when litigation is begun, it normally ends in a negotiated settlement, not a judgment reflecting the entire process available. I focus on the "official" outcome-determining processes precisely because their grounding in culture—and their constructive power—has been wrongly ignored or denied. A close examination of the relationship is necessary to correct this imbalance. Informal processes also reflect social hierarchy, norms, and metaphysics and no doubt capture different ingredients of culture than the formal processes. But my purpose in this chapter (and this book) requires a primary focus on the formal, official processes. It is because those processes are reserved for important disputes that cannot be resolved informally, because they are public, and because they are held up as the correct and legitimate way of finding right answers to hard questions that such dispute institutions are so interesting to me.

Modern dispute resolution processing is as much a product of the culture and society in which it is found, and as influential on it, as the *benge* trial is for the Azande. Each serves a similar social function. Each provides a culturally valid, binding source of knowledge, thus assuring the disputants and onlookers of the neutrality and consistency of result. The Zande chief must decide in accordance with *benge*; the modern judge must decide in accordance with the law and the evidence. These different processes are similar socially and culturally in that they incorporate prevailing hierarchical arrangements, including those of status and gender, *and* they express through action deeply held beliefs about the universe the participants inhabit. Social arrangements, metaphysics, and ontology—in short, the way of understanding the world—informs and is informed by all aspects of these dispute processes.

The challenge of seeing the constitutive elements of one's own society is the how-do-you-describe-water-to-a-fish problem. It is here that the lesson learned by observing the "strange" culture—the Azande—is useful. Having seen the culture-disputing connection so prominently played out in that society, we are now able to better recognize the same dynamic in our own. Evans-Pritchard helps us by sharing his own effort to come to terms with the apparent paradox of the Azandes' intelligence and their total embrace of the oracle as the path to sure knowledge: "And yet Azande do not see that their oracles tell them nothing! Their blindness is not due to stupidity. . . . It is due rather to the fact that their intellectual ingenuity and experimental keenness are conditioned by patterns of ritual behavior and mystical belief."[4] Important as this insight is, Evans-Pritchard could have taken another crucial step. "What a difference if he had only allowed at this point that this description could apply to most individuals in any culture!"[5] So, too, "what a difference" if we apply that insight to ourselves. In this spirit I propose that the "intellectual ingenuity and experimental keenness" so prominent in modern disputing are similarly conditioned and sustained by something akin to "patterns of ritual behavior and mystical belief." It is when we see this that the culture-disputing connection is clearest.

The connection is revealed most starkly at the same point in both Zande and American disputing, the moment of judgment. In both societies we can observe rituals of social transformation in which a third party is invested with power to decide between disputants and profoundly affect their wealth, status, or liberty. In both cases, the umpire's exercise of that authority reaffirms the social arrangements that are the source of the power. For Americans and Azande, the special authority over disputes is derived from a relationship with the predominant political authority— state power or tribal power. Despite their many differences, each of these societies has developed relatively formal institutions by which they resolve disputes according to settled norms following well-defined procedures. In both societies the facts of the matter are important. Formally at least (and with some exceptions), it is not the status, network of relationships, or reputation of the litigants that is decisive.

Americans and Zande therefore confront the dilemma faced by all societies in which a neutral is empowered to judge the disputes of others: how to legitimate that person's decisions so that compliance is likely, so that the constituting authority is not (by unacceptable decisions) delegitimized, and so that the decision maker does not become an object of revenge by the losing party. As societies in which disputes are resolved in whole or part by determining "what happened," they face a special difficulty, for the truth about a contested past is ultimately unknowable. Yet the umpire must not only find the facts but do so through a process that is convincing to the disputants and observers.

Legitimacy can be threatened when the decision is seen as personal to the decider. "Pressures of one sort or another can be brought to bear on the adjudicator in order to influence, even to control, his decision: bribery, flattery, appeal to prejudices, threats to his own interests, and the like."[6] Particularly in societies in which revenging a wrong is expected, the losing party, convinced of the rightness of his cause, will see the judge as an ally of an enemy, and be inclined to seek retribution.[7] If the judge's decision is seen to be compelled by some neutral force, this problem is attenuated. A process that depersonalizes the decision must resonate with the culture in which it is found in order to be successful. If it does not, it cannot be "legitimate."[8]

Some legitimization is provided by the person of the umpire, who usually enjoys superior political status of a general nature. For the Azande it was the king, prince, or local chief, whose very status was seen as a source of valid rulings. But closer observation shows that the personhood of the decider is apparently not enough: in his "judicial" role even the Zande king must consult *benge* to decide disputed facts. This takes us to the importance of role in legitimization. Many societies achieve the depersonalization of the umpire's decision making by delineating a particular role for that person. The role assumption involves more than simply exercising the power to decide the dispute. It requires the person in this role to follow a particular process in which he is guided by sources other than his own personal reaction in making the decision.

A common feature of this role is the umpire's duty to apply defined social norms to the dispute. Compliance with this duty has an obvious depersonalizing effect—"it is not me that is doing this to you, it is the Law." The umpire can even express disagreement with the norm that is applied. It is the judge who applies an unexpected or inappropriate norm that is seen as injecting an individualized persona into the matter. The duty to apply norms is only a partial solution because the applicability of a norm may be contested; a conflict of norms may itself be the cause of the dispute. Or, the disagreement may be about the facts. In the Zande trial described earlier no one argued that adultery was permissible; they contested whether it had in fact occurred.[9] Given the importance of fact determination to many systems of triadic disputing, it is important that it, too, be seen as resting on more than the umpire's unfiltered personal reaction. Otherwise the depersonalization will be incomplete.

Regardless of the sources invoked by the umpire in a given society, depersonalization of the judge is commonly aided by ceremony and ritualization,[10] such as installation ceremonies. These have the intention and effect of changing both the self-perception and the social perception of the actor. By participating in the ceremony, the person agrees, usually in some public and sacred way, to act differently in this role than in other life roles. Specifically, for the umpire this includes a commitment to resolve disputes in the culturally prescribed manner. The immediate and vicarious audiences implicitly accept this commitment and embrace the belief that the decisions will be role governed.[11]

Even if the umpiring role is temporary there will often be at least a modest ceremony to mark the change of position, as when, to take a modern example, a commercial arbitrator takes an oath to properly perform the office[12]—or, in the Azande case, when the consulter of *benge* undergoes a period of personal deprivation prior to consulting the oracle. The depersonalization is also signaled by the ritual manner in which the umpiring task is performed. The regularity of behavior is itself reassuring to participants and audience.[13]

I will return to the subject of ritual in chapter 7. Here I want to look more closely at what I have previously called the pillars of modern dispute processes—law and evidence, using the same outside-the-system anthropological cast of mind with which we observed disputing among the Azande. I suggest that reliance on law and evidence is no more or less a product of culture than *benge*. These norm and fact referents are not ordinarily justified as a culture-bound way of solving the social issues inevitably raised by triadic dispute resolution, but are seen by participants as a matter of course, as "only natural" or "only logical." This is, paradoxically, the surest sign that, like all "common sense," they are deeply culturally imbedded and contingent.

"Oracles" in Modern Disputing

To provoke the desired outside-the-system stance that allows us to see modern procedure as a culturally determined dispute-way, I will argue that its practitioners use devices that uncannily resemble in function the Zande consultation of oracles. I will argue that "the law" functions much like an oracle to reveal the norms properly applied to a dispute and that "the evidence" functions similarly for the facts. From inside the system the modern versions of these constructs are not thought of as oracular (*pace* Blackstone, to whom I return shortly); they are rather seen as part of a fair and rational system for deciding disputes. Yet, at a minimum these referents must be understood as modern solutions to the social dilemmas inevitably confronted when dispute resolution is given over to a neutral third party.

Why, then, do I depart from my own culture's way of understanding itself and adopt this troublesome stance? First, I do so precisely because our own constructs seem to us so obviously right that we need a metaphor from another world to shock us into seeing their cultural dependency. Like the Azande, we embrace the validity of these sources of dispute-resolution guidance and "display great ingenuity in explaining away the failures and inequalities of the [law and evidence] oracle and experimental keenness in testing it."[14] It is here important that the Azande themselves do not, as far as I can determine, use the word "oracle" in describing *benge*. It is not irrational, in their worldview, to consult *benge*. It is, rather, for them simply a window onto reality, perhaps analogous to a microscope. I hope that the proposed viewpoint is liberating: "Understanding the constructed character of the rule of law allows us to see its contingent character and to understand that law's claim upon us is not a product of law's truth but of our own imagination. . . ."[15] Law's truth has a claim precisely because it is a product of our imagination.

My second reason for using the oracle trope is that it helps us understand the way law and evidence address the legitimacy problems already described. Each provides a source of decisional authority that is represented as existing outside the decision maker, who is subject to its control. Third, this vision underscores the enormous power of law and evidence, as concepts, to retain their hold over us generally despite well-known lapses in the particular. Thus, to observe the ways that law and evidence function as oracles helps reduce our cultural hubris, which is alone not a bad goal.

The Law Oracle

Blackstone, the eighteenth-century expositor and champion of the English legal system, said, without a bit of anthropological detachment, of the common law judges, "They are the depositories of the laws; the living oracles, who must decide in all cases of doubt, and who are bound by an oath to decide according to the law of the land."[16] Blackstone's famous passage captures something of the sacred that infuses our respect for law, and something of the divination process at the heart of judging. In Weber's discussion of Blackstone, he takes a different tack. For him it was "the decision," the "English precedent," that is the oracle.

> [T]he role played by decision as the indispensable and specific form in which the common law is embodied corresponds to the role of the oracle in ancient law: What was hitherto uncertain, viz., the existence of a partic-

ular legal principle, has now, through the decision, become a permanent rule.[17]

I too think it is better to understand "the law" itself as the oracle[18] and the judges as the diviners, the consulters, the intermediaries between the oracle and the world; they are like the operator through which *benge* speaks. As was said in the African context, "the diviner who pronounces the oracle's inspired words declares himself and is by definition declared not to be the subject of enunciation. It is not the diviner who speaks in his own name. . . ."[19]

The point is made graphically by the ancient urn showing King Aigeus consulting the oracle at Delphi through the goddess Themis. "She is seated on a tripod in an attitude of meditation, and gazing with the fixed stare of the clairvoyant into a bowl of water she is holding in the palm of her left hand."[20] Themis divines the revelation of the oracle as do our modern judges.

Blackstone in fact understood that judges were no more than well-schooled diviners, as we see from another portion of the passage quoted previously: the judges' oath binds them to "decide according to the law of the land." On this view, the judges do not create the law; they merely announce it. Lon Fuller captured this when he said, "The acceptability of the judge's decision may be enhanced by the fact that he seems to play a subservient role, as one who merely applies rules which he himself did not make."[21] This is so whether the source of law is the legislature, an administrative agency, or a higher court.

Fuller, who was a legal realist, says that the judge "seems to" play a subservient role, thus implying that in fact the role is much more active. At its most robust, the realist claim holds that legal rules are only a minor ingredient in the decision making of courts; Jerome Frank claimed that one of "the chief uses" of legal rules "is to enable the judges to give formal justifications—rationalizations—of the conclusions at which they otherwise arrive."[22] Debate about the actual and proper role of law in judicial practice continues.[23] It is not necessary for me to take a position in this debate for present purposes. Law functions as oracle whether or not it is an autonomous body of rules and principles that, properly applied, compel particular results. In other words, like *benge*, law's oracular status does not depend on its power to withstand empirical testing. The recognition that judges are guided by policy preferences as well as legal materials does not make them any less diviners. It only changes the pool into which they

The goddess Themis divines the judgment of the oracle at Delphi.

gaze. G. Edward White put it this way: "The judge, in this view, was simply a mouthpiece for the rational policy choices of his time. Although he no longer 'found' the law, he made law by 'finding' public policy."[24] But the judgment would still invoke the law, as by claiming that the correct policy decision was what the legislature intended. At the least the judge will assert that the decision was sufficiently grounded in law to allow policy to play a role.

Like other divination systems, law provides answers to difficult questions, and its pronouncements are often ambiguous, "delphic," as it were. Its wisdom is accessible through those diviners granted access to it by virtue of their training and completion of certain rites. Consultation is characterized by the use of special language and ritual, which are "techniques for suppressing the subjecthood of the judge."[25] Law as oracle relieves the diviner of responsibility for the judgment. In most legal opinions the judge speaks as if the decision was compelled by the legal authorities cited, which is what the audience demands and expects.[26] "The issue is what does the law require, not what outcome will a decision maker favor."[27] We want the oracle's judgment, not that of the person who consults it.

How can we square this notion with the issuance of dissenting opinions by American appellate judges? Is that not proof of judicial "free will"? In a curious way the practice reaffirms the oracular status of law because the dissenter claims not that the majority was prejudiced or corrupt but that it misunderstood the law. This is not so different from the way the Azande resolve conflicting judgments of *benge*. They admit that a particular *benge* decision can be wrong, perhaps because of intervening witchcraft or improper performance of ritual, but this does not shake their faith in the poison oracle as a legitimate institution.

It may be objected that the judge who delivers the judgment of the law is not like the diviner because the judge/law relationship is not mystical; law consultation does not directly invoke the supernatural. The rebuke makes apparent sense only because it wears cultural blinders. For us the oracle of the Azande (or of Delphi) is mystical; but it is not so for them. *Benge* is for the Azande simply a way of knowing the world. There is nothing "mystical" in the sense of requiring a suspension of disbelief. And so, in modern societies, the consultation of "law" is rational, and disbelief is not consciously suspended. It is rational in that it "tries to proceed upon the basis of general principles and to maintain consistency in the sense of avoiding contradictions within itself."[28] But law is not successful in its effort to maintain consistency. Viewed from outside the cultural system of which it is a part, law, with its impenetrability, its ambiguity, its ever changing responses, is as imagined and socially constructed as *benge*, even if it does not seem so to us. Its capacity to maintain the stance of rational consistency at the very moment it has departed from it is, as Stanley Fish has demonstrated, the "amazing trick" that keeps it in business.[29] Perhaps because on some level it is aware of this quality, law has not given up its grounding in the realm of the sacred. Its physical space, its codes of dress, its manner of speaking, and its reliance on oaths are all attempts to ennoble its operation with an other-worldliness. This is a theme developed more fully in the chapter on ritual.

The power of oracles is revealed only when they are consulted; and law is therefore asked to speak authoritatively only in the context of disputing. Whatever hold law has on our imagination is dependent on disputes. In this sense, disputes create law. Law is then itself constitutive of still later disputes because it creates new claims or new bases on which to resist old claims.

Law, or in my metaphor, the law oracle, guides the judge who must determine which norms apply to the dispute. Since the argument of this chapter is that modern disputing reflects culture, it is not enough for me to suggest that law has oracular power and is a culturally contingent way of legitimating the decisional process. I need to show the connection between law and the modern cultures that produce and use it. I need not engage at a high level of abstraction in the ongoing debates about the nature of law. I must only distinguish what is called law in modern societies from the order of custom that has prevailed in traditional, typically small-scale societies. For this purpose modern law is defined as an institutionalized and complex set of norms intended to guide behavior through sanctions and incentives. As we have already observed, the rules that comprise the law are elaborate, so as to be obscure to all but trained technicians. As H. L. A. Hart described it, modern law (or state law, as he referred to it) includes more than norms that govern behavior. It includes as well three kinds of "secondary rules": rules of recognition that allow the judge to decide which norm is relevant, rules of change that allow appropriate authorities to legitimately introduce new norms, and rules of adjudication that govern the means by which the norms are applied.[30] The complexity inherent in such a system—recognized by Hart[31]—necessitates a set of values and institutions that will produce and support the persons equipped to administer it. Once we accept these features as common to modern legal systems and as distinguishing such law from custom, the connection between law and the culture of the societies in which we find it is inescapable. The peculiar form of dispute processing we call a legal system "mirrors" society without regard to the specific content of the norms applied by a particular legal regime. That legal functionaries, admittedly differentiated from broader society in certain respects, pursue their own interests and apply their own beliefs in constructing the details of the legal institutions in a modern state cannot be the source of a serious objection to my point.[32] Those functionaries could not exist in their current form or function as they do but for the fundamental attributes of modern culture. As we shall see, the relationship is reflexive in that the complexities of dispute processes support and encourage the development of those features.

Evidence as Oracle

If law is the oracle from which the judge divines norms of decision, where does she turn when the facts are contested? The legitimacy of the system depends as much on the finding of facts as on norms. Where is our "fact" *benge*? In the American case, we are initially drawn to the jury, which replaced trial by ordeal, oaths, and combat, and which thus "took the place of the oracle, and indeed it resembles it inasmuch as it does not indicate rational grounds for its decision."[33] The jurors find the facts, much as the judge finds and pronounces the law: after passively receiving the evidence presented to them, the jurors retire for their private, collective deliberations. When they pronounce a verdict it need not be explained or justified by them. The parties may not even inquire into the method by which the decision was reached. On the other hand, there are limits on the powers of the jurors that also limit validity of the metaphor. For one, not all civil cases are tried to a jury—the case may be tried to the judge because the parties have not asked for a jury trial, or because the proceeding does not fall within the category of cases in which jury trials are available. For another, the jury verdict is not necessarily determinative. If the judge finds that there is "no legally sufficient evidentiary basis [on which] a reasonable jury" could have reached the verdict actually returned, the verdict may be set aside and judgment granted to the other party, a process authorized as "judgment as a matter of law."[34] Even if the verdict is supported by legally sufficient evidence, the judge may set it aside and order a new trial before a new jury because the verdict is, in the judge's view, "against the weight of the evidence."[35]

The civil jury, it must also be observed, is almost as idiosyncratically American as *benge* is Azande. Outside of a narrow range of cases in England, it is found only in the United States and some provinces of Australia and Canada.[36] It cannot be used as an exemplar of modern disputing.

It is "the evidence" that constitutes the pool into which the diviner (juror or judge) must gaze to find the truth. With respect to the facts, it seems, the judge and jury jointly serve as diviners of the truth, but the evidence is its source. In common with the judges (and with Azande diviners) jurors are ritually purified by their oath taking, by the examination of them to eliminate the biased, by restrictions on the kind of evidence that may be presented to them and the form it must take, and by the judge's carefully prescribed admonitions as to their behavior. The latter, most importantly, instructs them to decide the case according to the evidence presented.

To speak of "evidence" as though it were an oracle even remotely comparable to the *benge* of the Azande seems absurd largely because evidence examination does not directly enlist mystical or supernatural forces. It is part of a formally rational system of fact finding in that it is dependent on sensory information. Although the kinds of information accepted as evidence vary among legal regimes, all modern systems rely on a specially filtered category of documents and statements through which an agreed-upon version of the past is constructed. I connect evidence to the oracular to emphasize the cultural connectedness of fact-finding methodology and the unknowability of a contested past. Every society does the best it can with the tools at hand. For the inhabitants of modernity it is plausible to believe that the best method of determining the truth about a contested past is through human agency, shaped by whatever rules of evidence apply. This belief is a product of culture and history.[37] In its application of reason to observable facts, it approximates the methods of science that have dominated Western thought since the end of the Middle Ages. It is not coincidental that the church banned the use of ordeal in trials at the Lateran Council of the twelfth century; it was a recognition of a new paradigm of the truth-finding process. As Damaška observes, "momentous" transformations in Western disputing took place in the late Middle Ages.

> Spearheaded by the Church of Rome, Continental jurisdictions responded to the erosion of magical proof in radical fashion, rejecting medieval fact-finding institutions in favor of a system of judicially conducted witness examinations. England, on the other hand, responded by adapting ancient institutions of its own to changed circumstances: the voice of God, as revealed in trials by ordeal, was eventually replaced by the voice of the countryside, as expressed in the verdict of the Angevin jury.[38]

Although the jury retains some aspects of that role, subsequent centuries have seen it restricted to a passive recipient of the evidence allowed by a judge.

To acknowledge that evidentiary fact finding is a product of the general a-mystical metaphysics of Western culture is to be only partially inconsistent with the claim that it is oracular. Yet the fact examination that takes place in courts is very different from that of the laboratory. Indeed, it must be, for the courts cannot use controlled experiments to determine past events. In every modern legal system, however, the rationality of the process is undermined by rules that inhibit accuracy in search of other values. The American reliance on the lay jury is the most prominent example, but all systems restrict the kinds of information that may reach the fact finder in ways that undermine the reliability of the product. The refusal of the civil law system to allow extensive pretrial discovery probably creates as much factual uncertainty in its courts as the jury does in the American. It is law that determines whether a statement or document will be received as evidence, and it is law that determines the weight given to a particular kind of evidence. Legal processes tell the decider how the real must be sorted from the false. This is what it means to say that law is a "distinctive way of imagining the real."[39]

Rules that restrict the reliability of the process are not the only weakness of our fact finding. Jerome Frank's observations of its weakness more than half a century ago still stand up. Eyewitness testimony, on which all systems rely to a greater or lesser extent, is subject to error at many points, including the witness's initial observation, later recollection of the event, and recounting of it months or years later. The recounting is itself troubled by restrictions on what the witness may say and how it may be said, not to mention by lawyers' badgering and "tricks." It depends too on the fact finders' power to listen to, make sense of, and apply to the task at hand all of the conflicting versions to which they are exposed.[40] Our collective knowledge of the deepest weaknesses in our fact finding is largely suppressed in favor of an ideology of belief. In fact, the system is celebrated precisely for its supposed accuracy, as when Wigmore pronounced cross-examination the greatest engine for the discovery of truth ever devised. We suspend our disbelief for the same reasons as do the Azande. We need a way of resolving disputes and we have managed to create a way of doing so that meets the needs and expectations of our culture.[41] We have created "oracles" in which we can believe, but the belief ironically depends in part on denying their oracular qualities. Our devotion to the rational demands this denial as a price of legitimating our dispute-ways.

And yet there is another side to this coin. It is the skepticism that is also an aspect of modernity and that to some extent defines the "postmodern." The contingency, the relativity, the subjectivity of belief cannot be completely suppressed even in a process devoted to the discovery of a truth on which much of value depends, for these doubts are another ingredient of the cultural mix. Available truth- and law-finding techniques are fallible and on one level seen to be so. How is this reflected in the operation of the modern dispute-resolution system? It may underlie the well-documented fact that in the vast majority of lawsuits brought in the United States judgment is never pronounced, for they are resolved by settlement. Resolution by agreement has many causes, but among them is the uncertainty of outcome that counsels half-a-loaf acceptance.

Doubt about the accuracy and hence the validity of modern dispute-resolution oracles helps explain the rise of alternative dispute-resolution techniques, particularly mediation, that promote agreement as preferable to judgment. This movement "gathers pace . . . in the mid-1970s" and "begins to take institutional shape . . . from the early 1980s."[42] A "failing faith" in the adjudicatory process[43] cannot be only coincidentally related to the postmodern skepticism of true belief. We should not be surprised if challenges to a culture's way of knowing impact on its way of dealing with dispute. I will explore the cultural origins of ADR in chapter 6.

It is nonetheless the trial, with its invocation of law and evidence, that is the paradigm for reaching judgment when agreement fails. I return to that paradigm to explore the ways in which, like the Zande *benge* consultation, it in turn influences or constructs the culture in which it lies.

Law and Evidence as "Constructive"

These pillars of modern systems of disputing affect the societies in which they are so important, beyond providing tools to govern conduct. Their influence may be seen at many points in American culture. One obvious influence is of a piece with the differentiation I have earlier described. Technical sophistication, an extensive body of knowledge, and the bureaucracy that supports it are indispensable attributes of a modern legal system. The set of institutions and trained persons that is necessary to the operation of a modern legal system in turn requires an underpinning of other social arrangements, such as law schools, and values, such as the importance of abstract reasoning, that are inescapably cultural. Law, without which the modern state could not exist, then produces social facts that are identified with life in that state. Law's effects are not confined to the differentiated sphere of legal functionaries, at least not if theories that trace economic development to the "rule of law" are accurate. It is not too much to claim that the complex and enormously productive modern economic system is itself traceable to law. Some specialists in economic development argue that it is virtually impossible without the rule of law.

The ripple spreads. The emphasis on a kind of linear logic that is so much a part of legal reasoning reinforces similar mental processes in other areas of life. Law's judgment is obtained largely through logical reasoning, despite Holmes's famous dictum to the contrary. The task of the judge in the overwhelming proportion of cases is to determine whether rule a, b, or n applies to the dispute at hand. Which line of cases is this case most like? What analogies are most compelling? Consequently, the diviners of the law oracle must successfully pass through an extensive initiation. Successful passage requires abilities not shared in equal degree by all members of society, namely, analytic reasoning, comprehension of texts, facile writing, memory, and other skills. These values are not arbitrary once law comes into being. They reflect the nature of the legal process and therefore the tasks that judges and lawyers are called upon to perform, such as synthesizing complex and voluminous materials. Since financial rewards and social prestige follow success in the arena of disputing through law, its demands help create an elite social group—part of the meritocracy with which we are familiar. Those who come to prominence in the arena naturally extol the worth of their own virtues. The nature of the task comes more and more to reflect them. In this way, the disputing system "naturally" rewards and reinforces social stratification. It is this dynamic that in part explains the attack of traditionally underrepresented minority groups on barriers to the legal profession that reflect the purported manifestation of such skills.

American dispute-ways have been closely intertwined with the role of gender in social life, as they have elsewhere. It is a mark of patriarchy that women were excluded from authoritative roles in the formal dispute resolution process. Recall that *benge*, which was the most trusted truth-finding instrument for the Azande, was also an institution through which female sexuality was controlled. Only *benge* could render unassailable judgments of adultery, yet women were excluded from participating in *benge* consultation, whether it concerned adultery or any other dispute. In our terms, this exclusion was a badge of inferiority. Closer to home, women did not gain a decisional role in the American legal system until the twentieth century. Women had been excluded from jury service, from the judiciary, and even from many law schools.[44] The vast changes in the role of women in the American dispute-ways are symbolized by the presence of two women on the Supreme Court. This sea change no doubt reflects much broader changes in society attributable in large part to the feminist movement. At the same time, the ceding of legal authority to women has symbolic value that changes the way society understands the very nature of femininity. Between 1963 and 1993, for example, the percentage of women in American law schools rose from under 4 percent to over 40 percent[45] and today is at approximately 50 percent. As they in turn have achieved professional status and their own decisional authority, traditional attitudes that underlie patriarchy increasingly lose their hold. Because of the importance of linear logic in the American legal system, women's success in this realm undermines essentialist notions of female mentality.[46] So even apart from changes in the profession itself, increasing female decisional authority can be expected to change intrafamily relations and even the self-perception of girls coming of age in the society.

More generally, the concept of law's rule is central to the legitimacy of many—perhaps all—modern states. The United States is prototypical. Crucial to the American self-construction is the idea that "ours is a government of laws and not of men." This credo is deeply embedded in American legal and popular culture. It is not too much to say that it is the bedrock principle on which rests the entire system. It is the embrace of the rule of law that allows Americans to accept the exercise of political authority even when the results are personally disagreeable. The courts' "contribution to the legitimacy of government" has been called their "most profound social function."[47] They could not perform this function if their decisions were seen to be the product of the individual judge, unconstrained. The centrality of law is expressed in a variety of iconic American documents, such as the Declaration of Independence (which is largely a cataloguing of the lawlessness of George III), the Constitution (especially the Bill of Rights), and the Gettysburg Address, among many others. As Paul Kahn put it so well, "From an internal perspective—i.e., from the perspective of the citizen—the historical unity of this community is, in large part, the rule of law as practice and belief."[48] Law protects us from raw political power, even as it creates political institutions. When it subjects us to them it is seen as right, "legitimate," that it do so. It is this belief in law's legitimacy that accounts for the general quotidian acceptance of established order. Critical Legal Studies scholars argue that this legitimacy is fraudulent, that it rests on a false claim of legal neutrality, when in fact law was and is developed precisely to undermine the existing unjust society. The critique acknowledges the immense constructive power of law as an institution and concept.

Law contributes to the individual's conception of self as an "individual." Law performs this function through its embrace of a concept of the person as expressed in values such as the dignity of the individual, the jural equality of all members of the polity, and protection from arbitrary action by elites. Legal rights, not honor, protect us from perfidy and anger. Although it takes an extreme form in the United States, law's rights emphasis resonates throughout the modern world.[49] It contributes to the belief in an individual as a human being with "an opportunity to choose a style of life . . . developing a unique personality, a self unlike all other selves."[50] Some social critics, recognizing the constructive power of law, have attacked the emphasis on rights precisely because it enhances individualist consciousness at the expense of a more communitarian spirit. The centrality of the modern legal system, a culturally specific tool for addressing disputes, is obvious, wherever one comes out in this debate.

The process through which law is administered models many of our micro-interactions: "Let's hear both sides of the story," we tell our squabbling children. "I am owed an explanation," we tell an offending supervisor, or colleague, or even a lover.[51] We examine the evidence, the sensory "facts," to make up our minds. We invoke them to convince our opponent.

The training of citizens to see themselves as ruled by law "extends throughout the culture, including all those practices and institutions in which belief is formed and reinforced . . . [W]e need to study the prominent rites of transformation through which an ideal image of the subject under law is constructed: moments of public, self-definition of the legal subject."[52] Whatever the many ways that law and evidence help us organize our social and internal lives, recall that dispute is its life breath. No moment is more prominent or important than the ceremony of social transformation that marks our dispute-ways.

As in other cultures, modern disputing processes and institutions reflect the deeply held normative values, authority relations, and metaphysics of the society that produced them. At the same time, by privileging a particular way of knowing in the resolution of disputes, it helps maintain those ingredients of social life. At a minimum, the repetitive resort to a particular mode of inquiry by a respected individual acting in public on momentous occasions will reinforce the validity of their methodology; and in revolutionary times new procedures will facilitate a transformation. In chapter 8 I will elaborate on the social and psychological processes through which dispute institutions influence the broader culture.

4

American "Exceptionalism" in Civil Litigation

In the previous chapter we saw how the main features of "modern" disputing—the reliance on law as a source of norms, and evidence as a source of fact—were culturally situated. The cultural connection with disputing practices is obvious when we juxtapose modern systems with those of cultures that rely on supernatural methods of obtaining truth, such as oracles or ordeal. But in this chapter I will make a more difficult point—that variations in disputing practices even *among* modern states are traceable to underlying cultural differences. I will connect the considerable differences between disputing in the United States and in other modern systems to differences in culture and will thus show the cultural origins of those procedural variations. Once again we will see how limited is the notion that dispute-ways are solely the product of legal specialists, somehow insulated from the culture in which they operate.

The relationship between a nation's culture and its court procedures has intrigued procedural comparatists and social theorists for decades[1] but remains controversial.[2] Notwithstanding at least some acceptance of such a relationship, its relevance to the pragmatic work of procedural reform has not been appreciated. The importance of the issue has grown as the globalization of business and personal activity has created incentives to transplant or harmonize procedures across borders.[3] This trend is reflected, for example, in the American Law Institute/UNIDROIT project on transnational rules of civil procedure, for which a distinguished group of international scholars has drafted a set of principles and rules that combine features of different major legal systems. They are intended to "offer a system of fair procedures for litigants involved in litigation arising from transnational commercial transactions."[4] Other efforts to harmonize adjudication systems include the proposed Hague Convention on the Enforcement of Judgments,[5] and the litigation rules proposed for the nations of the European Union.[6]

Any proposal to borrow procedures from another society should prompt a cultural inquiry. One reason for this is instrumental: Will the borrowed approach work in a new social setting? Processes that are successful in one place will fail in a society where they offend deeply held values. A more important—if knottier—issue is raised by the reflexivity of culture and disputing: How will the new procedures impact on the society that adopts them?[7] What broader cultural changes—for good or ill—may be set in motion? Underlying these concerns are the subsidiary claims that (1) the formal procedures of dispute resolution found in any culture reflect and express its metaphysics and its values, an argument I have already made and will expand upon in this chapter; and (2) dispute procedures, because they are so public, dramatic, and repetitive, are in turn one of the processes (rituals, if you will) by which social values and understandings are communicated and are therefore critical to the ongoing job of transmitting and maintaining culture. I take up this point in chapter 8. Now I want to show how official procedures in specific modern states reflect the fundamental values, sensibilities, and beliefs (the "culture") of the collectivity that employs them. I will use the United States as the case in point because the well documented idiosyncrasies of American culture are reflected in the rules that govern civil litigation.[8]

I maintain that the many differences between litigation in the United States and elsewhere are not wholly, or even predominantly, a matter of "legal culture" as opposed to a more general culture, i.e., a set of values and understandings generally shared by the population that constitutes the nation.[9] I do not deny that the professional corps of lawyers and judges that operate the legal system have far more influence over its practices than the layman, nor do I deny that they create practices that reflect their interests and professional enculturation ("habitus," in Bourdieu's term). Ordinary citizens seldom experience the civil justice system directly and popular accounts of even famous cases are unlikely to focus much on the details of procedure. People are inclined to defer to the experts out of respect for their knowledge and status. This leaves legal specialists a good deal of room within which to shape court procedures. Professional self-interest and parochialism is, however, cabined by broad parameters imposed by the people subject to and served by the system, at least in any democratic state. Further, the professionals are themselves a product of the same culture and cannot readily escape its basic values and beliefs. If this chapter is successful, it will help the reader appreciate the limits of elite control by demonstrating the depth of the disputing-culture connection even in modern states. Although the architects of a sophisticated dispute-resolution system enjoy some ambit in designing it, the culture in which they function limits the range of options available to them and inclines them in certain directions when choices are presented.[10]

In his meticulous exploration of the distinctly adversarial features of the American legal system, Robert A. Kagan avoids direct reliance on culture. Preferring institutional and political explanations, he maintains,

> American adversarial legalism, therefore, can be viewed as arising from a fundamental tension between two powerful elements: first, a *political culture* (or set of popular political attitudes) that expects and demands comprehensive governmental protections from serious harm, injustice, and environmental dangers—and hence a powerful, activist government— and, second, a set of *governmental structures* that reflect mistrust of concentrated power and hence that limit and fragment political and governmental authority.
>
> Adversarial legalism helps resolve the tension. In a "weak," structurally fragmented state, lawsuits and courts provide "nonpolitical," nonstatist mechanisms through which individuals can demand high standards of justice from government.[11]

Kagan does not appear to reject cultural explanations and in that sense his approach and mine are inconsistent only in that I trace the institutional qualities he identifies, and which are explored below in this chapter, to a more general and deeply held set of values.

A description of the link between the culture of any collectivity and its way of disputing requires some description of those dimensions. I will first identify the salient features of American culture. I will then show how cultural predilections dominant in the United States are reflected in four important aspects of civil procedure that are peculiarly American: the civil jury; party-dominated pretrial fact investigation; the relatively passive trial judge; and party-chosen expert witnesses.

American Culture

Generalizations about the culture of any nation-state are problematic. The United States presents particular difficulties. Large in area and population, diverse ethnically, racially, and regionally, it may seem a risky subject for exegesis. I plough ahead nonetheless, supported by several considerations. One, there is a respectable body of empirical and other work in cultural studies that takes nation-states as the objects of examination and finds that national boundaries do matter.[12] Two, the reader will keep in mind that any claim about culture does not assume invariance within a population. It is a generalization, with all the utility and limits that the word connotes. As such, it can describe the attitudes and preferences shared most of the time by most of the population. Third, whether because of its long geographic isolation or the peculiarities of its history, the United States has been identified quite strongly with particular cultural attributes.

American exceptionalism has been observed and remarked upon at least since Alexis de Tocqueville published his observations of American society over 150 years ago. "Tocqueville is the first to refer to the United States as exceptional—that is, qualitatively different from all other countries."[13] The qualities that struck Tocqueville, such as individualism, egalitarianism, and a readiness to pursue disputes through litigation have persisted over time and been observed by other students of society. A leading modern proponent of the "America as unique" thesis is Seymour Martin Lipset, who recently developed his argument in *American Exceptionalism: A Double-Edged Sword*.[14] Because Lipset so successfully captures this standard description of American culture, I will center my discussion of it around his work, but the reader should keep in mind that Lipset is only one of many scholars who have identified similar American characteristics.[15] This is not to deny the heterogeneity of American society. Subcultures of region, race, ethnicity, and gender may exhibit the cultural traits observed as generalities more or less robustly. Differences among particular individuals will also be found within this or any other culture; a generalization about a collectivity is not a prediction about any single person in it. These caveats notwithstanding, there remains persuasive evidence that an American culture exists.[16] Indeed, the successful assimilation of generations of immigrants into a system of belief and symbol is itself a large part of the American story. Americans share an "emphasis on fair procedure, having one's day in court, and broad acceptance of the myths and rituals associated with the legal and political process."[17]

Lipset describes the societal and institutional manifestations of distinctive American values, reports modern survey results that show the continued strength of those values, and provides an account of their sources. While the exceptionalism thesis has not gone unchallenged,[18] and while "[s]keptics may remain unconvinced," Lipset's argument "certainly is compelling and is backed up by a very wide range of survey data and examples."[19] As we shall see when I later turn to an account of its system of civil procedure in comparative perspective, American disputing provides another instance of its exceptionalism and is consistent with Lipset's description.

According to Lipset, America's "ideology can be described in five words: liberty, egalitarianism, individualism, populism, and laissez-faire."[20] As Lipset notes, egalitarianism in the United States "involves equality of opportunity and respect, not of result or condition."[21] Thus, American egalitarianism is consistent with individualism and laissez-faire.[22] "The emphasis in the American value system, in the American creed, has been on the individual."[23] It is the emphasis on the individual as a person equal in status to all other citizens that produces populism, rights orientation, and laissez-faire (or antistatist) attitudes.

Lipset argues that these values explain many distinctive features of American society, including some that are far from admirable, such as high crime rates. More ambiguous effects are those seen in the nature of governmental institutions and practices. He notes the relative weakness of the American central government and its modest involvement in the economy. The Constitution, he observes, "established a divided form of government . . . and reflected a deliberate decision by the country's founders to create a weak and internally conflicted political system."[24] Almost all other modern states have parliamentary systems under which the majority party exercises power that is virtually plenary. As Mirjan Damaška said about American government, "Most astonishing to a foreign eye is the continuing fragmentation and decentralization of authority."[25]

Individualism, liberty, and laissez-faire values also explain the comparatively low levels of American economic and social regulation (except for the strangely coexisting puritanism that has led to strict legal regulation of sex-related conduct and drug use).[26] The comparatively meager American governmental support of welfare-state projects, be they cultural activities or universal health care, is also typically laissez-faire and individualist and is reflected even in constitutional incongruity. Many European constitutions contain provisions that impose welfare-state obligations on the government, but the American one does not.[27] According to Mary Ann Glendon, these constitutional differences "are legal manifestations of divergent, and deeply rooted, cultural attitudes toward the state and its functions. . . . [C]ontinental Europeans today, whether of the right or the left, are much more likely than Americans to assume that governments have affirmative duties."[28] At the same time, the Bill of Rights incorporates the American ideal of a citizen as possessing the right to be "let alone" by government. As Jerold Auerbach has it, "Law has absorbed and strengthened the competitive, acquisitive values associated with American individualism and capitalism."[29] If this is true of law in general it is even more true of dispute procedures in particular.

Since America's values strongly influence its governmental arrangements, it would be odd if these same values did not also contribute to an American exceptionalism in disputing. "[D]ominant ideas about the role of government inform views on the purpose of justice, and the latter are relevant to the choice of many procedural arrangements. Because only some forms of justice fit specific purposes, only certain forms can be justified in terms of prevailing ideology."[30] Although Lipset does not discuss procedural details, he does connect values and the operation of the legal system. He notes, for example, that in the United States, judges are either elected or appointed by elected officials, whereas in most other countries judges are specially trained professional civil servants who enter the position through a competition and generally serve in the judiciary for their entire career.[31] The American approach (election or political appointment) is one of many manifestations of the populism that has its roots in the egalitarian ideal.

American individualism and egalitarianism, Lipset also claims, underly the emphasis on a rights-based legal discourse, and help explain high rates of litigation in comparison to other industrialized nations.[32] "In America . . . 'egalitarianism is based on the notion of equal rights of free-standing, rights-*asserting* individuals.'"[33] But this apparent attachment to courts suggests, perhaps, a weakness in the claim of American antistatism. Courts are governmental institutions, so a resort to courts to resolve disputes unavoidably invokes governmental authority. This suggests a "fundamental paradox [because while] the use of law . . . empowers the individual . . . [O]n the other hand it increases his dependence on the institutions of the state."[34] Indeed, as I explain in chapter 6 when I look at the rise of alternative dispute resolution in the late twentieth century, there is some reason to believe that an increasing suspicion of government in the United States has led to a privatization of disputing. Still, going to court in furtherance of one's interests is not wholly incompatible with laissez-faire attitudes. Compared with most governmental institutions, courts are responsive to individualized pursuit of personal claims. Consider that private litigation is for the most part controlled by the litigants, who provide its impetus, its direction, and, often, its ultimate resolution through settlement. Unlike other branches of government, courts neither meddle nor rescue unless called upon to do so, and then paradigmatically act only for the litigants before them. And, as we shall see in more detail, the values of a distinctly American culture underlie the forms and structures of adjudication in America and have contributed to an American exceptionalism in disputing that parallels that of its culture. Perhaps this "fit" makes the resort to litigation less forbidding than it might otherwise be.

American Adjudication in Comparative Context

In this section I will show the many ways in which formal, official, American adjudication reflects the culture in which it functions. To follow the argument the reader must also follow me through the thicket of formal procedural rules, both American and other. I therefore begin with some helpful map drawing.

The modern legal systems of the world are often categorized as belonging to either the "common law" or the "civil law" family.[35] The United States is a member of the common law group, like other nations that trace their legal, linguistic, cultural, and political roots to England. Most other countries fall into the civil law category; they trace their history to Rome and to Roman law. The character of a particular nation's system may be the result of prior colonialism (as with North and South America) or conscious adaptation from foreign systems (as with Japan and China). Although there are significant differences in the historical development and styles of legal reasoning between the common and civil law systems, most important for present purposes are the variations in the rules governing adjudication. (It will be helpful to bear in mind that by a quirk of legal terminology, the word "civil" has dual and sometimes confusing meanings. "Civil" procedure is the process used for typical private disputes such as tort or contract and is distinguished from the procedures used to prosecute crimes. The word "civil" has an entirely different meaning when used to differentiate between the "common law" and "civil law" families. In the latter situation, "civil" refers, as already noted, to the legal system originating in Continental Europe.) That the United States is in the common law camp suggests a cultural connection between its culture and its processes, for the reasons that follow.

Differences in the rules of civil procedure between the common law and civil law groups have led to the controversial labeling of these procedural systems as "adversarial" or "inquisitorial." Some commentators refer to procedure in common law (Anglo-American) countries as "adversarial" because this system vests a good deal of control over the proceedings in the parties and their attorneys, which allows for a sharper clash between adversaries in the courtroom. Under the civil law system, on the other hand, the presiding judge has in many ways a great deal more authority, even including responsibility for questioning witnesses—this prompts the "inquisitorial" label. Many observers emphasize this differential allocation of authority between the parties and the judge as the defining distinction between common law and civil law procedural systems. The literature also, however, sharply criticizes this terminology, in part because the categories are imperfect at best—differences between nations within a category can be considerable. Thus, although the United States and England share the "common law" heritage and have "adversarial" procedural systems, one finds many differences between them, as I will show.

Moreover, the words "adversarial" and "inquisitorial" are mischievous in this context in another way: many Continental lawyers deny, sometimes vehemently, that their system is "inquisitorial" in any pejorative sense. They reject any implication that their processes are similar to the infamous Inquisition of the medieval church.[36] And it is certainly the case that the dispute-resolution procedures of all modern states share such deep principles as the right to be heard and to present evidence, the right to representation by counsel, and the right to an impartial adjudicator.

Nonetheless, the labels serve as useful shorthand, so long as we recall their limitations. Mirjan Damaška, who criticizes too simplistic a reliance on this division, agrees that "the core meaning of the opposition remains reasonably certain. The adversarial mode of proceeding takes its shape from a contest or a dispute: it unfolds as an engagement of two adversaries before a relatively passive decision maker whose principal duty is to reach a verdict. The non-adversarial mode is structured as an official inquiry."[37]

The inclusion of the United States in the adversarial group suggests the connection of its procedures to liberty, individualism, egalitarianism, populism, and antistatism—in sum, to the "competitive individualism" so highly valued in America.[38] As I will now take pains to show, the American dispute process—like its values—is exceptional even when measured against its siblings in the common law family. So let me turn to specific procedural rules that reflect these values.

Some Features of American Procedural Exceptionalism

My claim that there is a culturally constituted American "procedural exceptionalism" turns primarily on four of its features. They are (1) the civil jury; (2) litigant-controlled pretrial investigation; (3) the relatively passive role of the judge at the trial or hearing; and (4) the power of the litigants to choose their own experts to testify on technical matters.

1. The Civil Jury

"The jury is one of America's venerated institutions."[39] It has achieved and maintained an importance in American trials that is unparalleled elsewhere in the world. While the jury retains a lively role in criminal cases in most English-speaking nations (but not in the rest of the world),[40] it is striking that in no other nation does the jury play the role in civil litigation that it has in the United States. The right to a jury trial in civil cases in the United States is historic and iconic: it was added to the federal Constitution by the Seventh Amendment as part of the Bill of Rights ratified in 1791.[41] In 1938, when the Federal Rules of Civil Procedure were promulgated, its drafters thought it desirable to include a provision reminding readers that "[t]he right of trial by jury as declared by the Seventh Amendment to the Constitution or as given by a statute of the United States shall be preserved to the parties inviolate."[42] The Seventh Amendment and the Federal Rules apply only in federal litigation, but the right to a jury in civil cases is found in state constitutions as well. Typical is the provision of the New York Constitution: as adopted in 1777, it provides that the jury trial right "shall remain inviolate forever."[43]

Contrariwise, juries have never been used in civil cases in any of the countries that follow Continental procedure.[44] The power of the jury in the American tradition has been called "[t]ruly astonishing in the Continental view."[45] And England, where it originated, has abandoned the civil jury in all but a very few kinds of cases.[46] Other common law jurisdictions have followed suit.[47]

It is not hard to see how the historic American attachment to the jury is bottomed on core American values. It is quintessentially an egalitarian, populist, antistatist institution. It is "strongly egalitarian"[48] because it gives lay people with no special expertise a fact-finding power superior to that of the judge, despite all of his or her training and experience. Although it is true that the judge presiding at the trial may overrule a jury verdict and grant judgment "as a matter of law" against the party favored by the jury, this power is circumscribed. It can be exercised only if "there is no legally sufficient evidentiary basis for a reasonable jury to find for that party. . . ."[49] The jury is also egalitarian in that jury service is a duty of citizenship imposed on all. Furthermore, every juror has an equal vote regardless of education or social status. Indeed, it is strikingly an institution that plunges people, willy-nilly, into an arena in which communication and cooperation across distinctions of race, ethnicity, and wealth are mandatory.

The civil jury is populist, "an avatar of democratic participation in government,"[50] because it allows the people to rule directly.[51] A jury in a products liability case, for example, can determine that a particular product was designed or manufactured in an unreasonably unsafe manner and award damages against the manufacturer. There is a resulting incentive to change the product to avoid future lawsuits. The jury is thus setting safety standards that might otherwise be governed by statute or regulation. Jurors are well aware of their power to act as a "mini-legislature" in such cases. According to a recent article in the journal of the American Bar Association, "Like no time before, the 12 people seated in the jury box regularly demonstrate an increasing willingness—even a clamoring—to force basic American institutions, such as government, business and even private social organizations, to change the way they operate."[52] The article lists a number of cases in which juries awarded large verdicts in order to "send a message" to the defendant and its industry that certain behavior was not acceptable.

Although the civil jury is of course an organ of government, it nonetheless has an antistatist quality because it allows the people to decide matters differently than the other institutions of government might wish. Both in the civil and criminal spheres, this is no mere theoretical matter, as demonstrated by the debate over jury nullification, the sometimes claimed power of the jury to ignore the law as a way of "doing justice," which continues to the present.[53]

The jury's connection to American individualism is not as obvious as its egalitarian and populist qualities. In some sense it is anti-individualist because the jury operates as a collectivity. Moreover, people do not volunteer to serve as jurors but are compelled by force of law to do so. On the other hand, the role of the individual is apparent because the number of persons on each jury is small, twelve or less, and as few as six in some jurisdictions. Where, as is traditional, a verdict depends on unanimity, a single hold-out can abort the trial and effectively command a new one.[54] The individualist value that underlies the civil jury is better appreciated when we take the viewpoint of the litigants. For the individual citizen whose liberty or property is in its hands, the jury may be seen as a protector of rights in a way that the judge, an official of the state, is not.

It is striking and revealing that the egalitarian American ethos and the jury as a device for protecting individual rights developed together. Reverence of the jury in American life emerged at the same time as the American people took on their exceptionalist values. It was in the period around the time of the American Revolution that the jury became "so deeply embedded in American democratic ethos."[55] By the mid-eighteenth century, as Americans increasingly distinguished themselves as a separate people, juries had become a means of resisting the Crown's control over colonial affairs, and British attempts to circumscribe jury powers were seen as a further cause of grievance.[56] Tales of courageous jurors who stood up to tyrannical English government have ever since been an important part of the American self-image: "Most American history books hail the trial of [John Peter] Zenger for seditious libel in 1735 as the leading case for freedom of the press and as an example of a victor of the people over an aristocracy."[57] Zenger, the publisher of a New York newspaper, was prosecuted because of the journal's sharp criticism of the appointed English governor of the colony. Andrew Hamilton, who defended Zenger, wove together a substantive claim—the right of the people to criticize their government— and the procedural point that the jurors had the power to protect that right. "Jurymen are to see with their own eyes, to hear with their own ears, and to make use of their own consciences and understandings in judging of the lives, liberties or estates of their fellow subjects."[58]

Although the hagiography surrounding the Zenger case has arguably idealized the participants, the case "did help to establish unique American views on the jury and its place between law and those governed."[59] The jury's continuing role in the construction of the American ethos was observed by Jefferson, who called jury service the "school by which [the] people learn the exercise of civic duties as well as rights,"[60] and by Tocqueville: "The jury, and more especially the civil jury, . . . is the soundest preparation for free institutions. . . ."[61] Modern scholars contend that the

jury continues to serve as an influence on the moral reasoning of participants.[62] An example of the jury/values connection is provided by the ac-
quittal of John DeLorean, the entrepreneur who claimed that police en-
trapment had led to the charge of drug dealing. One juror explained the
verdict: "There is a message here. . . . It's that our citizens will not let our
government go too far. . . . It was like the book *Nineteen Eighty-Four*. They
set one trap after another for DeLorean."[63]

It is telling that the right to vote and the jury trial have been called the
two institutions of American democracy that it "seems simply unthinkable
to criticize."[64] Both are icons of American values. Despite the hyperbole,
no institution is beyond criticism, and the attachment to the jury has not
been shared by all Americans. Jerome Frank, a prominent federal judge,
was famously scathing in his skepticism of the jurors' ability to judge
facts.[65] Like the culture in which it is found, the role of the jury has not
been static, but contested and dynamic. Its powers have ebbed and flowed
in response to changes in social life.[66] In one sense the story has been one
of diminution, both in the frequency in which civil cases are tried to a jury
and in its power in respect to the judge.[67] In another, as we have seen, jurors are still willing and even eager to exercise their broad powers when
they have a chance.[68] Whether the American civil jury will, like its English
ancestor, atrophy to irrelevance depends in large part on the continued vi-
ability of those ingredients of the collective American psyche that have
sustained it so far.[69] Surveys of attorneys, judges, and the general public
show that the civil jury continues to enjoy very wide support in the United
States.[70]

2. PARTY CONTROL OF EVIDENCE GATHERING: PRETRIAL DISCOVERY

Individualism, egalitarianism, laissez-faire, and antistatism are also evident in another disputing practice that is particularly robust in America
and not duplicated anywhere else in the powerful form it takes there: pretrial "discovery." This is the power that is granted to the adversarial parties
to control the investigation of facts prior to trial. Again, the contrast is in
sharpest relief when the United States is compared with Continental systems.

American rules of procedure authorize a bag full of devices with which
the litigants' attorneys may pursue evidence outside the courtroom and
yet be backed by the authority of the court in demanding the cooperation
of opponents and witnesses. Each party has the power to require an oppo-

nent and other potential witnesses to submit to oral questions under oath outside the presence of the judge (a deposition), to answer written questions under oath (interrogatories); to produce its files for inspection by the adversary (document discovery), and, where physical or mental condition is in issue, to submit to a medical examination by a physician of the demander's choosing.[71] As one British practitioner put it, "An American is incapable of handling a case without discovery and deposition. Discovery is his shower and deposition is his breakfast."[72] Other than setting a time limit for completion of the process, the judge will ordinarily get involved in it only if one of the parties requests a ruling on the propriety of a particular request or response. Nothing approaching this out-of-court fact discovery is permitted by civil law courts: "The weakness of Continental 'discovery' mechanisms is proverbial. . . ."[73]

It may be argued that the difference in discovery rules is best explained not by underlying cultural differences but by institutional differences in the nature of the fact-finding process. The concentrated trial familiar to Americans does not exist in countries using the civil law system. Instead, the "first instance proceeding," as they call the process of fact determination before the court of original jurisdiction, consists not of one continuous proceeding but of a series of appearances before the court by the litigants and their witnesses.[74] The role of the jury may in turn underlie this difference of process: a concentrated trial is virtually mandatory when lay people are required to take time out of their own work lives to collectively hear and decide a dispute, but is hardly necessary when the facts will be heard by a professional judge who will be at the court daily. As a practical matter there is thus less need for "pretrial" preparation in the Continental scheme because of the episodic approach to proof taking. The readiness by which hearings may be scheduled for future occasions obviates the concern that surprise evidence will "ambush" a party to the detriment of the truth-finding process: the surprised party will have an opportunity to present rebuttal evidence at a subsequent session. Pretrial discovery is, contrariwise, important to American litigation because a substantial delay in the trial to gather new evidence is inconvenient or, in a jury case, virtually impossible.

But there is far more to the issue than scheduling differences: the Continental jurists view discovery with repugnance not only because they find it unnecessary but also because they think it inappropriately intrusive for one private party to be able to rummage through the files of an adversary simply because they are involved in litigation.[75] In civil law countries compulsory production of evidence is viewed as more properly a governmental function and discovery is objectionable because it allows the litigants to exercise powers and functions that should be reserved for the court. In this view the formal questioning of witnesses, for example, should be done in court—not at a deposition in some lawyer's office. "Quite predictably, attempts by American attorneys to conduct depositions on the Continent are treated there as offensive to the prerogative of the state to administer justice and are now outlawed in several European countries."[76]

Moreover, the purely instrumental scheduling explanation is undercut because American discovery practice differs from that of other common law countries in which concentrated trials are still the norm. Like the jury, the American approach to pretrial party-dominated discovery has roots in English practice.[77] The power to compel discovery was first developed by the English court of chancery.[78] But here again, it was in America that it was transformed into an "exceptional" practice—a set of mandatory investigation tools available to private litigants not duplicated in the United Kingdom or elsewhere. As a result, "American discovery practice sometimes appears 'exorbitant'—'fishing expeditions'—to lawyers in other common law countries."[79] The key difference between American and English practice is thus in the breadth of the demands that can be made on the adversary party. In England pretrial requests for documents have been limited to those concerning facts alleged by the pleadings more strictly than in the United States. According to Jack Jacob, "if there are in truth other facts which would show or prove he has a well-founded claim or defense, he is not entitled to discover them to frame or reframe his case on their basis."[80] The recent reforms of English procedure have limited document discovery still further.[81] Moreover, the American style discovery deposition is not available in England, where the out-of-court taking of oral testimony is available only by court order and is largely limited to situations in which a witness will be unable to attend the trial.[82]

Party-controlled pretrial fact gathering, American style, promotes the values I have identified as central to American culture. It is egalitarian because it "levels the playing field" in that discovery gives an economically weaker party the means to make a deserving case that would otherwise be hidden in the files of a wrongdoer. A common example is a products liability action by an injured user who can find proof of improper cost cutting in the manufacturer's own files. The egalitarianism expressed by discovery is of the American kind in that it offers equality of opportunity, not of result: party-driven discovery also means "party-paid" fact gathering. The process can be very expensive, because it is labor intensive and much of the labor is performed by attorneys. Although the American contingent-fee rules, which allow lawyers to advance the expenses of litigation, moderate this effect somewhat, there are still litigants of limited means who will be subjected to oppressive discovery demands by the opposition. This is less likely to be encountered in countries where the judge takes on much of the investigative labor. The rules of extrajudicial discovery are thus egalitarian in the sense identified by Lipset; they are not dependent on a government agency to pick up the cost and thus even out the disparity of resources. As in other areas of life, American egalitarianism blinks at disparity of resources and focuses on formal equality of opportunity.

Party-controlled discovery also expresses the populism, laissez-faire, and antistatism so pronounced in American culture. For Americans there is nothing wrong with a procedural device that allows citizens and their attorneys to exercise substantial litigation powers without obtaining judicial permission.

The relationship between discovery and individualism is arguably more complex. On the one hand, discovery reflects competitive individualism in that it allows each attorney to create and pursue a discovery program tailored by an assessment of the best way to proceed in the particular case, without much judicial supervision and only loosely cabined by the rules of procedure. From the point of view of the party (or witness) from whom discovery is sought, however, the intrusions of the prying opponent can feel like a violation of self. Consider on this score that a plaintiff claiming damages for physical injury may be subjected to a medical examination conducted by a physician chosen by the defendant.[83] The plaintiff must accede, or suffer a dismissal of the case. (Of course, the decision whether to sue in the first place is up to the plaintiff, who can protect against such an intrusion by refraining.) Moreover, the very idea that one must assist an adversary with case preparation rests uneasily in an adversary system that otherwise exemplifies "the 'each person for himself' mentality."[84]

It seems that the discovery system accords more weight to the individualism encapsulated in a party's power to obtain discovery than to that of the resisting party. Of course, in most cases the parties will at various times be in both of these positions, so the system both advances and restricts their personal freedom of action. One explanation of the outcome lies in the recognition that in an economic system built on competitive individualism there are powerful if lamentable incentives to cut corners and shade the truth to advance one's cause in litigation as elsewhere. The rules of the game must be designed to reveal such chicanery, and party-directed discovery is an important part of that design. Interestingly, this justification of the discovery devices assumes that the self-interest of the parties will lead to a truth-finding process that will promote social welfare in general. In this deep sense, the reliance of the rules of discovery on personal initiative is consistent with the American ideology of individualism.

3. The Role of the Judge

A significant difference between American litigation and that used in the civil law countries concerns the role of the judge: the American judge remains largely passive during the trial except when called upon by the parties to make a ruling, whereas the Continental judge plays a much more active role at the hearing.[85] At the American trial it is the attorneys, not the judge, who decide what evidence is needed, and it is the attorneys who present the evidence through the examination of witnesses and presentation of documents. A fictional American lawyer once caught the predominant view admirably when he offered the opinion that an American judge "is sworn to sit down, shut up, and listen."[86] (English judges have traditionally shared the American inclination to let the parties run the show, but it appears that the reforms of the English Rules of Civil Procedure in 1999 will lead to a more controlling and active posture.[87])

John Langbein accordingly claims that the "'grand discriminant'" between the American and Continental legal cultures is "adversarial versus judicial responsibility for gathering and presenting the facts."[88] Germany, which is in this regard typical of many civil law countries, can accordingly serve as a basis for examining the point in more detail.[89] The German judge has a statutory "duty" to clarify issues,[90] which involves the court deeply in the development of the case.

> Always examining the case as it progresses with understanding of the probably applicable norms, the court puts questions intended to mark out areas of agreement and disagreement, to elucidate allegations and proof offers and the meaning of matters elicited in proof-takings. . . . The court leads the parties by suggestion to strengthen their respective positions, to improve upon, change, and amplify their allegations and proof offers and to take other steps. It may recommend that the parties take specific measures in the litigation.[91]

The court, acting on recommendations from the parties, decides whether to hear a particular witness[92] and the order in which the witnesses will be heard and documents presented.[93]

"One of the most notable differences" between the process at the common law trial and the oral hearing in the civil law process "is the method of interrogating witnesses."[94] In the civil law countries it is the judge who alone or predominantly questions the witnesses. Even if the attorneys are allowed to put some questions, and even if, as in Italy, the questions are actually drafted by the attorneys and submitted to the judge for use, vigorous cross-examination by counsel is a rarity.[95]

Like other Continentals the German judge has a control over the actual interrogation of the witnesses that is particularly telling:

> In the ordinary case there is relatively little questioning by the lawyers or parties. What there is of it is generally conducted direct rather than through the court. . . . For the lawyer to examine at length after the court seemingly has exhausted the witness is to imply that the court has not done a satisfactory job—a risky stratagem.[96]

Thus, what is arguably the most important role of the American trial lawyer—examination and cross-examination of witnesses—is almost entirely ceded to the Continental judge.[97]

To be sure, recent changes in American litigation rules have tended to enhance the role of the court in relation to the parties: the whole concept of "managerial judging" centers on the power and responsibility of the judge to move the case along, to promote settlement if possible, and at the very least to get to the trial promptly.[98] One could argue that in this respect there has been a convergence between the systems, a point made forcefully by Adrian Zuckerman.[99] But the critical difference, "the grand discriminant," remains constant. It is still the American lawyer—not the court—that is responsible for gathering and presenting the proof. It is still the American lawyer—not the court—who is responsible for choosing the witnesses and for questioning and cross-examining them.[100] Notwithstanding the ritualized elevation of the American judge—through honors of place, dress, and forms of address—it is the parties, through their lawyers, who dominate the trial itself. Note, too, how the differential in the American and Continental judicial powers parallels the differential in their powers to find the facts—the weaker American judge must often cede power to the lay jury.

The case for common law/civil law convergence is much stronger when we use England as the exemplar of the common law and look at the new English Civil Procedure Rules. Neil Andrews, describing "extensive . . . modification of the adversarial principle,"[101] notes that the new rules not only include greater pretrial managerial powers but also grant the British judge more power to control the trial, to prescribe the evidence required, and to prescribe the means of its presentation. Judicial questioning of witnesses will apparently become much more frequent.[102] This is not the case in the United States.

When we look at the power of the judge to find and determine the law applicable to the case, we find that the American judge has a power that is at the heart of the common law system—the power to make law by developing and applying new legal norms. The common law tradition allows the judge to help shape the law through legal decisions that become part of the corpus of *stare decisis*. The civil law counterpart, considered to be merely "*la bouche de la loi*," is theoretically limited to applying the law as set forth by the legislator. She cannot "make" law. Is the greater role of the Continental judge at trial trivialized because in law-making the American judge is the more powerful? In my view, this difference does not contradict my central point that in the courtroom, as between the judge and the litigants, the former is more powerful on the Continent. The point is also buttressed by the Continental judge's authority to take note of and apply law that has not been argued by the parties, whereas the U.S. counterpart is in general limited to deciding the case on the basis of law actually relied upon by the parties.[103] Importantly, the American judges' common law powers come at the expense of the legislature, and are best seen as an example of that fragmentation of political power, noted by Seymour Martin Lipset and discussed above, that is wholly consistent with the antistatist, antihierarchical ideal.

Once again, the procedural practice (here, the role of the judge at trial) rather obviously accords with deep cultural proclivities. Michele Taruffo argues that the allocation of authority between the parties, on one hand, or the court, on the other, reflects such cultural factors as

[t]he trust in individual self help rather than in the State as a provider of legal protection; the trust in lawyers rather than judges, or vice-versa; different conceptions of the relationships among private individuals and between individuals and the public authority; different conceptions of whether and how rights should be protected and enforced and so forth.[104]

The American case provides ample support for this view: the individualist, egalitarian, laissez-faire American would not abide the degree of judicial domination of its trial that is perfectly acceptable in parts of the world where those values are less important.

4. THE ROLE OF EXPERTS

Compared with the rest of the world, the American use of expert testimony in the judicial process is also exceptional. In American courts an expert normally appears as a witness "for" one of the parties. The expert, who has been chosen by, prepared by, and paid by the party, will be offered as a witness only if that party thinks the testimony will help him. Dueling experts thus offer conflicting opinions and it is the job of the jury to decide which version of reality is more persuasive. True, the applicable rule allows the judge to modify this practice: rule 706 of the Federal Rules of Evidence specifically permits the court to appoint a neutral expert beholden to the court alone. But this power is seldom invoked, and party-selected experts dominate the American courtroom when technical issues are in dispute.[105] In the civil law courtroom, matters are very different. The normal practice is for the judge to choose a neutral expert who will ordinarily be the only expert to testify on the issue. There is no "duel."

As John Langbein has put it,

> The European jurist who visits the United States and becomes acquainted with our civil procedure typically expresses amazement at our witness practice. His amazement turns to something bordering on disbelief when he discovers that we extend the sphere of partisan control to the selection and preparation of experts. In the Continental tradition experts are selected and commissioned by the court, although with great attention to safeguarding party interests.[106]

The American approach has been compared unfavorably to that prevailing in the civil law countries.[107] A major concern is the incentive of party-chosen experts to tailor testimony to please the hand that feeds them. But for present purposes let us put aside an instrumental view of the matter and note the cultural aspects. I think that poor reception of the neutral expert in the United States is in large part due to the deep-seated values already identified. The public display of dueling experts in opposition to the anointing of a single authority signifies both discomfort with political hierarchy and—even more important—a cultural preference for a pluralism that extends even to views about how to determine reality. A society that requires court experts to submit their divergent opinions to the ultimate judgment of a lay person (whether judge or jury) is endorsing the idea that truth is elusive. Reality is understood to be uncertain. It is contingent: the subject of debate. The public spectacle of experts who disagree is not, in this sense, an embarrassing weakness but an expression, here in a metaphorical way, of the familiar American suspicion of authority and of orthodoxy. Given the multicultural heterogeneity of American society, it is not surprising and may well be necessary. It resonates with the pluralism so evident in the American Constitution.

Much as the reliance on the verdict of an oracle in Zande trials reflects and reinforces reality dominated by magic, the dueling American experts reflect and reinforce an understanding of reality as democratic, that is to say, created and understood by each person according to his own lights, each suspended in a web of his own spinning. It is consistent with the antistatist, egalitarian, and populist values that we have seen to underlie the jury, party-conducted pretrial discovery, and the party-dominated courtroom.

American Exceptionalism and "The Faces of Justice"

The themes explored so far are also captured when we examine American disputing in the context of the nuanced and very influential schema of the world's procedural systems developed by Mirjan Damaška.[108] Although not easy to summarize, Damaška's work is pursued here because it offers a highly regarded account of procedure that explores the links to broader political features and supports the argument of this chapter.

In *The Faces of Justice and State Authority: A Comparative Approach to the Legal Process*, Damaška offers an alternative to the much criticized adversarial/inquisitorial categorization of procedural systems. He posits two dimensions along which relevant types can be plotted. One concerns the "structure of government", i.e., its "character" of authority. The second "concerns the legitimate function of government—more specifically, views on the purpose to be served by the administration of justice."[109] He argues that a nation's procedures will reflect these fundamental attitudes about government and that this dynamic is observable, albeit imperfectly, in the real world.[110] Damaška does not undertake a country-by-country comparison of procedures, but he often distinguishes between Continental and Anglo-American systems (sometimes separating the "Anglo" from the

"American") and he refers to particular nations as exemplars. He shows how particular processes flow from basic predilections about the form of governmental organizations, and that these vary with historical experiences of particular places. Damaška thus shares the view that the cultural grounding of modern disputing institutions is very deep. It is for this reason that, as he notes, what appears "normal" in one system can seem "grotesque" to another.[111]

DAMAŠKA'S "CHARACTER OF AUTHORITY": HIERARCHICAL VS. COORDINATE

To describe the character of procedural authority, Damaška distinguishes the hierarchical ideal from the coordinate ideal.[112] According to Damaška, the structure of the authority (hierarchical or coordinate) informs the process used by that authority.[113] The hierarchical ideal "essentially corresponds to conceptions of classical bureaucracy. It is characterized by a professional corps of officials, organized into a hierarchy which makes decisions according to technical standards."[114] This ideal embraces a "strong sense of order and a desire for uniformity"[115] through the use of specialists or professionals motivated by an "ethic of cooperation" reinforced by supervision from above,[116] and by rule-bound decision making.[117] "Private procedural enterprise is thus almost an oxymoron in the lexicon of hierarchical authority."[118]

In contrast, the coordinate ideal is "defined by a body of nonprofessional decision makers, organized into a single level of authority which makes decisions by applying undifferentiated . . . standards."[119] The machinery of justice is "amorphous."[120] Authority is vested in amateurs, "roughly equal lay officials" who may be assisted by professionals, but whose decision making will suffer from a lack of consistency. "A cast of mind that aspires to the ideal of coordination must be prepared to tolerate inconsistencies—and a considerable degree of uncertainty—more readily than one attached to the hierarchical vision of authority."[121] Thus, responsibility for proof taking and other preparation is not vested in officials but in the parties and their representatives.[122]

Hierarchical authority, with its emphasis on "the authority of rules," would be antithetical to American values of populism, individualism, and egalitarianism, whereas the coordinate authority model would be commensurate with them. As we would predict given what we know about American culture, Damaška finds that "the American machinery of justice . . . continues to be more deeply permeated by features embodied in the coordinate ideal than are the judicial administrations of any other industrial state in the West."[123] The Continental model, contrariwise, has long had[124] and still retains "a very pronounced bureaucratic hierarchical flavor, especially when observed from the common-law perspective."[125]

Damaška's "Dispositions of Government": Reactive vs. Activist.

The second determinant of process according to Damaška is the "disposition" of the government to be "reactive" or "activist."[126] Governments inclined to the reactive approach simply provide a framework within which citizens pursue their own goals. The administration of justice is typically engaged in conflict solving. Not so the activist state. It embraces a particular model of the good life and strives to achieve it. Policy implementation is an important goal of adjudication in such a state. As a result, "The legal process of a truly activist state is a process organized around the central idea of an official inquiry and is devoted to the implementation of state policy."[127] Extreme examples include the former Soviet Union and Mao's China.[128]

Damaška argues that the different dispositions of states (reactive or activist) impact on the way procedural authority is organized and implemented. He notes that "[p]rocedural arrangements follow ideas about the purpose of government" and express "fundamental tenets of a political doctrine," as where the "ideal of personal autonomy" is transferred to the administration of justice in the reactive state.[129] Since the conflict-solving mode of procedure fits best with a laissez-faire state, it is hardly surprising that "[t]he American legal process allocates an unusually wide range of procedural action to the adverse parties, especially in trial preparation, creating opportunities for free procedural enterprise unparalleled in other countries."[130]

The Damaškan Synthesis

After exploring the separate procedural consequences of his two different sets of antipodes (hierarchical versus coordinate authority and the reactive state versus the activist state) Damaška offers some thoughts on how they combine. In his view there is no necessity that an activist state should embrace only hierarchical arrangements of government or that the reactive state should only be comfortable with coordinate arrangements. Space prevents consideration here of the subtleties of these interactions. What is interesting for my purposes is the degree to which American processes conspicuously replicate features expected when the reactive state embraces the coordinate model.[131] Even when American government adopts some "activist" purposes (as in the aftermath of the New Deal or in the embrace of "public interest" litigation), "it is one of the most striking facets of the American brand of state activism that the state apparatus continues to be permeated by features attributable to coordinate authority. These surviving features—especially in the machinery of justice—are more pronounced than in any other modern industrial state."[132] Damaška's great achievement was to create "a framework . . . within which to examine the legal process as it is rooted in attitudes toward state authority and influenced by the changing role of government."[133] While insisting that political factors "play a central role in accounting for the grand contours of procedural systems,"[134] he adds that a government's choice of procedural arrangements is limited by "existing inventories of moral and cultural experience, the fabric of inherited beliefs, and similar considerations." We thus share an appreciation for the cultural connection of even modern-state disputing institutions. What I add to the Damaškan analysis of procedural forms is, first, a more detailed analysis of the American "case" in cultural context and, second, a more direct reliance on culture (i.e., deeply held values and beliefs) as the primary determining variable. Social preferences for coordinate arrangements and for a reactive state are not separate from the more general values of a society; they are in no small part its product: the place of American disputing in Damaška's matrices flows from the egalitarianism, individualism, laissez-faire, liberty, and populism identified in so many areas of America's social life.

Empirical Evidence Linking Procedural Values and Culture

At the outset of this chapter I offered empirical support for my claim that culture helps to explain the idiosyncrasies of American civil procedure. I cited numerous studies showing that American values differ from those of other countries. The second part of the argument—that American procedures reflect those values—has been the subject of the interpretive and analytic approach just concluded. It is more difficult to support empirically. There are, however, some helpful investigations of the connection between culture and disputing that have been conducted by scholars working in the field of social psychology of procedure.[135] These scholars use the tools of empirical psychology to explore the process preferences of persons engaged in disputes. To the extent that they have tested process values cross-culturally, their work has obvious relevance to the present chapter.

While it is by no means uniform, much of the evidence emerging from studies of the social psychology of procedure tends to support the claim that there is an important cultural determinant underlying personal evaluations of procedural fairness. In 1988 Lind and Tyler reviewed the relevant literature and found that there was "growing evidence that, contrary to some of the earlier procedural justice findings, there are cultural differences in some procedural justice effects."[136] The most robust cross-cultural differences observed in the psychology of procedure literature emerge when the cultures studied are those generally understood to be more diverse from each other across the board: studies comparing the preferences of Chinese and American subjects showed the former more likely to prefer mediation to adversary disputing, as well as more likely to prefer inquisitorial processes to adversarial.[137]

Studies using subjects from Western countries reveal closer accord in procedural preference judgments. One study used American, French, German, and British respondents and asked them to rank preferences among, *inter alia*, pure adversarial and pure inquisitorial processes. All showed a marked preference for the former.[138] That the Continental subjects were less attracted to judge-dominated models than a cultural explanation might have predicted may be explained by the nature of the procedural models the respondents were given. The "pure" inquisitorial process was represented by "adjudication with the third party acting as both investigator and judge," whereas the "pure" adversarial process involved "a binding third-party decision procedure with two investigators selected by the disputants and responsible for developing and presenting the case of the disputant."[139] Observe that the adversarial model constructed by the experimenters is similar in its bold strokes to the actual adjudicatory processes of *all* of the nations involved. The inquisitorial model presented is, on the contrary, so extreme that it differs so sharply from anything any of the respondents would have encountered that it is no wonder that they tended to reject it. It would have been objectionable in the cultures of all the respondents. In my opinion the study therefore cannot reveal different levels of preference for systems that were relatively more or less adversarial or inquisitorial.

What does seem constant across cultures is that the fairness of procedures is important to people, although they may find differences in the processes they believe contribute to fairness.[140] Indeed, one of the most important and robust findings of the psychological investigation of procedural preferences is that people value fairness independently of the results of a particular outcome. Satisfaction with a process is enhanced if it is perceived as fair, regardless of whether the individual won or lost.[141] Moreover, the investigators account for these results by a group value model that "assumes that many procedural justice values and beliefs are instilled through socialization."[142] Thus, "[l]ike other such attitudes, for example, liberalism, racism or authoritarianism, procedural preferences might be acquired during the childhood socialization process and come to acquire their own affective base."[143]

Lind and Tyler offer the results of numerous studies in support of the socialization effect. One type of evidence is the finding that "people who are involved in a procedure that they think is fair do not change their assessment of that procedure's fairness if it produces a poor or unfair outcome."[144] This adherence to a procedural form suggests that ideas of fairness are deeply held. Second, there are studies "finding that judgments about the meaning of procedural justice are consistent across members of the same culture."[145]

This understanding of the origin of personal preferences for dispute-resolution processes is, of course, consistent with the argument put forth in this chapter because it would explain why Americans would prefer procedures that differ from those preferred elsewhere.

I leave this chapter satisfied that the connection between American values and its formal dispute-resolution system is clear. Because my concern has been with the cultural meaning of these formal and ideal processes, it is irrelevant that most disputes are not brought to courts or that the vast majority of lawsuits are settled and so never involve a jury or an expert witness. In chapter 6 I will examine the cultural origins of some less formal means of dispute processing used in the United States: "alternative dispute resolution," or "ADR."

Also yet to be reached is a fuller discussion of the reflexive nature of culture and disputing. Is it all one way—from values to processes? Or, as I contend in chapter 8, is there a reciprocal flow as well?

5

The Discretionary Power of the
Judge in Cultural Context

In this chapter I examine a problematic development in American disputing: the striking rise of discretionary judicial power over legal procedures that began early in the twentieth century and continues into the twenty-first. This phenomenon constitutes a case study of the interplay of cultural and professional influences on American procedure. I will argue that the concept of judicial discretion, which is classically distinguished from the concept of law, is in part a rhetorical construct rather than a decisional process of a special kind. The key background fact, however, is the marked and unquestionable growth of judicial procedural authority that is defined as "discretion." To be sure, the range of judicial discretion has increased at many points in the American legal system[1] as well as in the systems of other nations,[2] and there may well be commonalities in the causes of this movement that cross subject-matter and even national boundaries. Here I seek to account for its twentieth-century expansion only in the particular realm of American civil procedure, where it has been looked upon with special favor.

The most significant moment in the movement from rules to discretion was the adoption of the Federal Rules of Civil Procedure in 1938. An authoritative treatise on the rules tells us, "It is not an exaggeration to say that the keystone to the effective functioning of the federal rules is the discretion given to the trial court. The rules grant considerable power to the judge and in many contexts only provide general guidelines as to the manner in which it should be exercised."[3] One scholar lists thirty-six examples of Federal Rules of Civil Procedure "that lend themselves to, or specifically provide for, judicial discretion."[4] Illustratively, they include the scheduling of the trial and pretrial matters,[5] regulation of the scope of pretrial disclosure,[6] relief from the consequences of error,[7] the admissibility of many types of evidence,[8] and even the question whether the court should hear the case at all or dismiss it for prosecution in another forum.[9]

I offer an account of this expansion that turns on changes both in the wider culture and in legal culture. These began in the first decades of the twentieth century and have continued to be influential to the present day. I argue that the legal specialists in charge of procedural rule making were influenced by shifting public attitudes and values *and* by needs internal to the profession. The two twentieth-century developments on which I focus are, first, the triumph of "businesslike" efficiency and flexibility as a widely shared institutional value and, second, the loss of faith in the rule of law and the professional anxiety attendant on this loss. This chapter therefore serves as another piece of my argument against the notion that "legal culture" is the exclusive preserve of the professional elite. Without losing sight of the dynamics internal to the profession, I will show that even a highly technical doctrine, probably understood only by lawyers, is nonetheless deeply connected to, and influenced by, the social and symbolic worlds they inhabit.

There is a copious literature on the role of discretion in legal systems generally, but as far as I can determine, its twentieth-century explosion has not been studied as a cultural phenomenon.[10] The cultural study depends on the observation of behavior and the beliefs that underlie it. "Inquiry must begin with a thick description of the legal event as it appears to a subject already prepared to recognize the authority of law."[11] Before developing the cultural perspective, I will therefore engage in some hopefully not-too-thick description of the doctrinal elements of discretion—the "legal event"—and will note some peculiarities of its place in the U.S. law of procedure.

Discretion and Its Problematic Relation to the Rule of Law

That judges sometimes exercise a kind of decisional authority, called discretion, which differs from and is more expansive than their power to find and apply law has long been familiar in the common law world. Discretion is the power to choose among a range of options.[12] The breadth of that range varies according to the instance of discretion. As with all legal doctrines, a general statement of the concept of discretion only begins to describe its boundaries and actual function. It is well recognized that the degree of authority conveyed by a grant of discretion is variable and context specific.[13] Discretion at its most robust means the power to make decisions unrestricted by legal standards and unreviewable by higher authority. This robust version of discretion is seldom encountered in American law. Perhaps the only true examples of discretion unrestricted by law are those in which the highest court of a jurisdiction has been vested by a legislature with discretionary authority over some matter. Most prominently, when the Supreme Court decides to grant or withhold review of a decision, it exercises unreviewable and totally discretionary authority. Some states, such as New York, have given a similar power to their highest court. Perhaps uncomfortable with this departure from law, the courts often purport to impose standards on themselves.[14]

Yet for all its apparent familiarity, the notion that American judges have "discretion" or "discretionary authority" over some kinds of issues has always rested uneasily in a legal system that purports to embody a "rule of law."[15] Discretion is particularistic; law's rule requires overarching commands that bind all judges deciding like cases. As Lon Fuller put it, law is "the enterprise of subjecting human conduct to the governance of rules."[16] In short, "discretion" and "rule of law" are antithetical.[17]

The growth of judicial discretion over procedural matters thus begs explanation. Particularly is this so in the American context because of the importance of law to the American polity. In a system that prides itself on its adherence to a "rule" of law, how can discretion be not only tolerated but embraced? The primary responses offered in defense of discretionary authority in a legal system can be summarized as necessity, on one hand, and limitation, on the other. That is, discretion is necessary if the system is to function, and is acceptable as long as properly circumscribed. I will now describe these defenses in more detail and will argue that, far from providing a satisfactory account of the concept, they show that discretion is a construct whose separation from law requires a cultural account.

Kenneth Culp Davis, a leading commentator on discretion, thought that discretionary authority was an essential aspect of governing and of the judicial process in particular. For Davis it is in fact an inevitable component of it: "Rules without discretion cannot fully take into account the need for tailoring results to unique facts and circumstances of particular cases. . . . Every system of administration of justice has always had a large measure of discretionary power."[18] For this reason, Davis criticized what he called the "extravagant version of the rule of law [which] declares that . . . legal rights may be finally determined only through application of previously established rules."[19]

Davis thought that this "extravagant" version of the rule of law was not only impractical but also an inaccurate account of the American legal system. To prove its falsehood he offered seven examples of the exercise of discretion that contradict the claim that anything like the extravagant version characterizes American law. His third and fourth examples illustrate how, for Davis, discretion is embedded in the rule of law itself. As they are important to my argument, I will set them out:

(3) The Supreme Court of the United States overrules a batch of constitutional precedents. The only relevant "rules" are directly opposed to what the court decides.

(4) A common-law court decides a case of first impression. No statute governs, and no precedent is applicable. Broad principles that bear on the problem pull both ways.[20]

These examples are startling in that neither court would, I am quite sure, accept the claim that its action was discretionary. Each would say, I suspect, that it was applying the law, even if it had to rely on the most general of principles to find the law.[21] But since Davis defines discretion broadly to mean the power to choose among a range of options[22] he is, in a sense, correct to say that the courts in the examples given had such power; they were not subject to reversal by a higher authority. Still, that power is not ordinarily characterized as discretionary. "The most popular conceptions of law allow no room for judicial discretion within the rule of law."[23] Moreover, most judges, even of supreme courts, do not see themselves as free of legal constraint, even in hard cases. As a realist, Davis focused on what he thought the courts are actually doing, not on what they say or think they are doing. For Davis, courts resolving hard legal issues are exercising the same general kind of authority as an administrative agency that, acting under a statute that specifies no standards, grants one airline an overseas route in preference to another applicant.[24] Although everyone would agree that the agency is exercising discretion, our allegiance to the rule of law blanches at the judicial example.

But by observing that discretion is embedded in and therefore conflated with law's rule, Davis invites us to ask, "Why, in the society observed, is a similar kind of decision making called law in one context and discretion in another?" We can agree with Keith Hawkins: "Thinking about the relationships of rules and discretion draws attention to tensions, ironies and contradictions."[25]

A second source of discretion's legitimation within the rule of law is the bounds that law itself draws. It is said that judicial discretion has "wide latitude" but that the judge's decision may be reversed if she goes beyond the accepted parameters. Reversal is justified because the discretion has been "abused." An abuse of discretion is sometimes said to create an issue of "law." Thus, even an appellate court that has no jurisdiction to review the exercise of discretion is by this sleight of hand seized with power to review the claimed abuse.[26] Most instances of discretionary authority in American procedure are the limited type; the ambit of permissible action is defined by the abuse-of-discretion standard. Descriptions of discretionary authority are bound up with statements of limitation.

Consider the statement quoted earlier from the treatise on civil procedure to the effect that the discretionary authority of the judge is the "keystone" of the Federal Rules of Civil Procedure. A few lines further on the same authors tell us, "However, the judge must exercise his discretion soundly and with restraint because a construction that ignores the plain wording of a rule or fails to view it as part of the total procedural system ultimately may prove to be as detrimental to the system as an arbitrary or rigid construction. . . ."[27] Similar qualifications are found when we examine the trial judge's discretionary authority over evidentiary matters. In discussing Rule 102 of the Federal Rules of Evidence,[28] the leading treatise tells us, "This flexible approach to applying the rules of evidence . . . implies a considerable grant of discretion to the trial judge."[29] But the authors quickly add,

> The large discretion in applying the federal rules of evidence afforded the trial judge by Rule 102 does not imply that the judge may do as he or she wishes. Any determination . . . must be in accord with the broad principles specified in Rule 102, which underlie the whole body of rules and our entire system of justice. . . .[30]

So Rule 102 is paradigmatically read simultaneously to give and to limit discretionary authority.

How meaningful is discretionary power of this limited kind? To what degree does it differ from the judge's power to determine law? This question is not easily answered because in so many instances American "law" consists not of specific rules but of "factors" to be "balanced." Our understanding of the role of discretion in the American legal system as a cultural system is enhanced when we focus on the similarities, rather than the differences, between the judicial application of that doctrine and that of law. The collapse of "discretion" and "law" into each other is striking.

To illustrate the point, I will compare the way in which the courts approach the "discretionary" doctrine of *forum non conveniens* (sometimes referred to as the doctrine of the "inconvenient forum") with their handling of the "law" of judicial jurisdiction over persons. This essay into the detail of procedural canon is an essential part of the thick description: although both doctrines restrict the plaintiff's choice of forum, they do so in different and supplementary ways. Personal jurisdiction involves a limitation provided by "law": in order to exercise adjudicatory power over the defendant in the particular case presented, a court must have been granted authority to do so by a statute. The statutory authority must not exceed the constitutional limitations found in the Due Process Clause of the Fourteenth Amendment of the Constitution. *Forum non conveniens*, however, is a discretionary doctrine that allows the court to dismiss an action—notwithstanding that it has jurisdiction—because the forum is in some way "inconvenient" for the defendant, the witnesses, or the court itself. An important practical difference between the doctrines is that if a court grants dismissal on *forum non conveniens* grounds, it may impose conditions on the defendant, such as to agree to accept the jurisdiction of another allegedly more convenient court elsewhere.

As opposed to the effect of the two sets of limitations, the process of decision making in the application of these doctrines is surprisingly similar, despite ritualistic distinctions between law and discretion. I will demonstrate the process similarities by comparing two decisions of the Supreme Court, one dealing with the discretionary doctrine of *forum non conveniens*, and the second dealing with the issues of law raised by a challenge to the exercise of jurisdiction.

The Supreme Court explicitly endorsed the *forum non conveniens* doctrine in the federal courts in *Gulf Oil Corp. v. Gilbert*.[31] The lawsuit grew out of an explosion that destroyed a warehouse in Virginia that belonged to Gilbert, the plaintiff. Although Gilbert was himself a Virginia resident, he brought the action in a federal district court in New York. Defendant Gulf Oil was unquestionably subject to jurisdiction in New York as it did business there and had appointed a local official as its agent for the service of process. Nonetheless, the trial court had dismissed the action on *forum non conveniens* grounds. After reviewing the various factors in some detail, the Supreme Court held that the District Court had properly exercised its discretion in dismissing the action so that it could be brought in Virginia.

"The doctrine" said the Court, "leaves much to the discretion of the court to which [the] plaintiff resorts. . . ."[32] It then went on to describe guidelines for the exercise of that discretion:

> An interest to be considered, and the one likely to be most pressed, is the private interest of the litigant. Important considerations are the relative ease of access to sources of proof; availability of compulsory process for attendance of unwilling, and the cost of obtaining attendance of willing, witnesses; possibility of view of premises, if view would be appropriate to the action; and all other practical problems that make trial of a case easy, expeditious and inexpensive. . . . The court will weigh relative advantages and obstacles to fair trial. It is often said that the plaintiff may not, by choice of an inconvenient forum, "vex," "harass," or "oppress" the defendant by inflicting upon him expense or trouble not necessary to his own right to pursue his remedy. But unless the balance is strongly in favor of the defendant, the plaintiff's choice of forum should rarely be disturbed.
>
> Factors of public interest also have place in applying the doctrine. Administrative difficulties follow for courts when litigation is piled up in congested centers instead of being handled at its origin. . . . There is a local interest in having localized controversies decided at home.[33]

The Court then went on to apply the listed factors to the case at hand and, as I have said, upheld the dismissal.

Now let's compare the Court's approach to *forum non conveniens* with the constitutional law governing personal jurisdiction. As noted, the exercise of jurisdiction over any person is limited by the defendant's rights under the Fourteenth Amendment to the Constitution. The Due Process Clause does not in explicit terms set forth any such rule, but the Court has reasoned that protection from suit in a distant court is an aspect of the right to a "meaningful opportunity to be heard" that is the essence of the due process guarantee. It is not "discretionary." The defendant has a constitutional *right* to be protected. In a series of cases over the past decades, the Court has defined the situations in which defendants could be sued outside their home state and has set forth some general principles that govern the inquiry. One of these, which is elaborated in the *Asahi* case, is that "[t]he strictures of the Due Process Clause forbid a state court to exercise personal jurisdiction over [a defendant] under circumstances that would offend 'traditional notions of fair play and substantial justice.'"[34] This broad proscription must obviously be more narrowly defined if litigants and lower courts can look to it for guidance. Rather than set forth any rules to that end, the Court instead described the "factors" that must be considered in applying the stricture:

> We have previously explained that the determination of the reasonableness of the exercise of jurisdiction in each case will depend on an evaluation of several factors. A court must consider the burden on the defendant, the interests of the forum State, and the plaintiff's interest in obtaining relief. It must also weigh in its determination "the interstate judicial system's interest in obtaining the most efficient resolution of controversies; and the shared interest of the several States in furthering fundamental substantive social policies."[35]

Similar formulations may be found in many other cases dealing with the issue. It is obvious enough that the factors considered in analyzing due process defenses to jurisdiction are hardly distinguishable from those relevant to *forum non conveniens* decisions. They involve fairness to the defendant but also consider the interests of the plaintiff, the forum state, and the effect of the locus on sound adjudication. An appellate court reviewing the decision of a trial court would face the same sorts of questions whether the issue presented went to one or the other of these standards. Did the lower court properly weigh the factors? In fact, this is exactly what we find. Whether and to what extent the fact that one is a matter of discretion and the other of law affects the mental processes of the reviewing court is impossible to tell if we ignore the labels.

Consider the Supreme Court's ruling in *Asahi*, the due process case quoted above. The Court held that California, the state in which the action had originated, could not assert jurisdiction over Asahi, a Japanese corporation that had manufactured a component that was alleged to have caused a motorcycle tire blow-out and accident. The Court said, "Considering the international context, the heavy burden on the alien defendant, and the slight interests of the plaintiff and the forum State, the exercise of personal jurisdiction by a California court over Asahi in this instance would be unreasonable and unfair."[36] Thus, the lower court was required to dismiss the action. It was not within its discretionary authority to hear it.

What if the issue had been *forum non conveniens*, rather than jurisdiction, and the reviewing court had thought that it was "unreasonable and unfair" to have the case tried in California? It is extremely unlikely that it would have gone on to say, "but since it is a matter of discretion, we will not disturb the result below." A revealing example is *Piper Aircraft Co. v. Reyno*, a suit that grew out of an airplane crash in Scotland and was pending in a federal district court in Pennsylvania, which had jurisdiction. The district judge, exercising his discretion, had granted the defendant's motion to dismiss the case on the grounds of *forum non conveniens*. The court of appeals reversed, finding an "abuse of discretion." The Supreme Court, disagreeing with the analysis of the factors there employed, reversed *that* court.[37]

I do not mean that there is no "within the system" difference between *forum non conveniens* and the limiting law of personal jurisdiction imposed by the Fourteenth Amendment. Indeed, speaking as a legal technician, I must note that it is only when jurisdiction is proper that a case can be dismissed because the forum is "inconvenient." Courts will not have discretion to reach the *forum non conveniens* issue unless they are satisfied that, as a matter of law, they have jurisdiction. What I do argue is that because the method of reasoning under each inquiry is not rule bound but open ended and impressionistic, law and discretion in this instance are operationally no different. From outside the system, the actual effect of calling an issue "discretionary" seems less important than its opposition to "law" would seem to imply. This makes it still more interesting to the student of dispute-ways.

To summarize, the two defenses that discretion offers to critics who invoke the rule of law against it are necessity (that discretion is necessarily embedded in a system of rules, willy-nilly) and limitation (that discretion is in fact cabined by law to prevent abuse). These defenses create an ironic mirror. Discretion and law come to resemble each other because of the now apparent similarity of decision making under discretion and under law. On closer examination we see discretion and law are distinguishable primarily in the label that the legal system accords to a particular instance of judicial decision making.[38] The irony here is not only that law and discretion are so much alike but that it is the defenders of discretionary authority—notably Davis—that make us see this by his conflation of the two.

One may oppose this story with a more orthodox account. The latter suggests that the distinction between law and discretion is not a fiction and that a judge exercising discretion really does have greater decisional freedom. Note, however, that if we accept this claim, we do not avoid the need for a cultural explanation: if discretion "really" is a separate realm, then it "really" is opposed to law, and we must nonetheless ask why its domain expanded so much by the middle of the century just ended and continues to do so.

The Cultural Component

Social practices often "make sense" when viewed from within the culture that creates and sustains them. The consultation of the *benge* oracle makes perfect sense to a Zande chief.[39] The gift of overwhelming amounts of food to an enemy makes perfect sense to the Massim.[40] But to an observer from outside the society, these practices appear bizarre and culture specific. A legal anthropologist from an exotic land would equally be struck by the anomalous nature of the doctrine of discretion, and might wonder whether it serves other symbolic or functional purposes that explain it. She might ask more specific questions: Why, if there is a surface conflict between the rule of law grant of discretion, has the latter been permitted to expand so much in American procedural law? The question is not answered but compounded if in fact law and discretion are claimed to be not distant cousins but twins. Why is discretion necessary as a separate category if discretionary authority is already embedded in law?

Rules or practices that appear anomalous in the context of the system in which they are found are intriguing. The way that an apparent anomaly is handled and explained by local practitioners can reveal complexities and conflicts within the culture. The concept of discretion is such an anomaly in the context of the American procedural system. The conflict between the rule of law and the freedom of discretion parallels a conflict between the American values of individualism (which is promoted by the flexibility of discretionary decision making) and egalitarianism (which is promoted by an even-handed application of law). So what nudged the American dispute system in the direction of flexibility? It was an expression of two broader developments. The first is the increasing status accorded to effective organizational functioning—businesslike efficiency—in the late nineteenth and early twentieth centuries. Second, the embrace of discretion was part of the legal regime's response to intellectual attacks that threatened its legitimacy: it was a paradoxical but successful effort to preserve the mythic status of the autonomy of law.

Discretion in the Service of Efficiency

My argument here rests on the view that as the nineteenth century ended a new technocratic and corporatist paradigm against which organizations would be measured emerged and triumphed. It valued output at the lowest cost possible. Its virtues were efficiency and flexibility. Adherence to traditional but inefficient practices was devalued. An organization that failed to adopt the "modern" values would face disparagement and marginalization. Despite whatever privilege or "insider" position they might have had, the architects of the judicial system (legislators, lawyers, academics, and judges) were certainly aware of the shifting values and internalized them sufficiently to inspire a new design for dispute resolution.

The expansion of the discretionary authority of the judge over procedural matters was an important ingredient of the development of twentieth-century procedure. Formalism, discretion's opposite, had been championed by David Dudley Field, the influential drafter of the 1848 New York code of civil procedure.[41] Field feared that elasticity in procedure would undermine the rule of law. "For Field, a carefully constructed procedure, with defined prescriptions and proscriptions, was needed to enforce the rights to be contained in the companion substantive code that he had envisioned."[42] Thus, although a triumph of the Field Code was its success in merging the law and equity courts, Field opted where possible for the procedural rules previously applicable to actions at law, as opposed to the more flexible equity rules.[43] The Field Code was influential and by 1890 it had been adopted in about half the states.[44]

A key event in the turn toward flexibility in American procedure was Roscoe Pound's famous speech to the American Bar Association in 1906,[45] "The Causes of Popular Dissatisfaction with the Administration of Justice."[46] It sounded a "basic theme [that] remained as a constant in the movement. Formal procedural rules were no longer appropriate. . . . Instead, procedure was to step aside and let the substance through. In short, judges were to have discretion to do what was right."[47] For Pound, "The most important and most constant cause of dissatisfaction with all law at all times is to be found in the necessarily mechanical operation of legal rules." He observed that a system with formal rules that required cases to be thrown out for technical reasons "is out of place in a modern business community." Pound sparked a professional introspection that eventually led to passage of the Rules Enabling Act in 1934 and the promulgation of the Federal Rules of Civil Procedure in 1938.[48] The Rules marked the triumph of equity—and hence discretion—in American procedure.[49] Field had sought to "bind judges with rules, while the Federal Rules expand[ed] judicial discretion."[50]

A change in legal process as significant as the move from the formalism of the Field Code to the flexibility of the Federal Rules undoubtedly has multiple causes,[51] but surely underlying the change in procedures was the new vision of the modern: the desirable institutional operation model was typified by the successful business. Organizations were to be managed rationally, according to scientific principles. Christine Harrington has documented the pervasive critique of the courts along these lines during the Progressive Era.[52] She quotes one judge, who lamented in 1917,

> In the past fifty years we have revolutionized our methods of the conduct of private business, and largely also the conduct of public business; our methods are more direct, exact, and to the point; they minimize the possibility of error, eliminate "lost motion" and cut "red tape." Yet to all this improvement in method our judicial procedure has paid substantially no heed.[53]

David Dudley Field and his later antiformalist critics invoked science in support of their visions of procedure—but they held different notions of the scientific.[54] For Field, law was a science that depended on a "system of rules and conformity to them. . . ."[55] For Charles Clark, a weighty proponent of flexibility in procedure, however, science was skeptical of rigid categories. "Balancing tests replaced attempts at categorization and definition."[56]

Wolf Heydebrand and Carroll Seron chronicle the influence of modernist efficiency-oriented values on the development of American procedural law and judicial organization.[57] They describe a decades-long process of a "technocratic rationalization of justice," with its emphasis on cost-effectiveness and productivity.[58] This model is impatient with rigid procedures at the same time that it demands streamlining and routinization. "[T]he new administrative ethos also sought to introduce a degree of flexibility in order to loosen the hold of formal procedures."[59]

Supporters of procedural liberalization invoked the early-twentieth-century admiration of the corporate model:

> There was an almost quaint attraction to being modern. The new judicial procedure was to be scientific, flexible, and simple. Commerce and busi-

ness believed in such simplicity. Businessmen got things done by cutting through technicality, and by not letting rigid, antiquated rules get in their way. Procedure should have been equally straightforward.[60]

Heydebrand and Seron argue that the triumph of the technocratic approach is traceable in part to a squeeze on judicial resources resulting from a rising caseload combined with a relative reduction in financial support for the judiciary.[61] They also note the morphing of the state during the New Deal into a provider of social services on a scale that created unprecedented budgetary demands.[62] Because increased taxation is resisted, "there is further pressure . . . to transfer business methods from the private to the public sector and to introduce labor-saving technology and other measures of efficiency, budget control, and cost effectiveness to public and governmental organizations."[63] Judith Resnik has also argued that criticism of judicial inefficiency led to increasingly more managerial techniques.[64]

But pressure on the ability of the courts to function adequately need not have inexorably led to an expansion of discretionary authority. A range of responses to the increased demands for judicial services was possible, including toleration of greater delays, a large increase in personnel, or an increase in the cost of access to the courts.[65] From the standpoint of cultural analysis we should ask why the course adopted, the turn to discretion as part of a technocratic, efficiency-oriented "business" solution, was chosen. That it seems to us now to be quite reasonable and perhaps the only "logical" course may reveal only that we, too, are viewing the matter from within the web of the same culture that produced this outcome. The cultural explanation points to a connection between apparently technical legal doctrine and widely shared values, beliefs, and symbols. The shift from formalism to pragmatism would, I believe, have occurred after 1900 even in the absence of the ecological pressures on the judiciary. It is telling that when Roscoe Pound launched his attack on formalism in 1906 the caseload of the federal courts was actually falling.[66] It is not accidental that Pound's call was heeded by 1938 during the acme of the New Deal's empowerment of administrative agencies. Discretionary authority was at the heart of their functioning. A prominent proponent of this development, James Landis, argued that the officials who ran them needed flexibility and wide discretion, just like the business managers to which he compared them.[67] In short, efficiency, flexibility, and therefore discretion were "in the air." No less than those of other organizations and institutions, the guardians of the courts wanted to create a system that would be efficient and be seen to be so. Discretion was a necessary element of that vision because it enabled the relevant manager—the judge—to manage.

The change in the image desired by and for courts is also illustrated by developments in the architecture of the courthouse in the past century. Beginning in the eighteenth century and continuing into the twentieth, American court buildings made a conscious reference to icons from other domains. One variation imitates the classical Greek temple. The Supreme Court of the United States, although in fact a rather late but familiar example, is striking in this regard, with its high, broad front staircase and its massive pillars.[68] The ancient Athenians were much admired in eighteenth- and nineteenth-century America for their brilliance in many fields, including democratic government. By associating themselves with the buildings of the Greeks, American courts exude a sense of both ancient permanence and governmental wisdom, important claims to authority both. This style is found in large and small cities across the country.[69] Where, as in smaller towns and villages, the Greek temple was not invoked, reference was often made to the Protestant-style church or meeting house, thus implicitly claiming the authority of the divine. This was the old regime.

As the twentieth century progressed the image of the courthouse changed to reflect the new values. Many American courts constructed in midcentury and after evoke not the Greek temple but the corporate headquarters.[70] In this context visitors to New York may wish to compare the new, very functional, and "corporate"-appearing federal courthouse on Pearl Street with its older neighbors on Foley Square, the state supreme court building and the "old" federal courthouse.

So one explanation of the peculiar doctrine of discretion and the form it takes in American law is that it is a presentation by and to the courts and to the public. It is a statement about the nature of the courts and the way they conduct their business. They legitimate the social order as the vehicle of the rule of law, at the same time as they are efficient, pragmatic, "modern" institutions. The shift from formalism in procedure to discretion is thus an example of the responsiveness of official dispute-ways to changes in the generally held values that help define a culture.

Discretion as a Response to Law's "Age of Anxiety"

A second account of the rise of the American form of limited discretionary authority takes a more speculative, interpretive approach. It traces the phenomenon more directly to the needs of the legal specialist community. Simply put, the argument is that the discretion doctrine developed as it did in response to and as a means of dealing with the anxiety caused by a threatened loss of faith in the rule of law.

Faith was undermined by two related developments. First, there was the general shift in legal reasoning from rule-bound formalism to the kind of factor-weighting policy-analysis approach illustrated by the *Asahi* case described above.[71] This well documented turn away from formalism affected virtually every area of American law. The leading thinkers of the formative period were quite open about it. From Cardozo's *Nature of the Judicial Process*:

> It is true, I think, today in every department of the law that the social value of a rule has become a test of growing power and importance. This truth is powerfully driven home to the lawyers of this country in the writings of Dean Pound. "Perhaps the most significant advance in the modern science of law is the change from the analytical to the functional attitude."[72]

"A fruitful parent of injustice," said Cardozo elsewhere, "is the tyranny of concepts."[73]

Looking back on the period, Atiyah summed it up:

> In the first half of the nineteenth century, I suggest, the courts were inclined to resolve the conflict [between principle and pragmatism] by adhering to principle. They were less concerned with doing justice in the particular case and more concerned with the impact of their decision in the future. In modern times, by contrast, I suggest that the courts have become highly pragmatic and a great deal less principled.[74]

Whatever the reasons for this intellectual revolution (and no doubt among them was the appeal of flexibility that I have connected with the rise of discretion), it will be seen that decisions based on judicial weighing of factors in the context of particular issues and cases looks less like the platonic ideal of a rule of law than did the regime it replaced: the application of specific rules to the facts presented. Although this revolution occurred more or less at the same time that discretionary judicial authority increased, one must distinguish the two, because the legal culture certainly did so. That is, judges maintained a distinction in their opinions between cases in which they applied discretion and those in which they were subject to law, even though they brought a similar mode of analysis to the different tasks. The promise of the new mode of legal reasoning was that it would lead to judicial decisions that made better public policy. Its problem was that it looked more like politics than law and therefore threatened law's primary claim to legitimacy, its autonomy.

This brings me to a second and related cause of the loss of faith, the attack of the legal realist movement that came to the fore in the thirties and forties and has remained influential ever since.[75] No more than painting, psychology, or physics was the "science of law" immune from the modernist intellectual attack on inherited certainties.[76] The realists claimed that the apparent certainty of legal formalism was a mirage. They argued that while legal rules could be stated and were invoked by courts to justify holdings, the question which rule was applicable to a particular case was usually contingent and debatable. Hence, the actual outcome of cases depended more on the judge's view of the right result as a matter of social policy or personal predilection. This was because the judge would (consciously or not) choose a rule that dictated the preferred end.[77]

If the realists were correct, it meant that not only was there no longer "law" in the sense in which it had been understood by the formalists but also that there never had been such law.[78] Given the importance of the belief in law to the American polity, a loss of faith in it must have been a source of social anxiety. This would be true as much for the practitioners of law—judges, lawyers, and law reformers—as for the general public. Their socially privileged position is dependent on the general acceptance of their importance in and necessity to the operation of the rule of law. More important, their professional sense of self-worth is dependent on the very same role. All this seems to me unarguable. A harder question is how this relates to discretion.

To explain, I need to first reprise and emphasize the importance of the rule of law to what American society imagines itself to be. As I suggested in chapter 3, the belief that "ours is a government of laws and not of men" is a critical aspect of legal and popular culture in the United States. "From an internal perspective—i.e., from the perspective of the citizen—the historical unity of this community is, in large part, the rule of law as practice and belief."[79] The courts' "contribution to the legitimacy of government" is thus seen as a "most 'profound social function.'"[80] It is in large part the apparent adherence to formal legal processes that enables the courts to effectively play this role. Lon Fuller captured this when he said, "The acceptability of the judge's decision may be enhanced by the fact that he seems to play a subservient role, as one who merely applies rules which he himself did not make."[81] I disagree with Fuller here only in that he does not go far enough. The acceptability of the collective product of the judiciary is not only "enhanced" by the belief in law as its source (rather than the judges); it is dependent on it.

A challenge to the rule of law threatens the American ideal and puts the society in a state of intellectual and psychological disequilibrium. Grant Gilmore put his finger on it when he titled his chapter on the legal realist period "Age of Anxiety."[82] That is why all political power must be seen to operate within the ambit allowed by the rule of law.[83] On this view there is no place for discretion—which creates a gap in the law—in the American legal system. Even the attraction of corporate-style efficiency might not have been enough to allow the turn toward discretion. A more complex motivation was also at work. Paradoxically, it is found in the very anxiety occasioned by the threats to "law."

One of the most common defenses against anxiety is denial. We deny reality when it is less painful to do so than to accept it. Denial is therefore a familiar phenomenon in many areas of human life, including the most painful: serious illness, religious doubt, relations with others, and even death. It should be obvious that I do not here mean intentionally lying but rather a psychological process that operates unconsciously and unintentionally.

Denial is practiced collectively by societies as well as by individuals.[84] The enslavement of Africans, for example, was made possible for people who maintained a belief in their own morality by denying the common humanity of their victims. Denial need not be so malign. Social and personal strain is endemic, caused as it is by the functional problems every social arrangement inevitably faces.[85] As Geertz argues, "All [social arrangements] are riddled with insoluble antinomies: between liberty and political order, stability and change, efficiency and humanity, precision and flexibility, and so forth."[86] These contradictory claims on consciousness lead to social and personal anxiety, one response to which can be the invocation of ideology as a vehicle of denial and in the service of anxiety reduction.[87]

Denial, therefore, can be seen to facilitate the operation of legal regimes as well. Vernon Palmer has suggested that the use of equity by French judges is systematically denied because its exercise is not considered legitimate within the French legal system.[88] In the United States, denial operates as a defense against the anxiety caused by the attacks on the reality of the rule of law. This is both conscious and unconscious. On the conscious level, arguments and examples are invoked that show that judges really do follow precedent and that the outcome of legal disputes can be predicted. Unconscious denial allows legal scholars to observe that "hard" cases do not have predictable outcomes but to argue that nonetheless there are "right" and "wrong" answers to such questions. Or that the rules are clear and it is only the application of the rules to the facts that is difficult. Or, most of all, unconscious denial allows judges and advocates to proceed as if the resolution to every contested legal issue depended on correct reasoning from *stare decisis*.

Duncan Kennedy also argues that denial plays an important role in dealing with the tensions inherent in the application of the rule of law in the American legal system.[89] Kennedy finds a source of anxiety and the ensuing denial in the "role conflict" experienced by American judges: "For judges, the goal is 'justice under law' and the conflict is between that idea and the categorical exclusion of the 'personal,' in the sense of the ideological, from the decision process."[90] In other words, an irresolvable conflict is built into the very process of judging. "These judges are in a bind"[91] and are or would be made anxious to the degree that they allow the conflict to rise to consciousness. The solution is to deny that they allow the ideological to guide interpretation.

Other participants in the legal system, such as legal academicians, share and support this denial for reasons of their own. In addition to their own stake in commitment to the system (to which I have already alluded), Kennedy observes that this specific experience of simultaneously holding the contradictory elements is an instance of a larger human project. Quoting Freud—both Sigmund and Anna—Kennedy reminds us that the battle between opposing mentalities is an inevitable part of mental life and that denial is one of the ways it is resolved.[92] Vicarious participation in the role conflict resolution through denial is comforting.

My genealogy of the denial-raising anxiety differs only somewhat from Kennedy's. It is not necessary to attribute the anxiety only to the conflict he identifies, though he surely describes a bind felt by many judges. I think the driving conflict is more general and pervasive in the work of judging than the pull of "law" against "ideology." It is the conflict between belief and disbelief. Most judges hold and express the view that they are in fact the servants of the law. Each legal opinion is crafted as an affirmation of that faith. And yet their own experience of interpreting texts must test that faith every day because interpretation is always an individual practice. Unease—at a minimum—is the price of affirming with each legal opinion the existence of a binding law that is in fact only sometimes plainly "binding" but is instead the product of interpretation informed by methodological predilection. Here denial enters by aiding the maintenance of faith.

Regardless of its source, the invocation of denial theory in this context begs the not-so-flippant question, "Just what denial are we talking about? The nudity of this particular emperor has been pointed out ad nauseam since the already-mentioned legal realists of the thirties." Ah, but those assaults on "law" not only made denial all the more important; their manifest failure underscores its power. The attacks of the realists and their critical legal studies successors have at best dented the armor of the rule-of-law ideal.

One of the difficulties encountered in American legal education is to get students to adopt the profession's denial of the role of existing social relations in dictating the outcome of contested rules. This is accomplished by ruling out of order all claims of social justice, and rewarding arguments that fit the paradigm of "legal" reasoning. This is called teaching students to "think like lawyers." It means reasoning logically from existing statutes or cases. Students resist this project intellectually and psychologically because many of them bring to the study of law a belief that law reflects existing social relations and a desire to use law to change those relations. But this inculcation of denial is not malign, because one cannot function successfully as a legal professional without it. I think the most successful legal education allows students to recognize the separate spheres of reasoning and to operate in each sphere independently, but to synthesize them in those instances when synthesis is possible within the legal paradigm.

Denial is made difficult by the emergence of facts inconsistent with the desired paradigm. This problem can be solved by making the exception fit the paradigm, i.e., by ascribing a function and place to it. The exception can then even be made to support the paradigm. "The exception proves the rule," as the saying goes. This form of denial operates importantly for most, perhaps all, metasystems, especially those that operate on faith. In religion, for example, human suffering is not seen as disproof of a benevolent deity but rather as further proof of divine existence, i.e., as proof of the god's power to chasten wayward children, or simply of its incomprehensibility to humankind. I suggest that something of the kind is at work with the American treatment of discretion. It is the exception to the rule of law that affirms its validity. This gives our society psychological support by relieving the anxiety caused by the often unconscious fear that law is not in fact what we consciously claim and hope it to be. Discretion was embraced in part because it could do the work of "proving the rule." I think that a variant of the same point is made by Paul Kahn, who explores the way our concept of the rule of law accounts for discretionary authority given over to the realm of politics. Kahn argues that by a "jurisdictional trope," "[p]olitical action becomes 'discretion,' legally assigned to particular decision makers."[93] It is law's rule that allows the action, so the rule of law remains paramount. The line between law and action (or discretion) is never settled, says Kahn. "Indeed, the line itself is a part of the construct that we bring to the phenomena."[94] Exactly so. And as the line is constructed, it is shaped by the social forces I have tried to elucidate.

More, the line between law and discretion provides a vehicle for safely displaying that "reality" about our rule of law that we usually wish to disguise: its contingency. The display is confined in the various ways already described and therefore safe. I invoke an example from very far afield indeed: In "Deep Play: Notes on the Balinese Cockfight"[95] Clifford Geertz addresses the puzzle of the prominent place of cock fighting in Balinese culture. He observes how the uncontrolled aggression and violence of the dueling fowls seems "a contradiction, a reversal, even a subversion of [their normal social life], as the Balinese are shy to the point of obsessiveness of open conflict." But, according to Geertz, beneath the placid veneer are feelings of envy and aggression. The cock fight,

> [a] powerful rendering of life as the Balinese most deeply do not want it . . . is set in the context of a sample of it as they do in fact have it. . . . The slaughter in the cock ring is not a depiction of how things literally are among men, but, what is almost worse, of how, from a particular angle, they imaginatively are.[96]

I suggest that the embrace of discretion operates in a similar fashion, if hardly as dramatically, for the American legal system. The development of discretion was at once a display of and denial of the frailty of law as a body of positive and knowable rules. "Discretion" became, as it were, a foil for law. The open adoption of a limited form of discretion created an arena of legal activity that is not "law." It therefore helped prove that there was an-other regime, which was "law." The dynamics I have described in this sec-tion arose largely from the needs of legal practitioners and in that sense were internal to the system. But this is not to say that there was no con-nection with society at large. The collapse of verities in the law was part of a much wider shift in the worldview of the society in which it is located. I will return to the "loss of certainty" that accelerated as the century wore on in the next chapter when I take up the rise of alternate dispute resolu-tion. The response of the legal domain was specific to its own problems and used the tools at hand.

Discretion and "American Exceptionalism"

The rise of discretion and "managerial" judging does not sit easily with all of the values that were said in chapter 4 to underpin the formal model of American disputing. As discretion expands, the judge is not as constrained by a rigid version of the rule of law. The litigant is thus seen as subjected to a more personal kind of power, anathema to the foes of authority and hierarchy. It is no surprise that institutions do not move in lock step with even deeply held values. Culture itself is always contested by interest groups and in some cases responsive to them. Perhaps this mushrooming judicial power was tolerated because the efficiency game was worth the candle.

Nor are the "exceptional" American values necessarily consistent with one another. Observe, then, that discretion fits rather well with individual-ism. It is, after all, the facilitation of individualized justice that is discre-tion's claim to legitimacy. A litigant might well accept even dramatic growth of authority if convinced that it would lead to more respect for his particular condition. And if we look at the world from the judicial per-spective, discretion seems especially reflective of individualism. The judge is also an "individual." An increase in the power to do justice tailored to her convictions will sit well with her sense of self. Nor would she see this power as conflicting with the parties' interests or rights, for it was they who were the beneficiaries of particularized justice.

Examining discretion in cultural context helps explain its growth in American law during the twentieth century. It was both a conscious adap-tation by legal specialists to a society-wide change in attitudes about institutions generally and their unconscious response to anxiety about the very validity of law. The rise of discretion provides an example of a significant change in the details of process profoundly influenced, though not solely determined, by forces external to the profession. As we will see in the next chapter, overlapping as well as further changes in values impelled the alternative dispute resolution movement.

6

The Rise of ADR
in Cultural Context

Another puzzling and controversial shift in American dispute processing was the turn away from the formal courtroom adjudication described in chapter 4, and towards Alternative Dispute Resolution. ADR took off later in the twentieth century than the expansion of discretion described in the last chapter and was responsive to societal currents that only partially overlapped those described there. Was it the result of a "crisis" in the courts? If so, what were its ingredients? I will argue that quite apart from a perceived litigation crisis, the move to ADR in the late twentieth century had institutional, political, and cultural causes. More specifically, it was dependent on the sometimes conflicting late-twentieth-century value shifts involving distrust of government, privatization, humanization of large-scale institutions, social progress through individual improvement, and postmodern skepticism about an objective reality. These themes echo the broader categories discussed in chapter 4 and identified there as fundamental to American culture: liberty, individualism, populism, egalitarianism, and laissez-faire. Developments in these cultural currents were reflected in—or exploited by—political and institutional actors.[1]

In the first part of this chapter I will sketch out the rise of ADR in the last quarter of the twentieth century. I will then provide an historical perspective on the use of ADR in the United States. In the third part I will explain the institutional, cultural, and political changes that gave life to the ADR movement. The fourth section takes up the claim of some adherents that ADR will lead to beneficial changes in American social and personal life. This final section introduces the reflexive power of dispute institutions, a matter that I consider in much more depth in chapter 8.

Preliminarily, ADR takes many different forms because the generic concept includes any process that is an "alternative" to judicial adjudication.

In the United States ADR has included a potpourri of processes—negotiation, mediation, arbitration, med-arb (a combination of mediation and arbitration), early neutral evaluation, and summary jury trials.[2] I will use the term to refer only to arbitration and mediation, the most important and commonly used ADR methods. Although alike in that they do not contemplate a judicial determination of a dispute, these are very different processes in that arbitration involves a binding decision by a third party, whereas in mediation the third party assists the disputants in negotiating and reaching their own resolution.

Variations in ADR types have attracted support from different sectors of society and have served different if sometimes commensurate goals. Mediation, because of its emphasis on consensual problem solving, has appealed to reformers for whom the values of communitarianism and self-actualization rank high. Arbitration has often been embraced by business interests for its supposed cost savings over adjudication, because the results can be shielded from public exposure, and because of its reliance on decision makers knowledgeable about the type of dispute to be resolved. Business has recognized that mediation shares many of these characteristics and has found it attractive as well. Court administrators have established court-annexed programs that employ *both* forms of ADR in the hope that they will ease judicial caseloads or otherwise improve the courts' power to meet the needs of disputants.

Though by definition an "alternative" to court adjudication, ADR is nonetheless relevant to my general argument that official dispute resolution reflects local culture. In many respects much of ADR has become part of "official" disputing not only because it is so often court annexed but also because it has undergone a process of legalization by virtue of its regulation by law and lawyers.

The Rise of ADR in the Late Twentieth Century

Troubling statistical gaps prevent accurate assessment of ADR use except in specific venues. For example, although it is reported that the federal district courts referred about twenty-four thousand cases to some form of ADR in 2001,[3] I have been unable to find anywhere a compilation of the number of federal cases resolved following reference. And while we know that the American Arbitration Association (AAA) reported an increase in arbitrations that it administered, from about sixty-two thousand in 1995 to some 230,000 in 2002,[4] and, further, that Professors Eisenberg and Hill found a "massive" increase in the arbitration of employment disputes in the 1990s,[5] it is not possible to find a total of all disputes arbitrated throughout the United States or even in any state. These concerns prevent us from fully appreciating the expansion of ADR, but they do not undermine the conclusion of many observers that there has been expansion and that it has been significant. More than twenty years ago, Richard Abel introduced *The Politics of Informal Justice* by observing that "[w]e are presently experiencing what may well be a major transformation of our legal system."[6] He was not far from the mark: by 2004, Richard Chernick could assert that

> ADR . . . is now thriving, energetic and poised for its most productive period. . . . Some of the more important results of this ADR revolution include the following:
> - Creation of neighborhood justice centers for the mediation of community disputes.
> - Court-annexed mediation of small civil disputes and later expansion into judicial arbitration and early neutral evaluation programs in many state and federal courts.
> - Numerous statutes and executive orders on the federal level mandating ADR in the courts and federal agencies.
> - Peer mediation programs in our schools.
> - Statutes requiring the resolution of professional disputes through dispute resolution. . . .
> - Routine use of mediation and arbitration in the settlement of class actions and in the distribution of settlement funds for mass tort claims.[7]

Deborah Hensler finds that "the ADR movement has had some success over the past twenty-five years in changing business and legal decision-makers' views of how to best resolve legal disputes."[8] She notes a decline in court caseloads in many jurisdictions, the rise in AAA caseloads I have already mentioned,[9] and the practice of many federal and state courts to offer or require attempts at mediation of disputes. According to Hensler, "more than half of state courts, and virtually all of the federal district courts, had adopted mediation programs for large categories of civil suits" by the midnineties.[10] As to mediation in general, it has been claimed that "[d]uring the 1980s, mediation's use would accelerate onto a flight path that would make its presence and use pervasive."[11] Hensler also reports intriguing web-related evidence of interest in ADR. A search engine she consulted found over one million pages referring to mediation, arbitration, and conflict resolution, and 274 sites related to dispute resolution.[12]

Whatever its underlying causes, to which I soon turn, the growth of ADR was enabled by changes in positive law effected by both the judiciary and the Congress. Let me mention the most salient.

(1) The Judicial Role in ADR Growth

The most obvious way in which the judiciary has contributed to the growth of ADR has been by establishing the already-noted "court-annexed" programs. These typically involve the creation of an arbitration or mediation service (or both) that is administered by the court. Cases can be referred to either of these in the discretion of the judge to whom the case is assigned. In some jurisdictions, cases are automatically referred to ADR and can come before a judge only if the parties are not satisfied with the result of the alternative process.[13]

An example of a court-annexed ADR system that uses both arbitration and mediation is that run by the federal district court in Brooklyn, New York.[14] All cases in which the amount claimed is less than $150,000 are referred to arbitration. (Certain kinds of cases, such as those raising constitutional claims, are exempt from the requirement.) The referred case will ordinarily be heard by a single arbitrator, who must be an attorney certified by the court as capable of serving. He or she listens to the testimony and other evidence and the parties' legal contentions, and makes a decision. The arbitrator's fee, which is set by the court rules and is currently $250, is paid from court funds. Following the issuance of the arbitrator's award, any party may request a new hearing before a judge, in which case the lawsuit proceeds as if the arbitration had not occurred. If, however, the requesting party does not obtain a more favorable result in court than from the arbitrator, that party must reimburse the court for the arbitrator's fee. Mediation is an additional option in this federal court: whether or not a case has been (or will be) referred to arbitration a judge may require the parties to mediate their dispute. According to the court's rules,

> Mediation is a process in which parties and counsel meet with a neutral mediator trained to assist them in settling disputes. The mediator improves communication across party lines, helps the parties articulate their interests and understand those of the other party, probes the strengths

and weaknesses of each party's legal position, and identifies areas of agreement and helps generate options for a mutually agreeable resolution to the dispute.[15]

Mediators are not paid; they are volunteer attorneys who have been trained in mediation. If the parties fail to reach an agreement by a date previously set by the court, the case returns to the normal litigation process. If they have agreed, the case will be concluded with a settlement.

In addition to ADR referral rules such as that just described, the judiciary has contributed to the ADR boom by vigorously enforcing private agreements. Most notably, in a series of relatively recent decisions the Supreme Court invalidated previously reliable restrictions on arbitration by invoking the pro-arbitration purposes of the Federal Arbitration Act (the FAA).[16] Although this statute had been enacted in 1925 to make arbitration agreements and awards enforceable in the federal courts, the Supreme Court was initially slow to fully embrace arbitration as a valid alternative to litigation. In 1953 it held in *Wilko v. Swann* that arbitration was not appropriate for making "subjective" findings and thus could not be used to resolve claims of fraud based on violations of federal securities laws.[17] This suspicion of arbitration was not to last. A change in direction was signaled when the Court held in 1967 that the FAA applied in state as well as federal courts.[18] By 1983 the Court announced that "any doubts concerning the scope of arbitrable issues should be resolved in favor of arbitration, whether the problem is the construction of the contract language itself or an allegation of waiver, delay, or a like defense to arbitrability."[19] The spirit encapsulated in this language generated an important wave of pro-arbitration decisions.

In the 1984 case of *Southland Corp. v. Keating,*[20] the Court held for the first time that state statutes that restricted arbitration of commercial disputes violated the FAA and would be struck down. *Southland* involved a California statute that made arbitration clauses in franchise agreements unenforceable against the franchisee. The plain purpose of the law was to protect the party in a weak bargaining position from an oppressive requirement that the franchisee forfeit access to the courts as a condition of the deal. Chief Justice Burger's opinion for the Court focused on the purpose of the FAA—to override anachronistic hostility to arbitration—and held that California could not invalidate arbitration agreements that would be valid under federal law. A later case reached the same result when the issue was whether the FAA overrode an Alabama statute that protected consumers from arbitration clauses in home-improvement contracts.[21] The Court struck the statute down, holding that the consumer was bound by an arbitration clause buried in the contract. Not surprisingly, the Supreme Court soon took another look at the anti-arbitration *Wilko* securities case described earlier and overruled it, holding that arbitration agreements would henceforth be enforced in securities fraud cases.[22] The Court denigrated *Wilko* as "far out of step with our current strong endorsement" of arbitration.[23]

Nor were employment agreements exempt from "the relentless federal policy favoring arbitration."[24] In the *Gilmer* case the plaintiff had sued his employer claiming that he had been fired because of his age, in violation of the federal Age Discrimination in Employment Act.[25] Upholding the employer defendant's contention, the Court held that the plaintiff's sole avenue of redress was arbitration. The courthouse door was closed to him because he had agreed to arbitrate claims relating to employment when he had been hired. Neither the fact that the underlying claim alleged violation of a federal anti-discrimination statute nor the admitted inequality of bargaining power between the parties, said the Court, would justify ignoring the agreement.

The result of this line of cases is that arbitration clauses are now common in contracts prepared by merchants for their consumer customers, in agreements prepared by brokerage houses for their trading customers, and by corporations for their employees.[26]

(2) The Legislative Role in ADR Growth

In the closing decades of the last century, federal and state legislation accelerated the growth of ADR by encouraging, funding, and sometimes requiring it in courts and agencies. Congress enacted no less than five pro-ADR statutes between 1980 and 1998. The Dispute Resolution Act of 1980 was an early example. It encouraged states, local governments, and non-profit organizations to develop "effective, fair, inexpensive, and expeditious" dispute-resolution mechanisms and provided financial assistance to those entities that improved or established them.[27] Then, in 1988, Congress authorized ten federal district courts to implement mandatory (but nonbinding) arbitration referral programs for "minor" cases by adopting the Judicial Improvements and Access to Justice Act.[28] Two years later the Civil Justice Reform Act of 1990[29] required all district courts to create and implement a plan for reducing costs and delay within four years. It explicitly permitted the use of alternative dispute resolution programs as one means of accomplishing this end.

The Administrative Dispute Resolution Act of 1990 mandated the use of ADR in resolving disputes in the context of administrative agencies.[30] In this act, Congress authorized using ADR in a wide variety of administrative programs in order to "enhance the operation of the Government and better serve the public."[31] The Department of Justice later expressed its desire to "make available every possible incentive to encourage greater use of ADR in any form by the executive branch agencies"[32] because it felt that it was in the public interest to encourage the use of ADR[33] in view of the "faster, less expensive, and less contentious"[34] resolutions of disputes in the private sector.

Most recently, Congress enacted the Alternative Dispute Resolution Act of 1998.[35] It requires all federal district courts to establish an ADR program, but lets courts determine the types of ADR to be used in their jurisdiction.[36] In explaining the new law, Congress stated that ADR "has the potential to provide a variety of benefits, including greater satisfaction of the parties, innovative methods of resolving disputes, and greater efficiency in achieving settlements [and] . . . may have potential to reduce the large backlog of cases now pending in some Federal courts throughout the United States."[37]

The combination of judicial and legislative support enabled but does not fully explain the growth of ADR. Before turning to the cultural domain, I will first provide the necessary historical background.

ADR in Historical Perspective

The roots of the ADR "movement" of late-twentieth-century America lie deep in the country's past. This point has been documented by Jerold Auerbach in his book, *Justice without Law*.[38] As Auerbach shows, alternatives to litigation have been a feature of the American way of disputing throughout its history. Enthusiasm for them has flowered in particular times and places, but even when largely put aside, these alternatives have remained a model to which critics of courts and lawyers regularly return.

Dispute resolution outside of court was an important aspect of the ethics and practice of the early English settlers. The colonists were motivated by a utopian religiosity that embraced an ideology of community: "For Zion to survive in the wilderness according to Puritan design, the dispute-settlement framework . . . must be communal, not individual. Its . . . spirit was religious . . . the style was consensual, not adversarial."[39] In this context, litigation was "explicitly discouraged" and it was expected that disputes would be resolved communally, preferably through mediation or, failing that, by arbitration.[40] As Auerbach also reports, however, this communal vision and practice did not survive the social changes brought by an increasing, spreading, and ever more diverse population. "By the end of the seventeenth century, communal harmony was substantially weakened . . . throughout New England." As a consequence, conflict was no longer suppressed, litigation increased, and law "reigned" by the eighteenth century.[41] To the extent that mediation retained vigor as a response to dispute, it was largely in various self-organized utopian communities and within the insular world of immigrant groups (such as the Chinese) that brought a deep distaste for litigation to the New World.

Arbitration was another story. It was early on embraced by a different community—the merchant class. The Dutch colonists who preceded the English in "New Amsterdam" had established arbitration as an alternative to litigation and its advantages were not lost on successor businessmen. "By the mid-eighteenth century, arbitration was favored by merchants for its speed and low cost," and the New York Chamber of Commerce established an arbitration tribunal in 1768.[42] Still, arbitration played second fiddle to the formal legal system. The "rule of law" was, of course, a fundamental tenet of the founders of the American republic and came to dominate the national disputing ethos. Until the twentieth century arbitration remained important largely within trade groups that constituted communities of their own.

A litigation "crisis" of the early twentieth century beset the courts with problems familiar to current observers: excessive delay and cost that exacerbated wealth-based disparities in the justice available.[43] The response, too, was familiar: "there was renewed interest in alternatives to litigation, especially conciliation and arbitration."[44] But the two alternatives—arbitration and conciliation—differed in the values they expressed and in their ultimate success. The differences to some degree reflected different economic interests. Conciliation (a term often used interchangeably with mediation) was urged as a solution to those whose claims were too small, or those who were too poor, to make full-fledged litigation a realistic option.

Too, the "rhetoric of conciliation emphasized harmony and amity as alternatives to conflict."[45] Yet conciliation was consigned to the "periphery" of the legal system, such as small claims courts.

Commercial arbitration suffered no such fate. It was embraced by the business community, not only as a way to exit backlogged courts and to escape the populist unpredictability of juries but also as a way to avoid the increasing governmental control of business that was a hallmark of early-twentieth-century reformers: arbitrators would be "drawn from the ranks of respectable middle-class professionals."[46] The 1920s saw two important developments that reflected and spurred the arbitration movement: the adoption of New York legislation that made arbitration agreements binding and enforceable (thus ending the prior and long-standing power of the courts to override such agreements) and the formation of the American Arbitration Association in 1926.[47] Interestingly, when the next wave of reformers came to power with Franklin Delano Roosevelt following the crash of 1929 and subsequent depression, they railed against the very escape from the "rule of law" that had attracted business to arbitration. But by then commercial arbitration was "too deeply entrenched to be dislodged."[48] Its secure position was in part due to the paradoxical reality that commercial arbitration had been colonized by the legal system. This happened not through active judicial oversight—that has long been minimal—but because lawyers penetrated the system. More and more were disputants represented by counsel, were lawyers serving as arbitrators, and were the processes of arbitration, as opposed to the substance of the award, subjected to judicial control. Nothing could better symbolize this legalization of informality than the publication in 1930 of Yale law professor Wesley Sturges's treatise on the law of commercial arbitration. I see this unlikely marriage of law to not-law as an imaginative stroke that at once captures and synthesizes the pervasive American conflict between laissez-faire individualism and the "rule of law as our deepest cultural commitment."[49]

But if conciliation was ameliorating the "periphery" of American law, and arbitration addressed the needs of the commercial world, what caused the renewal of calls for ADR in the late twentieth century? Was it yet another crisis of litigation delay and expense? Or was it something else? The remainder of this chapter explores possible cultural, institutional, and political answers to these questions.

Litigation Growth Does Not Account for the Trend

The simplest explanation for the turn to ADR after 1975 would see it as a rational response to a sharp growth in litigation in the preceding decade that threatened to overwhelm the judiciary and delay the resolution of disputes. Different players in the legal system would have had different motivations for moving to ADR. Corporations and individual disputants might have chosen arbitration or mediation instead of litigating for any number of reasons—to save expense, to avoid juries, to preserve privacy, or to seek speedier resolution. These would not always track the concerns of judges, court administrators, and legislators who imposed or created court-annexed ADR diversion programs. For the latter group ADR may have been seen as a way of avoiding crushing caseload burdens that were unresolved by whatever efficiency had been achieved by the increase in judicial power described in chapter 5. Let me first pursue the judicial perspective.

According to Richard Posner, "An economist would consider it natural that a surge in federal caseloads should have led the judiciary and the legal profession to seek to encourage substitute methods of dispute resolution for full-scale federal litigation."[50] That caseloads were mounting is demonstrable. Between 1962 and 1974 the annual number of civil cases filed in all federal district courts doubled, from about fifty thousand to over one hundred thousand. Annual per capita filings also doubled, from about 260 per million of the U.S. population to about five hundred per million. The increase in filings in relation to GNP was less dramatic but still significant—from twenty-one per billion dollars to twenty-five. Filings per sitting federal judge rose from two hundred to 250.[51] Comparable figures for the state courts, where the vast bulk of litigation takes place, are not available on a nationwide basis, but rising dockets and delay surely plagued many jurisdictions in the late fifties and after.[52] On the federal side the problem was compounded because the criminal docket of the federal judiciary also mushroomed, from thirty-two thousand dispositions in 1962 to forty-eight thousand in 1974. As federal judges handle criminal cases in addition to civil, and because the Speedy Trial Act of 1974 effectively required them to prioritize them, the time available for civil cases evaporated in crime-ridden districts. Much of the relevant rhetoric painted a frightening picture of a future of exponential increases and inordinate delay.[53]

The behavior of relevant legal institutions—the courts and the bar—met Posner's hypothetical economist's expectations in that there was some case-diversion effort. As I showed earlier, private arbitration expanded, while in the courts, the "felt need to increase the settlement rate in response to growing caseload pressures has led to innovative alternatives—collectively referred to as 'alternative dispute resolution.' . . ."[54] But a simple cause-and-effect model tracing the ADR growth to increasing litigation and delay must be rejected. Though the burdens on the courts were growing, the specter of delay was only that: nothing like the feared impact on litigation length could be shown. In 1960, when the case avalanche was first hitting the federal courts, the median time to disposition of cases tried was 17.8 months and showing little sign of dramatic increase—even by 1983 it had only risen to nineteen months, where it seems to have settled.[55] Such a slight actual impact should not have created so large a shift in process.

Moreover, if reduction of court burdens was the primary motive of the ADR proponents, the form of the diversion favored by court administrators was peculiar. It consisted largely of internal redirection through the establishment of court-annexed arbitration and mediation. This meant that employment of within-the-system resources of some kind would still be necessary. And unless these new processes reduced the overall amount of litigant and judicial time and effort to get to disposition, they would not serve the institutional purpose. It was possible that many disputes sent off to mandatory court-annexed mediation and arbitration would return to court because one of the parties refused to accept the result.[56] In 1975, when the claims on behalf of ADR diversion were coming to the fore, there was no empirical evidence that a conservation of judicial time would be realized. Since they had hardly been tried, how could there be? In the event, subsequent studies of the ADR impact have turned up a puzzling set of findings. The conviction that ADR is an effective tool of docket management is much greater than its actual effect:[57] lawyers and judges have largely continued to believe that overall time and cost was saved by court-annexed diversions, whereas the empirical evidence points quite strongly in the direction of no such saving. (Obviously, this does not mean that there were no success stories in individual cases, only that the aggregate of cases showed no benefit.) These findings not only undermine attribution of ADR growth to judicial crisis; they suggest that we look elsewhere for the source of the hard-to-shake but unsupportable belief in it.

Diversion to ADR was only one of a number of the available caseload palliatives. Many others were suggested. According to Judge Posner, the federal system resorted to three, apart from ADR: the number of judges was increased, the system of supporting personnel (such as magistrate judges) was augmented, and the judges simply worked longer hours.[58] He reports some success in managing the caseload as a result.[59] If these steps were not sufficient, Congress could have provided still more judges. Or it could have reduced the kinds of cases over which the federal courts had jurisdiction. Or it could have done nothing at all and allowed litigants and judges to endure the inconvenience.[60] In light of the variety of possible approaches, why create and use "alternatives" to traditional adjudication? There must be more to the story.

Turning to the situation of the disputants themselves, we should recognize that while their incentives would have been different from those of the court managers, the two sets of actors were interrelated. It was, we must recall, judicial decisions that enabled and encouraged the use of ADR by potential litigants. As we have noted already, a number of reasons might have led them to accept the judicial invitation: to save expense, to avoid juries, to preserve privacy, or to seek speedier resolution. But these incentives did not suddenly arise in the late twentieth century, as our historical survey has shown.

All of the proponents of ADR must have had other reasons for thinking it preferable. At a minimum, they needed a mindset that allowed that specific move. The ADR history recounted earlier provided a reservoir of techniques and the legitimacy of precedent. Yet there was also blowing in the wind of late modernity a set of mentalities that were widespread enough to count as culture as I have defined it. Two of these themes predominate. I will refer to them as "counterculturalism" and "hyperlexis critique." Each has some explanatory power. Each echoes themes that emerged at the very beginning of the history of disputing in America. I will add to the mix two other themes, the "loss of certainty" affliction of late modernity, and the growth of privatization as an ideal.

The "Hyperlexis Critique"

The hyperlexis critics believed that the courts were besieged by cases and litigants that should not be there. They saw (and see) the nation as suffering from "hyperlexis"—an overreliance on law to solve the many problems of society. In their view this was the cause of a mushrooming caseload and concomitant delay, but their concerns went beyond those institutional is-

sues. They also lamented the increasing reliance on legal institutions to resolve disputes and solve problems as threatening to more fundamental
values, because they saw it as undermining traditional authority figures or
other governmental agencies.[61]

The hyperlexis critics called for the diversion of some disputes to other
fora. Usually this meant diversion of claims of small monetary value, such
as consumer disputes, but it included as well other cases that were important to ordinary people, as opposed to large commercial interests.[62] It was
argued that the courts as constituted were ill equipped to handle these
cases at a reasonable cost, and that for various reasons they did not need
or deserve full-fledged adjudication. It was apparent that the proponents
of this view were ready to push some grievances and some rights out of
the courthouse and thus literally outside the rule of law.

The hyperlexis reaction was as much a political phenomenon as cultural because it was concerned with access to governmental power. Laura
Nader was onto something when she argued that the hyperlexis critics
"were more worried about *who* was litigating than about the amount of
litigation. . . . It began to look very much as if ADR were a pacification
scheme, an attempt on the part of powerful interests in law and economics
to stem litigation by the masses. . . ."[63] Consider in this vein a 1976 statement by the then solicitor general, Robert Bork:

> As a society we are attempting to apply law and judicial processes to more
> and more aspects of life in a self-defeating effort to guarantee every minor
> right people think they ought ideally to possess. . . . We are forced, I think,
> to the conclusion that only a reallocation of disputes among types of tri-
> bunals offers any long-run hope for the federal judicial system.[64]

Support for Nader's cynical view is found as well in the timing of the hyperlexis reaction. By the seventies the federal courts had been the site of
successful claims of new constitutional and statutory rights. Partly this
was inspired by the Warren Court, the continuing civil rights revolution
(by then including demands for economic rights), and the feminist claims
for gender equality. Added to a receptive judiciary was the new availability
of lawyers for the poor through the federally funded legal services program.[65] Resistance to the rights agenda took a variety of forms, among
them attacks on the legal services program, and at least for some of its
proponents, "diversion" of claims under the ADR rubric.[66]

It was the hyperlexis critique that dominated a pivotal event, a 1976 gathering of leading lawyers and judges convened by Warren E. Burger, then the Chief Justice of the Supreme Court. Officially designated the National Conference on the Causes of Popular Dissatisfaction with the Administration of Justice, it came to be known as the "Pound Conference" because it marked the seventieth anniversary of the famous lecture on judicial reform by Roscoe Pound that I described in the previous chapter. As discussed earlier, Pound's 1906 indictment of the legal system's antiquated formalism had pointed the way to an increase of discretionary judicial authority. In his keynote address seventy years later, Chief Justice Burger complained of continuing inefficiencies but acknowledged that the interim period had seen "major advances" in simplifying procedure, noting especially the implementation of pretrial procedures—a lively site of judicial discretionary activity.[67] Asserting that serious problems remained, he called for "fundamental changes and major overhaul."[68]

The call for alternatives to traditional adjudication was a highlight of the Chief Justice's speech. He encouraged the "consideration of means and forums that have not been tried before."[69] Claims of low monetary value, he suggested, might be handled by "tribunals" of ordinary people (but including a lawyer or paralegal) that could make binding awards. "New ways" should also be found to handle "such family problems as marriage, child custody and adoptions." He also called for "new ways to provide reasonable compensation for injuries resulting from negligence of hospitals and doctors" and for "new ways . . . to compensate people for injuries from negligence of others without having the process take years to complete and consume up to half the damages awarded. The workmen's compensation statutes may be a useful guide in developing new processes and essential standards."[70]

Arbitration was one of the most prominent of the "new ways" the chief justice recommended: "I submit a reappraisal of the values of the arbitration process is in order, to determine whether, like the Administrative Procedure Act, arbitration can divert litigation to other channels."[71]

Another presentation did even more to invigorate the move to ADR. This was the address by Frank Sander, "Varieties of Dispute Processing."[72] After quoting a doomsday scenario for the federal courts in which millions of cases would overwhelm them by the year 2010, Professor Sander asserted, "There seems to be little doubt that we are increasingly making greater and greater demands on the courts to resolve disputes that used to be handled by other institutions of society. . . . Quite obviously, the courts cannot continue to respond effectively to these accelerating demands. It becomes essential therefore to examine other alternatives."[73] He then went on to make a profound contribution to the shape of ADR by describing how different kinds of disputes and disputants could benefit from different processes, be they arbitration, mediation, adjudication, or some variant of these. As he put it,

> What I am thus advocating is a flexible and diverse panoply of dispute resolution processes, with particular types of cases being assigned to differing processes (or combinations of processes), according to some of the criteria previously mentioned. . . . [O]ne might envision by the year 2000 not simply a court house but a Dispute Resolution Center, where the grievant would first be channeled through a screening clerk who would then direct him to the process (or sequence of processes) most appropriate to his type of case.[74]

Although Sander and the Chief Justice seemed most concerned to protect the courts from the threatening litigation tsunami, they also invoked the potential of ADR to improve community relations. Sander described a Massachusetts court-annexed mediation program that enabled disputing neighbors to reach an accommodation without a trial. He added that

> more significantly, [the mediation] would have a therapeutic effect on the long-term relationship between these two individuals because it would permit them to ventilate their feelings, and then help them to restructure their future relationship in a way that met the expectations of both parties. In addition it would teach them how they might themselves resolve future conflicts. Thus there is a strong likelihood that future disputes would be avoided, or at least minimized.[75]

In the years that followed, much of the vision of the Pound Conference contributors did come to pass. Arbitration and mediation flourished as adjuncts of the courts and as private processes, as I described at the beginning of this chapter. We should not forget that among the various manifestations was the loss of court access by myriad employees and consumers. I have referred to this process as political. But it was also cultural, in the same way that the ideology and metaphysics of Zande disputing supported particular power relationships in their society.

It is not adequate to attribute the rise of ADR solely to a political move by elites. Both counterculturalism and hyperlexis critics contributed to this result. In my view, the former, the communitarians, provided legitimacy to the political project of the latter, especially regarding mediation. Ironically, the alternative justice idea had been embraced by the satraps of the very legal system that the counterculturalism movement was even then rejecting. Auerbach describes the result as the "legalization of community."[76]

Counterculturalism and ADR

Counterculturalism refers to the social movement of the sixties, famously identified as a "new consciousness" by Charles Reich in his *Greening of America*.[77] It was a time, evocative of Woodstock and Haight-Ashbury, in which traditional attitudes and authorities were challenged and shaken. Its leitmotifs were in general consistent with the long-standing American values of individualism, populism, laissez-faire, and egalitarianism even as its adherents gave their own meanings to them and rebelled against the institutional forms those values had taken.

Particular concerns were anti-authoritarianism, anti-intellectualism, self-actualization, and the realization of community.[78] Among the grievances against the America of the time were *both* the absence of community and the loss of self.[79] The stress on community that was expressed by calls for "power to the people" and "participatory democracy" recalls the communitarianism that underlay disputing forms in the earliest periods of the American experience, as discussed earlier in this chapter, but conflicts with its individualist strains. Reich argued that the conflict could be resolved if the individual maintained a "deep personal commitment to the welfare of the community."[80]

Counterculturalists were understandably hostile to the established court-based system of dispute resolution: the power of judges and lawyers offended their belief that "coercive relations between people are wholly unacceptable."[81]

The rational linear thinking of the legal process offended their deep suspicion "of logic, rationality, analysis and of principles."[82] And the adversarial quality of litigation offended their dislike of competition. "[T]hey do not see others as something to struggle against."[83] A call for the revival of alternatives to adjudication therefore "arose from the euphoric hope that burst forth during the sixties, when community empowerment became a salient theme of political reform."[84]

The "community justice movement," which arose in this period, had as an "animating notion . . . that formal legal institutions, including the courts, are mechanisms for maintaining the power of elite groups . . . and prevent community members (i.e., the non-elite) from learning how to master their own environments and ultimately, their own lives." Because these critics saw the formal court system as an obstacle to the achievement of a better society, their goal was to "build grassroots justice institutions that apply community-based norms to disputes, and rely on community members to resolve disputes."[85] This project was realized by the establishment of community justice organizations such as the community boards of San Francisco, which used mediation and like approaches instead of adjudication to address disputes. Mediation, they believed, "was more likely to nurture positive relationships . . . and seemed consistent with the power-sharing ethos."[86] Part of this aspect of the attraction of ADR was its exclusion of lawyers: "In contrast to the Federal Rules [of civil procedure], which tacitly posit the lawyer as central . . . the ADR procedures are designed to foster direct participation by litigants."[87] ADR can thus allow the disputants to escape the hierarchy of the lawyer-client relationship as well as that of the judge/litigant.

Visionary proponents of mediation as an alternative to litigation have urged that it has the capacity to change the selves that use it and the culture in which it is adopted.[88] In *The Promise of Mediation*, for example, Robert Baruch Bush and Joseph Folger advocate mediation as a means of making society less individualistic and more relational.[89] They see "the unique promise of mediation [as] its capacity to transform the character of both individual disputants and society as a whole."[90] Mediation's constructive power is based on its informality and consensuality, both of which "allow parties to define problems and goals in their own terms, thus validating the importance of problems and goals in the parties' lives."[91] According to Bush and Folger, the individual transformation that will accompany self-definition of problems and goals consists of two parts: empowerment and recognition. Empowerment results in "a greater sense of self-respect, self-reliance, and self-confidence" while recognition helps disputants humanize their adversary and "strengthen their inner capacity for relating with concern to the problems of others."[92] This transformation will not be limited to individuals, they argue. It can also have a constitutive effect on society as a whole. They theorize that mediation use will help to construct a more relational society, which "stresses the equal importance of both individuality and connectedness in human consciousness."[93] The promise of mediation is that it can "become a foundational part of a different, relational society that is not a utopian dream but a gradually emerging reality."[94]

Not the least of the reasons why Frank Sander's celebrated call for ADR at the Pound Conference was so successful was that it appealed to countercultural values in addition to those of efficiency.

Privatization

Other cultural developments were also at work. One was the move to privatize many sectors of the American polity. The election of Ronald Reagan to the presidency in 1980 was both a product and symbol of this triumph of the private sector over the public. President Reagan expressed the view that government was not the solution—it was part of the problem. This is not the place to explore the relevant history in detail. We can note that institutional changes designed to reduce governmental power and presence were effected in environmental regulation, labor relations, and social welfare.[95]

Dispute resolution was also influenced by this temper of the times (though not by specific proposals of the Reagan administration, which seems not to have mounted any initiatives in the area of dispute resolution). Privatization of disputing involved, of course, removing disputes from the relevant organ of government, the judiciary. Corporations that contracted out of judicial supervision by the use of arbitration clauses achieved a kind of economic deregulation. Rights-asserting litigants, contrariwise, could be "diverted" away from attempts to vindicate their rights in court.[96]

We have already seen how this move was operationalized. Congress (and many state governments) encouraged and even required the establishment of diversion programs. The Supreme Court, no doubt affected by a concern for the overloaded judiciary, relied on the Federal Arbitration Act (FAA) to rigorously enforce arbitration agreements. Corporations quickly took advantage of these decisions to insist on arbitration clauses in contracts of employment, sales, and brokerage. They were thus able to privatize the resolution of such disputes because under the FAA there is only very little judicial supervision of arbitration awards. Legal rules need not determine an arbitral award.

Court-annexed ADR programs also involve a kind of privatization, even though the mediation or arbitration, as the case may be, proceeds under the auspices of the court and perhaps in the courthouse itself. The arbitrator or mediator is likely to be a practicing lawyer or court clerk rather than a judge, and the result will not follow strict legal rules any more than would an entirely private proceeding.

The Loss of Certainty

A final influential cultural shift has been the failing of faith in certainty. The problem is much deeper than the special hobgoblins of legal procedures. Claims of certainty have evaporated in many fields of knowledge throughout the twentieth century. In his book, *From Certainty to Uncertainty*, F. David Peat describes this process in realms as diverse as art, physics, mathematics, and language.[97] Students of postmodernism are well aware that the very notion that reality is knowable has been challenged in the last years of the century. As David Garland puts it, "The positivist notion that there were widely shared observations, a universally experienced reality, a given realm of real facts, the possibility of a theory-free science— none of this seemed very plausible once pluralism and relativism became part of the cultural atmosphere."[98] Peat's conclusion is itself exemplary of the postmodern stance when he says, "ultimate explanations and totally objective observations may not really exist."[99] This unease was not limited to the intellectual elite. It was also part of the new consciousness described by Charles Reich in 1970.[100] "It [this consciousness] believes that thought can be 'non-linear,' spontaneous, disconnected. It thinks rational conversation has been overdone as a means of communication between people. . . ."[101]

This postmodern stance has contributed to a particularistic attack on the courtroom, not only in the service of institutional defendants seeking insulation from "crazy" verdicts. One-time secure methods of proof have come under devastating attack: eyewitness testimony, confessions, and even fingerprinting have lost their former panache of authority. Even death sentences have been shown so often to be tainted by factual uncertainty that the former governor of Illinois suspended the practice in that state. In short, the legal arena is particularly apt to be misled by "junk science," say some critics.[102] Skepticism is not limited to fact finding: first the legal realists and then the critical legal studies scholars argued that there was no such thing as objective legal decision making because the rules were inherently manipulable. While never entirely accepted, these claims remain unsettling. Underlying these trends in legal scholarship was the cognitive revolution of modern psychology, which demolished the notion that categorization was anything but a product of the human mind. The implication for formalist legal thinking, so dependent on a belief in categories, should be obvious.[103]

The legal world has not been immune to postmodern skepticism. The connection to ADR should be obvious. If courts can no longer convince us that their elaborate and expensive processes lead to accurate fact finding and law application, why use them? More important, if there is no "reality" to be found regardless of methodology, why seek it? Mediation becomes particularly attractive as an option because the result does not turn on the "rightness" of the matter, but on the outcome the parties reach with the mediator's help. Mediators are taught to get the parties to focus on their interests, not on what happened or did not happen in the past. Though arbitration, like adjudication, involves a decision by a third party nominally attentive to the facts and law, it is in this postmodern light better than adjudication because it (sometimes) saves time and expense and because an arbitrator who is unsure where the right lies may "split the difference" at least in part, a tactic unavailable to a judge.

When we turn to ADR, to again quote Peat, "We have left the dream of absolute certainty behind."[104] This is one more reason it has found favor in the late twentieth century.

The rise of ADR was a product of institutional demands, political maneuvering, and cultural movement. Widely held notions about proper interpersonal relations and the nature of reality surely informed this form of disputing. A remaining question is that of mutuality, or reflexivity. Has ADR use fed back into culture by affecting the beliefs and values of the society in which it is flourishing? We have seen that its most idealistic proponents hoped that engaging in dispute processes that were less hierarchical, linear, and adversarial than those of the courtroom would nudge society in the same direction. Evaluation of that claim will best be made in chapter 8, in which the issue of reflexivity of process and culture is parsed at some length.

7

The Role of Ritual

Whether it is the variety of mystical practices the Azande lavish on the collection, preparation, and use of *benge*, or the elaborate rules of speech, deportment, and place that regulate behavior in an American courtroom, disputing practices are replete with ritualized, ceremonial behavior. Why is ritual so prominent in the formal disputing practices of many societies? How does this ritualization of dispute relate to the themes of this book? I will make two specific claims in this chapter in the service of my central argument for the reflexive nature of culture and disputing. The first is that disputing institutions employ ceremonial practices in the service of legitimacy. For this to work, the ceremonies borrowed must resonate culturally through symbolic association with other institutions that are themselves revered. In this sense, as in others already described, official disputing draws upon and reflects culture. After discussing the concept of ritual and its power in social life, I will use the United States as an example, describing the particular ceremonial practices of its formal dispute processing and offering some thoughts on their symbolic place in that society. My second point is that over time the practices thus legitimated take on a ritual quality and symbolic power of their own. I use this point in the next chapter to support my view that official dispute-ways are reflexively influential on the culture in which they are found.

On Ritual and Ceremony

The concept of ritual is slippery, but there are some generally accepted core elements.[1] In *Ritual, Politics, and Power*, David Kertzer argues that ritual is important to the maintenance of political power in modern states. He defines ritual as "symbolic behavior that is socially standardized and repetitive. . . . It follows highly structured, standardized sequences and is often enacted at certain places and times that are themselves endowed with special symbolic meaning."[2] For Kertzer, it is symbolization that distinguishes ritual from other repetitive practices, which, lacking symbolization, he dismisses as "habit or custom."[3] Kertzer's distinction between ritual and other repetitive practices is useful but incomplete. It ignores the process by which repetitive actions become endowed with symbolic weight, and thus also elides the difficulty of finding the line between ritual action and the merely repetitive. If a symbol is, following Kertzer and Geertz, "'any object, act, event, quality, or relation which serves as a vehicle for a conception,'"[4] we must ask how an object or event becomes a symbol. The issue is important to our understanding of dispute-ways because, I argue later in this chapter, dispute processes acquire the power of ritual through use and through association with other symbols. They become symbols in their own right and are invoked in other social practices.

Catherine Bell eschews a hard-and-fast definition of ritual. She helpfully lists six major attributes of "'ritual-like' action." They are formalism, traditionalism, disciplined invariance, rule governance, sacral symbolism, and performance.[5] Like Kertzer, she sees that traditionalism and sacral symbolism make the standardized sequences of the ritual seem valid, even hallowed, rather than arbitrary. A successful ritual works in part because the meaning of the symbols it marshals are familiar to the participants. Rituals "always operate within a shared community of belief, grounding their practices within the social relations, authorities, and traditions of that community."[6] A black robe may suggest rectitude, sacrality, and power in one society; it will not do so in all. Our knowledge of the history and other uses of such garments thus allows us to see the claim to religious authority that helps sustain judicial power in the United States and Britain. When we sense that required standardized behavior or language lacks the elements of symbol and tradition, we denigrate it as ritualistic. Paradoxically, successful rituals are not "ritualistic."

Ritual usually involves performance, which implies an audience. In most rituals the leaders and audience must both participate physically. As Bell says, "the most subtle and central quality of those actions we tend to call ritual is the primacy of the body moving about within a specially constructed space, simultaneously defining (imposing) and experiencing (receiving) the values ordering the environment."[7] A ritual draws power through participation. Belief follows action even if it did not precede action.

These qualities of ritual empower it to affect human belief and behavior because it enlists emotion in the service of persuasion. "Successful ritual . . . creates an emotional state that makes the message uncontestable because it is framed in such a way as to be seen as inherent in the way things are. It presents a picture of the world that is so emotionally compelling that it is beyond debate."[8] According to David Garland, this emotional effect is at the heart of the "rituals of criminal justice" that manipulate emotion in the service of a system of values.[9]

The use of ritual that resonates with shared social values helps to legitimate a dispute process. As Freud observed in another context, it is possible through ritual to make behavior permissible that is otherwise forbidden.[10] The example he gave was marriage, which in Freud's time made acceptable sexual relations that would otherwise be sinful. Dispute resolution processes also authorize acts that are otherwise forbidden, such as the deprivation of property, the use of violence, or even the killing of one member of society by others. The ritual action that accompanies institutionalized dispute resolution in many societies is thus one source of its success. It may well be that some kinds of dispute resolution, particularly those in which a third-party umpire imposes a result that will disappoint or even enrage the losing party, cannot be managed without some ritual ingredient. "The repetitive elements of judicial ritual contribute to this sense of correctness and legitimacy, and symbolically tie the particular event to more general ideas and characteristics of social order. Procedural correctness lends validity to substantive action. It gives the sense that things are being done as they should be done."[11] Like religious rites, says the anthropologist Sally Falk Moore, "ceremonies of situational transformation are invalid and ineffective if improperly performed."[12] Although Moore was writing in the context of a tribal culture, her point about the necessity of adherence to ritual applies as well to modern societies, as illustrated by the following dialogue from a petty theft case in a magistrate court proceeding in England:

MAGISTRATE: Do you plead guilty or not guilty?

DEFENDANT: Yes, I did it.

MAGISTRATE: No, I'm asking you whether you plead guilty or not guilty. You must use either the words "not guilty" or "guilty."

DEFENDANT: [looking towards probation officer] She said "Say guilty."

MAGISTRATE: No. You must say what you want to say.

DEFENDANT: Yes, I'll say what you like. I did it.

MAGISTRATE: No, you must use the language of the court.[13]

The reported judicial proceeding has the flavor of ritual in that it is not enough that the meaning of the defendant's words are clear. The precise phrase prescribed for the particular ceremonial occasion must be uttered. Indeed, because of the slavish insistence on exact words to the disregard of clarity and understanding, the colloquy strikes us as ritualistic and thus loses some of the power that the ritual of the plea would otherwise convey.

Successful ritual addresses the problematic position of the judge whose decision will be imposed on the contestants. One danger is that the losing party will see the decider as an object of revenge ("kill the umpire"). I observed in chapter 3 that the judge can be protected from disappointed litigants if responsibility for the result is attributed to a culturally valid controlling force, such as *benge*, or law. Here I add the role of ritual to the mix. Sacrality, tradition, power of place, and standardized sequences all contribute to the solemnity and acceptability of the outcome.

The insight that dispute resolution processes could be understood as ritual or ceremony (terms she uses interchangeably) was developed by Moore. Her classic essay is on the role of elders' tribunals in resolving intrafamily strife among the Chagga, a tribe living in the vicinity of Mt. Kilimanjaro.[14] She notes that "[t]he process of hearing and decision can be interpreted as two parts of a *ceremony of social transformation* . . . [in which] the submission of the disputants to the authority of deciders, transforms the disagreement between the parties into an affirmation by others. What started as a dispute becomes a ruling."[15] In the first part of the ceremony, the hearing, the Chagga elders are transformed into adjudicators, whom disputants acknowledge as such. Then the judgment alters the rights and obligations of the disputants, perhaps even changing their entire social situation. "By the end of the judicial process the relative positions of the disputing parties are altered in relation to each other, in relation to the tribunal, and in relation to the community the tribunal represents."[16]

The ritual transformation described by Moore replicates the general pattern of rites of passage or transition observed by Arnold van Gennep[17] and Victor Turner.[18] In their view, all rites that accompany the passage from one culturally significant condition to another pass through three phases: separation, margin (or "limin"), and reaggregation. According to Turner, the first phase involves symbolic behavior that signifies the individual's separation from a "fixed point" in the social structure or from a "set of cultural conditions." In the next, liminal stage, the "ritual subject" is in an ambiguous position, one that is neither the past state nor that which is to come. Finally, when reincorporation is reached the subject "is in a relatively stable state once more and, by virtue of this has rights and obligations. . . ."[19]

This description is applicable in different ways to different participants in a dispute-processing institution. Disputants who become "litigants" have passed from a stable position of rights holders to the instability (liminality) of subjects of the ritual disputing process. The status of their rights and obligations is ambiguous in that the ownership of the thing or status that forms the basis of the dispute is now openly contested. Once judgment has been granted, the social situation of the litigants has been altered regardless of who wins, and each is expected to act accordingly.

The judge, too, will already have undergone a rite of passage, for to judge is to acquire a particular power or status within the social structure. In modern societies the necessary rites are intertwined with the mastery of learning and ideology that we call professionalism.[20] The "pre-judge" moves through the transitional state of student and law student to lawyer and from lawyer to judge, each step of the process being accompanied by well established rites. The new status, though powerful and prestigious, requires the judge to behave in accordance with relevant social standards. It is not a stretch to note how the liminal stage of the path to a judgeship involves the humbling provided by ritual hazing that has long been an element of the law school experience. "The same processes [of liminal humbling] are particularly vividly exemplified in many African installation rituals. The future incumbent of the chieftainship or headmanship is first separated from the commonality and then must undergo liminal rites that rudely abuse him before, in the reaggregation ceremonies, he is installed on his stool in final glory."[21] Turner argues that the ordeals often used in status elevation occasions serve various functions for the different participants. Striking in the present context is his claim that such ordeals serve "antithetical functions, on the one hand punishing the neophyte for rejoicing in liminal freedom, and, on the other, tempering him for the incumbency of still higher office, with its greater privileges as well as more exacting obligations."[22]

In the next section I turn from the general treatment of disputing rituals to the specific traditional and sacral symbolism that helps legitimize that peculiar ceremony of social transformation, the American trial.

Ceremony in the American Trial

The ritual aspects of triadic dispute-resolution processes should not obscure their fundamental utility. When people are at loggerheads it is important to them and to their society that the dispute be settled acceptably. The line between ritual and purely instrumental activity is therefore often blurry. To parse this divide it is useful to distinguish between "ceremony," i.e., actions that are purely symbolic, having no apparent instrumental purpose, and the instrumental: when a judge who must decide the facts listens to evidence, she is behaving instrumentally; that she wears a black robe while listening is ceremonial.

Such ceremonial features evoke deeply held values through the use of symbols appropriate to the task for that culture. As the judge is both instrumentally and symbolically the personification of state authority, it is not surprising that her activity is intensely ceremonial. Adherence to the details of the rites helps to maintain belief in the impersonal nature of the result. Otherwise puzzling behaviors are almost entirely in the service of depersonalization and sacralization.

The suppression of the judge's individuality is accomplished by the "ritualized uniformity of the courtroom."[23] The uniformity is not haphazard—it refers to other spheres of social life. Most obviously there is costume: whether on the Supreme Court of the United States or a local trial court, a judge will almost never appear in her judicial role without wearing a black robe, a garment not otherwise worn in the United States except on other ceremonial occasions, such as religious observances or academic exercises.[24] The robe thus implies that the wearer is both learned and divinely charged and that the occasion is somehow extraordinary.

Then there is place. The trial proceeds in a specially designed room that intentionally incorporates culturally recognizable expressions of authority. The judge's chair (or "bench") is higher and grander than all others. Everyone must thus "look up to" the judge. The courtroom itself is often of splendid construction. One or more reverential mottoes adorn the wall, typically "In God We Trust." For one perceptive juror, this invocation, in prominent brushed metal on the oak wainscoting panel behind the judge, "confirmed the sacral architecture: the altar like bench, the choir like jury box, the lectern like witness stand, the rood screen of the balustrade separating the congregation from the powerful seats beyond."[25] Flags emblematic of national and local authority are on display. As a general rule, the higher the court in the judicial hierarchy, the more magnificent will be the space of the court. This chamber is generally located in a building constructed in a particular architectural tradition that suggests a Greek or Roman temple or, more recently, as I have discussed in chapter 5, a corporate headquarters. The building may be decorated with icons suggestive of classical sculpture and figures traditionally representative of justice.[26]

Behavior changes in the presence of the judge. All must stand when the judge enters or leaves the courtroom—itself a sign of respect in American society. The judge's "bench" may not be approached without her permission. Special forms of speech are employed when one speaks to a judge in court. She is addressed as "your honor," a phrase redolent of the titles used by courtiers, such as "your lordship" or "your highness." Lawyers who argue an appeal are instructed to begin their presentation with these precise words: "May it please the court."

The "rhetorical techniques of judicial expression" used in American judicial writing serve both to depersonalize the judge and to enhance authority.[27] An example is the adoption by appellate judges of "a single, transgenerational, communal self" in their opinions. The author of an opinion will say, referring to that of a long deceased predecessor "as we said in the case of. . . ."[28] The use of "we" here emphasizes the timeless quality and apersonal nature of the decision. It is also a kind of self-honorific, like the royal plural. A striking instance of this multipurpose rhetorical stance was the opinion in *Bush v. Gore*,[29] which was not attributed to any author but was issued "per curiam" (i.e., "by the court") even though only five justices subscribed to the result. The archaic Latin phrase of course contributes to the sense of mystery, timelessness, and majesty. Unlike the Roman Catholic Church the American courts have yet to abandon Latin in their regular public discourse.

The culturally required depersonalization is so important that it requires even the individual who becomes a judge to reconstruct her persona: this happens upon investiture when the new judge swears an oath to uphold the law, thus implicitly leaving behind her previously individualized opinions.[30] It is also part of the ritual of judicial confirmation of federal judges by the United States Senate. A friend who not too long ago successfully underwent this process was asked, with great solemnity by one senator, whether she would decide cases according to the law or according to her own view of right and wrong. She recalled thinking to herself, and to her own amusement, "This must be some kind of intelligence test." But I wonder whether her "correct" response did not in some way impact on the way she approaches her cases, as it was no doubt intended to do.

Ceremony will also have been observed at key points in the making of the judge. These rites of passage include university and law school commencements, bar admission swearing-in ceremonies, and the investiture into the judicial office. In the United States the latter is a grand occasion, even at the trial court level. Some courthouses have rooms designated ceremonial courtrooms that are more elaborately decorated than the others and are reserved for this and other solemn events. Before an assembly of friends, family, and other judges of the court (suitably robed), the new judge is treated to orations about his or her virtues, makes some remarks that include assertions of humility in confronting the task ahead, and swears an oath of fealty to the law and its primary manifestation, the Constitution. The event closes with celebratory and convivial libations. The oath connects the new judge to the holy; the honorifics confirm his importance before the world.

The roles of other participants in the trial have obvious ceremonial aspects. The parties are forbidden to address the judge unless they are called as witnesses. They will ordinarily participate only through their attorneys, who are familiar with the special language, obscure body of knowledge, and prescribed in-court behavior that is required. Like the judges, the attorneys have undergone long training and ritual validation exercise. When in court they have privileges of movement and space not accorded others. Their lawyerly interrelationship is itself ceremonial—sometimes exaggeratedly deferential (e.g., "my learned friend") and sometimes highly combative (but understood by the "brother" attorney as a kind of acting). This enforced exclusivity of participation contributes to the sense of privileged ritual.

Jurors, unlike the judge and attorneys, are ordinary citizens, but their role is marked by ceremony nonetheless. They must take an oath to decide the case honestly and fairly, and they are required to behave in accordance with rules of silence and role. They are instructed, "Do not discuss the case, do not make up your mind until you have heard all the evidence," etc. Their space in the court, I have noted, is somewhat exalted: higher than the general audience, but not as high as the judge, and off to the side. They are addressed by the other participants with a ritually prescribed mix of deference and patronization. The latter is manifest through the rules of evidence, and by attorney efforts to manipulate their emotions. When they must decide the case they are instructed by the judge about what they must decide in the "charge," often presented from a quasi-legalese script from which little or no variation is tolerated. Their deliberations take place in a special room, shielded from all who are not on the jury. The manner in which they report their decision is itself prescribed by rules of ceremony, appropriately solemn and full of drama.

The participation of witnesses also begins with ceremony—they must take an oath to tell the truth, usually an oath "before God" and sometimes literally "on the Bible." Out of respect for religious freedom, an affirmation to tell the truth "under penalty of perjury" may be substituted for an oath. In my experience this option is rarely invoked by witnesses or jurors.

All of this ceremony has the effect of sacralizing and legitimating the social transformation that takes place in the courtroom. That so much of this ritual behavior incorporates symbols from other realms bears on the mirroring question that is one theme of this book and shows how intertwined but complex is the relationship between official dispute processes and culture. In one sense the symbols used can be seen as keeping the general public at a distance by creating an arcane and unapproachable authority. A freedom of internal action by the profession is thereby preserved. We might further surmise that the use of culturally hallowed symbols is only necessary because so much of the process is otherwise obscure to the public. On the other hand, this amplification of legitimacy through symbol borrowing shows that dispute processes are not a self-contained sphere of social life. That they are culturally specific and must allude to the symbolic life of the culture in which the court operates is clear. Imagine the reaction, for example, if an American judge were to appear in court wearing the wig that is de rigueur in Britain. In the end, it appears that the ritualization of disputing serves multiple purposes. What I want to emphasize is how deeply embedded and important are these symbolic practices.

The Ritual Power of Dispute Processes

Having described the ways in which culturally allusive symbols are employed to enhance the functionality of formal disputing processes, I turn to the second claim of this chapter: that dispute processes that apparently serve only the instrumental purpose of dispute settlement take on a ritual quality and symbolic power of their own. We ought not to unbendingly separate the signifying aspects of the processes from their instrumental activities. Like a holiday dinner, a formal dispute-resolution procedure operates in both spheres. At the feast hunger is sated at the same time that bonds of family and community are acted out and reaffirmed. In court, a dispute is resolved and a system of metaphysics and social arrangements is also reaffirmed through action.

David Garland captures the latter point by invoking the concepts of "signifying practice" to cross "the artificial divide between language and action, the mental and the physical, the ideal and the real."[31] Garland, whose concern is with the cultural agency of punishment in modern society, argues that "in penality the instrumental *is* symbolic."[32] So, too, for dispute processes, whether civil or criminal, and whether of the modern world or of another time or place. In other words, the repeated, procedurally prescribed, socially loaded act of resolving disputes is a ritual that influences and sustains the culture from which it grew.

The process of judging and the acceptance of the judgments by the community recreates the authority of the judge and the persons who have invested him with authority: "It is through periodical ritual practices that social sentiments maintain their force and vitality."[33] Where the judge is a prince or a chief, the ritual of judging by him or his delegate is one of the ways his power is constituted. The act of judgment ritually confirms his special status by its public and practical impact on others. Even in democratic societies, "there is both a governing elite and a set of symbolic forms expressing the fact that it is in truth governing."[34] The rituals of dispute resolution are part of the "set of symbolic forms."

Like most rituals, dispute processes have a conservative bent. They appeal to tradition.

Their repetitive practices tend, as I have argued, to support existing conceptions and arrangements. But we should not leave this discussion without acknowledging the way in which ritual can facilitate social change. Revolutionary governments, of course, will consciously create new rituals, such as "People's Courts," as a way of cementing their new status and of propagating their ideology. Existing rituals of dispute can also enable incremental change to take place in a nonrevolutionary situation. As we have seen, they are used to effect a social transformation involving the judge and the litigants. They can also be used to transform social norms generally by serving as the platform for announcing and effecting a new norm. Rituals help courts do this by providing a link to the existing society, its myths, its elites, and its traditions. The "repetitive elements" of the dispute ritual themselves lend a legitimacy to the result. Thus, the social anxiety likely to be produced by the unsettling announcement of a new norm may be moderated by the adherence to a ritual of process.

Applying the latter perspective to American disputing, one could argue that the Supreme Court, because of the ceremony that characterizes it, is well situated to announce such norm changes as *Brown v. Board of Education* or *Roe v. Wade*. This is a dimension of the debate about institutional competence that deserves more attention than it has received.

My discussion in this chapter has focused on the way ceremony helps official dispute institutions perform their instrumental tasks and on how the symbolically charged operation itself takes on the quality of ritual. In the next chapter I position ritual in a more comprehensive discussion of the influence of disputing on society.

8

How Disputing Influences Culture

The Construction and Maintenance of Culture

In the preceding chapters we saw how institutionalized disputing practices reflect the culture in which they are found. As defined in chapter 1, culture includes the "traditional ideas, values and norms" that are widely shared in a social group.[1] It encompasses normative and cognitive beliefs as well as the symbols that represent those mentalities for its people.[2] We saw that the specific features of formal dispute-ways involve a public acting out and affirmation of the beliefs and assumptions that unite that collectivity, including its shared understanding of the nature of reality, its gender relations, its social hierarchy, its political arrangements, and the symbolic rituals through which these are expressed. We are now ready to examine more closely the claim that the culture/disputing relationship is reflexive—that dispute-ways help "construct" or "importantly influence" culture as well as express it.[3] This is a specific instantiation of Melvin Spiro's thesis that the "cultural heritage" of a people influences their "psyches and actions." In this variation on that theme, formal disputing practices are the operative ingredient of cultural heritage.

Constructing a culture does not end when the edifice is in place. The process is ongoing because, to properly constitute a cultural system, the values, symbols, and beliefs must be widely shared within the relevant community and must be transgenerational. Children must be socialized or "civilized" into the culture.[4] Belief and adherence must be sustained throughout the lives of its members: society must somehow deal with the inevitable struggles over values, practices, and beliefs. Spiro helpfully unpacks this process. Social actors must, first, "*learn about* the propositions; they acquire an 'acquaintance' with them"; second, they must "*understand* their traditional meanings"; third, they "internalize" the propositions—"they hold them to be true, correct, or right" and they are thus "culturally constituted" beliefs. Once the cultural propositions have been thus internalized, they "inform the behavioral environment of social actors, serving to structure their perceptual worlds and hence, to *guide* their actions." Even more, they serve "to *instigate* action, that is, they possess emotional and motivational, as well as cognitive, salience."[5] The process is circular, for action motivated or guided by belief will, if successful, reinforce it. Successful action can mean achieving social approval, internal gratification, or some other desired outcome.

Didactic verbal instruction is the most obvious method of transmitting propositions of culture to new generations. But internalization requires more. Human variety in genetic makeup and personal experience create centrifugal effects that instruction alone cannot counter. In every society, a whole system of sanctions and rewards encourages at least outward acceptance of its fundamental propositions. But no cultural system can rely on such extrinsic motivators alone, or even primarily.[6] Internalization is required. Thus, in addition to schooling, "traditional values, ideas and norms are acquired by the novices indirectly, as a consequence of their observation of and participation in, social relations, religious rituals, and the like."[7] Once internalized, predominant values "seem right" and the predominant metaphysics becomes "common sense."

Challenges to "the way we do things" will come from contrary personalities, dissenting groups, technological change, and diverse models offered by other societies. Since individuals are not automatons, their own creativity will inspire them, Thoreau-like, to march to a different drummer.[8] As too many beats will destroy the social fabric, a minimal orchestration is needed. No culture is eternally constant, so these pressures for change must be accommodated, if not controlled. Continued faith in adults is encouraged through techniques like those with which children were enculturated, with appropriate modification: extrinsic control by positive and negative sanctioning still plays its limited part but now through a system more sophisticated than parental punishment. Formal schooling will have ended, but its work will be supplemented by ceremonial public profession of the culture's credo—especially by political and religious elites. Like sanctions, exhortation is unequal to the task of culture maintenance, not only because the audience is as capable of cynicism as of belief but also because the essence of culture is a set of shared symbols, practices, and beliefs that are so complex, interrelated, and fundamental that exhortation in support of its entirety is probably impossible, and conscious defense of its individual ingredients is usually superfluous.

The maintenance of essential cultural attributes is therefore ensured mostly by the living of them, the performance of basic cognitive and normative propositions in daily life and at important public occasions. That particular human societies maintain their cultures over time is to some extent the product of a kind of collective inertia. "Existence in history produces the marks of history."[9] This epigram suggests how, apart from education and compulsion, culture is transmitted. "History" offers the values, beliefs, symbols, and institutions that largely structure the choices available to each individual. The form in which that history is preserved and transmitted will itself vary with the culture in which it is found—the difference between oral and written encapsulations being only the most obvious of many possible polarities. In all cultures, to return now directly to the argument of this chapter, the "participation in the symbolic practices"[10] of the group will be critical.

That a set of social practices predominant in one area of human life, such as disputing, can importantly influence practices, beliefs, and norms in other areas of society has been recognized by, among others, Pierre Bourdieu. This is basic to his conception of law: "The law is the quintessential form of 'active' discourse, able by its own operation to produce its effects. It would not be excessive to say that it creates the social world, but only if we remember that it is this world which first creates the law."[11] As he describes this process, law transmutes "regularity (that which is done regularly) into rule (that which must be done)" and thus imposes "a representation of normalcy."[12] Since law is a product of dispute, and is simply an aspect of the dispute-ways of specific cultures, Bourdieu's position is close to my own. Law's operation is but a special case of disputing practices importantly influencing culture.

It seems intuitive that people take from their practices in one area of life a sense of how to deal with other situations. But why should that be so? How does the transmittal take place? J. M. Balkin uses the term "cultural software" to refer to the set of shared understandings and modes of thought that are communicated throughout the society.[13] While this "software" guides individual thought and action it allows adaptation and modification by each person.[14] Balkin's account of the spread of "cultural software" is helpful because it recognizes and invokes the limitations and powers of human thought, as developed by cognitive psychologists. An underlying axiom is that human beings "are by nature cultural creatures."[15] We are "*born with* the ability to absorb and communicate previously developed culture. . . ."[16] That is, we have an innate capacity to memorize and internalize ways of being and to express our knowledge and understanding to others. But human memory and creativity are finite, so other qualities of mentality become important. One of these is that the mind is economical. It uses the tools that are at hand—an idea encapsulated in the bit of folk wisdom that enjoins us not to "reinvent the wheel" when about to begin an unfamiliar task. We thus believe things because other people believe them, and act in certain ways because others do. In adulthood people expand the range of figures whose examples they are willing to follow from parents and teachers to institutional authorities.[17] Cultural traditions, as represented in public institutions, dominate thought and have inertial power over action.

Limits of human mental power also explain the propensity to use a concept or cultural tool in a new but different situation, sometimes referred to, after Levi-Strauss, as cultural bricolage. This is the practice of taking the tools at hand to solve the problem at hand, even if it is a new problem, or a different venue of life. The tools can be physical, as when a chair is used as a step-stool, or conceptual. Balkin gives the interesting example of democratic political concepts influencing the functioning of religious organizations. The bricolage is aided, in Balkin's account, by the human attachment to mental processes such as narrative, homology, and metonymic devices.[18]

Whether particular mentalities will spread depends in part on whether they are communicated. Communication increases in power as it enlists properties of mental functioning. Cultural mental units—widely shared knowledge, belief, and symbols—are therefore more likely to be successfully passed on if "they are salient, relevant to existing activities, attractive or entertaining, or if they generate strong emotions."[19] These qualities make them more likely to be remembered and to be communicated to others. Narratives have these properties and perhaps for that reason are an especially powerful means of communication.[20] The same qualities help explain the power of public institutional practices, such as religious ceremonies, to reinforce preexisting beliefs.

Because of the limits of human memory, institutional practices increase their influence in society the more they are repeated. "Constant communication and participation in common social activities are important ways to reproduce and reinforce cultural software in the members of a culture."[21] Consider a marriage ceremony conducted under religious auspices. Its primary function is to celebrate and create a particular social relationship, but in the course of doing so, the participants implicitly proclaim and embrace a particular worldview and set of traditions, cement or impair relations with kin, display attitudes towards gifts and food, and, of course, endorse or disclaim a source of sacral authority. The ceremony becomes a way of accomplishing all of those unstated purposes. To recognize that institutional practices construct culture is necessarily to recognize as well that to some limited but important degree they construct us as persons. Dispute-ways are exactly that kind of practice.

The Power of Disputing Practices

Disputing institutions perform a crucial role in the ongoing work of maintaining or reconstructing social practices and norms, particularly those of authority and epistemology. As Judith Resnik has it, a system of procedure is "a mechanism for expressing political and social relationships. . . ."[22] An institution that "expresses" relationships proclaims the way they are and, by acting them out, endorses them.[23] Hamilton and Sanders observed this process at work in their study of the relationship between values and dispute procedures in the United States and Japan. They found that "[t]he dispute processing options available to disputants in Japan and the United States reflect and preserve differences in the structure of relationships in the two societies."[24] I will return later in this chapter to the Japan-United States comparison as one example of the constructive power of dispute-ways, but I first want to explore the means by which dispute-ways are able to play a significant role. In brief, it is because (1) the importance of dispute resolution to the life of a society and its members insures close attention to it; (2) its methods and results are usually public—in many societies the airing of a major dispute is an occasion of widespread public interest; (3) it requires personal participation—the physical and mental acting out of one's part; (4) narratives are at the heart of dispute, as each contestant will tell a different story, and the resolution process becomes a story of its own; (5) the persons presiding over the process usually bring an authority that precedes their status in the dispute-way process itself; (6) it ritually calls attention to its operation and authority; (7) its processes are repeated over and over before many audiences; and (8) its outcomes are validated through action.

The public, dramatic nature of disputing has long been understood. Recall Homer's description of the trial scene that is part of the cityscape forged by the god Hephestos on the shield of Achilles:

A crowd was in the market-place, where a dispute was going on. Two men disputed over the blood-price of a man who had been killed: one said he offered all, and told his tale before the people, the other refused to accept anything; but both were willing to appeal to an umpire for a decision. The crowd cheered one or the other as they took sides, and the heralds kept them in order. The elders sat in the Sacred Circle on the polished stones, and each took the herald's staff as they rose in turn to give judgment. Before them lay two nuggets of gold, for the one who should give the fairest judgment.[25]

Homer captures in a few lines that combination of authority, sacrality, drama, and social consent that informs so many disputing institutions in various cultures. Millennia later and worlds apart, Kafka's Fräulein Bürstner admits to Josef K., "I'm fascinated with court matters. The court has a strange attraction, doesn't it?"[26] In some sense she speaks for Josef, for Kafka, and for us. Disputing indeed has a "strange attraction."[27]

What is it that accounts for the widespread gripping nature of disputing? These events are "dramatic" in that they are public and exciting. Replete with danger for the disputants, often performed by skilled rhetoricians or magicians, according to the requirements of the genre, their denouement is usually uncertain, and the drama is full of suspense. No wonder that in modern societies, trials are the stuff of legend, literature, and now TV dramas and newscasts. These dramatic qualities help to give dispute processes their constructive power because they engage attention and involvement.[28] This facilitates two means by which dispute-ways operate to "lay the bricks" in the bricolage process: *example* and *participation*.

Example works in part because dispute processes are endorsed and operated by cultural "opinion leaders," those figures who speak with political or sacral authority or, perhaps most often, a combination of the two. We have seen this dynamic in action among the Azande, for whom the oracle of the king was infallible. We see it too in modern systems, including the American. Though most prominently invoking state authority, the American courtroom suggests a link to the sacred through the judge's robe, the ritualized honorific, the separate oaths taken by judge, juror, and witness, and the imposing structure in which trials so often take place. It would be surprising if people did not take cues for correct behavior from these events, as often and effectively reenacted by respected figures as they are: "Nor is this a marginal or specialist activity. . . . It is literally the Law, the authoritative voice of society, using force and authority publicly to enact its basic terms and relationships and to impress them, like a template, upon the conduct of social life."[29] The officially endorsed method of disputing necessarily presents a model of the way authority figures and their subjects should relate, a model especially relevant when the enterprise before them calls for a determination of truth and of right from wrong. Justice Brandeis recognized the constructive function of legal institutions when, in dissent, he objected to a conviction based on illegally obtained evidence and argued that "[o]ur government is the potent, the omnipresent teacher. For good or for ill, it teaches the whole people by its example. If the government becomes a law-breaker, it breeds contempt for law; it invites every man to become a law unto himself; it invites anarchy."[30] The belief in cultural arrangements that is encouraged by the example of authority figures acting out the rituals of dispute is enhanced by ordinary citizens' participation in them. These practices engage more than reason; they convince through participation, whether personal or vicarious. Simply by submitting their dispute to a third party, the litigants acknowledge authority. "The whole process reaffirms both the actual power of the deciders and the presumed efficacy and correctness of the norms and values referred to."[31] Thus, the ritual nature of dispute processes should be reprised here because of its relation to the constructive process, even in contemporary courtrooms.[32]

Court procedures become ritualized through repetition, as we have seen: the way of doing becomes the correct way of doing. "Ritual action is repetitive and, therefore, often redundant, but these very factors serve as important means of channeling emotion, guiding cognition, and organizing social groups."[33] They do so through participation. "We perform in rituals, and doing becomes believing."[34] Or, as Geertz puts it, "How, given what we believe, must we act; what, given how we act, must we believe."[35] Belief precedes and informs action and action informs belief. Dispute processes are well suited to reinforce beliefs and arrangements that underlie them and are expressed in them in part because they are acted upon: when a Zande trial ends with a *benge* verdict, or an American trial ends with a jury verdict based on the evidence, the change in social relations that follows tends to solidify belief not only in the method but also in the values and metaphysics that underlie it. So strong is this acceptance that errors can be explained away by within-the-system reasoning, and fundamentals are left unchallenged.

But must we rely solely on intuition and interpretation, or is there empirical support—real-world instances—of changes in official forms of dispute causing or importantly influencing broader cultural changes? Notwithstanding the notorious difficulty of showing causality in complex institutions,[36] there is intriguing evidence that supports my claim. Disputing institutions have influenced both social relations and cognitive practices. In earlier chapters I sketched out some of the impact on ways of thinking and behaving. In chapter 2 I showed the connection between Zande disputing and social relations by linking *benge* rituals to social status, gender relations, and their entire system of epistemology. The social turmoil that followed the British imposition of a foreign system of resolving disputes was striking. In chapter 3 I argued that the twin pillars of modern dispute resolution, law and evidence, also influence other spheres of social life, including the definition of merit, the formation of the state, and gender relations. In chapter 4 I showed how the "exceptional" qualities of American culture, such as individualism, egalitarianism, and populism, contribute to its disputing practices.[37] And, as we saw with respect to the role of the jury, those practices have in turn reinforced the values they express. Those who shaped the American legal system themselves believed that the equality they valued would be encouraged by the participation of ordinary people in dispute resolution. Recall that the jury's continuing role in the construction of the American persona was observed by Jefferson and by Tocqueville.[38] The development of the jury as a dispute-resolution institution in Anglo-American law is an instance of the "cultural bricolage" I described earlier—the process in which people use the concepts at hand to deal with a new situation. Prior to the twelfth century, the English jury was made up of people who were familiar with the litigants and the background of the dispute. Their role was apparently supplemental to decision by ordeal or battle: "When Henry II and his advisers looked round for a rational and reliable mode of proof (and prosecution) the jury was the best they could find. . . . It was the voice of the neighborhood, the sense of the community, best informed about what went on there."[39] These early jurors were asked to give a verdict under oath, and thus still functioned more like witnesses than an impartial body of fact finders obliged to decide according to the evidence. Over time, "the old mechanical and oracle like process gave way before a more analytical enquiry [and] the jury gradually developed into a neutral and distant body of citizens coming into court with an open mind to give a verdict on the basis of the evidence (such as deeds and witnesses that the parties put before them)."[40]

It was only in the sixteenth century that this practice became general in England. As we have seen, the American colonists then used the jury as much for its political role as for fact finding and contributed to well re-marked features of American culture. So we see a double bricolage. In the first, the informal practice of consulting neighbors is modified into a mode of fact resolution. Then the sense of agency necessarily felt by the empowered jurors becomes one vehicle for developing a new relationship between governed and governor.

The reflexive relationship between disputing and culture is docu-mented in the Hamilton and Sanders study comparing legal institutions in the United States and Japan in the context of citizens' attitudes about per-sonal relationship. This work was enriched by the authors' close attention to the social structures and individual attitudes held in the countries stud-ied. Existing literature and their own cross-cultural surveys led them to state that "Japanese relationships seem both more highly solidary and more hierarchical than those of Americans. The *combination* of hierarchy and solidarity characterizes much of Japanese society."[41] It is apparent that these attitudinal differences are reflected in the respective legal systems.

The two countries are distinguishable with respect to "the set of rules establishing the terms and conditions under which people can use law."[42] Hamilton and Sanders's description invokes themes long dominant in comparisons of the two nations: the American system favors adjudicative proceedings, while the Japanese tilts toward nonadjudicative processes such as mediation and conciliation. In the Japanese paradigm, the "out-come is more dependent upon conciliation and the mutual agreement of the parties."[43] A set of institutions has been created that facilitate such out-comes while, at the same time, barriers to litigation have been erected that steer plaintiffs away from the courts. Hamilton and Sanders also point to differences in the procedures in the courts themselves. They adopt the fa-miliar dichotomy of adversarial American litigation as opposed to the rel-atively inquisitorial system of which Japan is an example. On each of these axes (adjudicative/conciliatory and adversarial/inquisitorial) we are struck by consistency with the observed value differentials. The Japanese proce-dures "parallel Japanese social structure in the sense that they tend to treat people as connected rather than separated, and to encourage solutions that minimize conflict and reduce the probability that relationships be-tween disputants will be permanently severed by the dispute."[44] Inquisito-rial procedures, by the same token, parallel comfort with hierarchy by em-phasizing the authoritative role of the judge.[45]

This convergence of social attitudes and legal systems is multideter-mined. The barriers to court use extant in Japan are partly the work of between-the-wars political elites who had no taste for a litigation-based rights agenda or for increasing litigiousness.[46] The path of Japanese law under the postwar democracy has not, however, substantially shifted direction; nonadjudicative approaches continue to flourish.[47] The Hamilton and Sanders study does not support a rigid top-down explanation of the differences between Japan and the United States. Rather, their survey results indicate a consistency between the values expressed by individual respondents and values expressed in legal institutions.[48] They conclude, "In the long run, we believe that the relationship between structure and culture is circular: Structural relationships affect cultural values, which in turn affect structural relationships. This mutual causality helps to create stability. Institutions and values tend to reinforce each other."[49] The conciliatory and inquisitorial features of Japanese disputing thus reinforce the values of hierarchy and social solidarity.

A similar claim is made by Richard Abel and is based on his study of sub-Saharan Africa. In his essay "A Comparative Theory of Dispute Institutions in Society," he explores the reciprocal influence between culture and disputing.[50] He addresses the matter primarily in the context of changes in the degree of formalism embraced by dispute-resolution systems in the postcolonial African nations that he studied. Abel claims that changes from an informal, "undifferentiated" disputing system typical of some tribal societies to a formal, specialized bureaucratic model typical of more technological societies would affect the local society in predictable ways.[51] Among these, "the internal coherence which characterizes the decisional process of some higher appellate courts may be elevated into an ideology as the rule of law, which in turn exerts pressure upon other dispute institutions to conform their behavior to the criteria of procedural due process."[52] The effect widens still further because "[t]he ideology may be seen as an idealization of the process occurring within [higher-level legal] institutions, which is then generalized as a value for a wide variety of other institutions which handle disputes, e.g., prisons, schools, universities, etc."[53] Contrariwise, a deformalization of disputing would, according to Abel, have the opposite effect. "We know from numerous studies of tribal societies that undifferentiated [informal] dispute institutions tend to preserve and strengthen multiplex, affectual, enduring social relations."[54]

As with social relations, cognitive processes are part of the interpenetration of culture and disputing. I have earlier described how the cognitive processes used in dispute resolution parallel those privileged in collectivities as diverse as the Azande and modern Western nations. Of course, we would expect any society to use its generally available tools of understanding when faced with disputes in need of resolution. To the degree that those tools are relied upon and credited in the disputing process, they are reinforced because of its public, dramatic, repetitive, and narrative qualities. This give and take is illustrated by Balkin in his exploration of the power of metaphor in culture.[55] He uses the example of rational argument as warfare and notes how the adoption of the metaphor structures our understanding of argument. We refer to our "opponent" and we "marshal" arguments with which we "demolish" their "positions." The metaphor adds power to a conceptualization; it thus suppresses alternative modes of thinking about truth seeking. According to Balkin, such metaphors have an effect broader than affecting our view of discussions about disagreements: "The metaphorical model also helps to constitute social conventions of argument and hence helps constitute social reality.... If argument is war rather than cooperation, we are likely to treat the people we argue with differently, and we will expect different treatment as well."[56] I would add that the metaphor also shapes our understanding of reality. It suggests that assertions are true or false and steers us away from shades of difference.

Balkin has thus helped us deepen our understanding of the way that dispute-ways can importantly influence culture. In this example, we see that the way people relate to each other in daily life is a product in part of the nature of their formal dispute institutions. The parent who tells her children that she must hear both "sides" of a sibling quarrel before resolving the dispute reflects and acts upon the process that she would herself expect in court. Without consciously thinking about it, she passes on a model of cognition and behavior. She constructs a culture in the shadow of a dispute-way.

In chapter 6, "The Rise of ADR in Cultural Context," we saw that the most idealistic proponents of ADR hoped—even predicted—that engaging in dispute processes that were less hierarchical, linear, and adversarial than those of the courtroom would nudge society in the same direction. They implicitly adopted the claim of reflexivity that is the subject of this chapter. Recall, for example, that Bush and Folger advocated mediation use as a means of making society less individualist and more relational.[57] For them, mediation's constructive power is based on its informality and consensus, both of which "allow parties to define problems and goals in their own terms, thus validating the importance of those problems and goals in the parties' lives."[58] They theorize that mediation use will promote a more relational society, which "stresses the equal importance of both individuality and connectedness in human consciousness."[59]

Some critics of the Bush-Folger transformation thesis have argued that American culture is too individualistic and fragmented to allow mediation to penetrate its psyche. For instance, in her study of mediation in small-scale societies, Sally Engle Merry noted that the use of mediation depended "on the existence of a cohesive, stable, morally integrated community."[60] Other critics accept the possibility of a metamorphosis but fear that it will not be benign. They worry that informal disputing magnifies, rather than diminishes, political power differences between parties.[61] Some research suggests that the use of nonadjudicative techniques actually increases the disadvantage of the weaker party, showing, for example, that women might be harmed by the mandatory mediation of domestic-relations disputes.[62] An examination of landlord-tenant proceedings in New York similarly reported that tenants were better off when their cases were adjudicated in a formal civil court rather than conciliated in an informal housing court.[63]

Informal disputing procedures might magnify the parties' inequalities because, ironically, many mediators stress the empowerment of the disputants in crafting a solution. Mediator neutrality is the preferred stance if that is the goal, even if one disputant might be using his power to take advantage of the other. While this neutrality might enable disputants to solve their own problems, "'neutrality' always expresses values and confirms existing advantages."[64] Thus, in their desire to maintain neutrality, mediators might actually be strengthening the bargaining power of the stronger party. Another way in which mediation may strengthen the position of the more powerful party is by deemphasizing the importance of rights. Many mediators believe that parties should be discouraged from asserting their legal entitlements in favor of more productive bargaining talk.[65] However, the rights that are deemphasized in mediation and arbitration are the same rights that protect against the naked application of social or personal power in a legal setting. By ignoring these rights in order to emphasize bargaining, ADR may be influencing culture in a way that makes Americans less rights driven, and in turn harms the least powerful citizens.

I cannot resolve the conflicting visions of the social metamorphosis that a paradigm shift in American disputing might bring to social hierarchies and interpersonal relations, but I must note and applaud the respect the debaters show for the connection.

. . .

This chapter began with a discussion of the maintenance of culture over time—its construction and reconstruction. I noted that many students of society accept the importance of public and repetitive action to the maintenance of belief. I then noted that this kind of action is a prominent feature of institutionalized processes for resolving disputes. Together with other features, the performative nature of official disputing makes it a significant medium through which culture is transmitted and influenced. I then described several instances in which this very process has been observed in societies as diverse as precolonial Africa, Japan, and the United States. It should be clear that regardless of the technical nature of much of formal dispute processing, its architects and practitioners operate within the constraints that affect all members of their society, and that their work will, in turn, impact the beliefs and symbols that constitute that culture. In the chapter that follows I will explain why this dynamic must be understood by procedural policymakers.

9

Conclusion

I have presented two claims about institutionalized dispute processes and society: first, that these dispute-ways reflect the culture in which they are found—its values, its social arrangements, its metaphysics, and the symbols through which these qualities are represented; and second, that the relationship is reflexive—that the processes by which disputes are addressed will be an influential ingredient in the ongoing social task of maintaining or "constructing" the culture in which they are located. If these contentions are valid, my theory of disputing will have both predictive and normative utility: it predicts that when the culture goes through substantial change, for whatever reason, the dispute-ways will eventually follow suit. The reverse is also true: changes in disputing will reverberate more broadly. As to normativity, my approach instructs policymakers thinking about the reform of local dispute-ways to be mindful of potential cultural impact. Procedural reform of any consequence cannot be considered under the bell jar of legal technicality.

I recognize that my first claim (that dispute-ways are culture bound) can be read as limiting my second (that they importantly influence culture). If disputing practice is locked in a pas-de-deux with culture, destined to follow its greater partner's lead, how can the process partner possibly effect a change that departs from what is already choreographed? The solution to this paradox lies in returning to the recognition that culture is neither eternal nor absolutely uniform in any society. It is continually contested and therefore subject to change. Competing tugs will whirl it this way or that. These tugs will stem from a clash of political interests, from new social and economic conditions, and from disagreement about how best to serve social needs. Max Weber confronted a variant of this problem in his discussion of the emergence and development of legal norms. If legal norms arise from social consensus and take on the character of coercion, "there arises the question of how anything could ever change in this inert mass of canonized custom which, just because it is considered as binding, seems as though it could never give birth to anything new."[1] He argues that a "new line of conduct" can emerge as the result of changes in individual behavior that, because of new conditions, spread through the society. Change can also result when one of several available arrangements is seen by the community to be best suited to dealing with new conditions. Change takes place in part through the unconscious treatment of new rules as variants of the old.[2] Weber's points apply to procedural change as well. Individual and institutional changes in that important sphere of social life can have cultural resonance and can move the society in a new direction.

Architects and reformers of processes must often choose one value at the expense of another. Thorough truth finding, for example, will exact costs in time and expense. I do not propose that a culture-sensitive analysis will necessarily dictate a resolution of such conflicts. I urge only that the constructive power of dispute-ways should be on the agenda.[3] The outcome should depend on an estimate of the cultural clash and constructive strength of a contemplated new direction and, even more important, the desirability of the value that will be served.

To illustrate this mode of analysis I consider a hypothetical proposal to abolish the use of civil juries in the United States.[4] Assume that it is argued that juryless trials are likely to take less time, to be less costly, and to produce more accurate results. The culturally sensitive analyst would ask how the change would affect the predominant understanding of citizens' relation to government, and how it would affect personal relation to authority in the society. If, as I do, one worries about the potential for authoritarianism in any society, and hence favors greater agency for individuals, one would oppose this change, even accepting the assumptions. Jury service contributes to a sense of empowerment, i.e., "the opportunity and the right to make decisions about one's own life and to participate in decision making on public issues."[5]

In *Crimes of Obedience*, their study of authoritarianism in American life, Kelman and Hamilton[6] seek to understand the social and psychological factors that lead people to comply with or resist directions to commit immoral or illegal acts. While too complex to report here in detail, they conclude in essence that the life experiences of the subjects vis-à-vis institutional and other authority figures are a critical factor in determining how they will respond to direction from authority. Because of their belief in the constitutive powers of social practices,[7] the authors argue that governmental and other institutions should be structured so as to enhance personal empowerment and efficacy. "Structural changes most conducive [to this] would involve the *dispersion of authority* within the society."[8] In addition to dispersal, the authors encourage "changes in social structures, educational experiences, and group supports that will ensure citizens and subordinates in bureaucratic hierarchies regular access to *multiple perspectives*, external to and independent from the authority. Exposure to alternative perspectives helps individuals increase their psychological distance from authority, thus enabling them to evaluate its demands with a greater degree of independence."[9]

The objects of authority—those who are expected to comply—are not the only audience that receives social signals about compliance. Authority figures are addressed as well. Their experience in and observation of the functioning of institutions characterized by dispersal of authority and multiple perspective will reinforce the sense of the agency of other members of society. Role performance that continually enacts an ideal of shared authority, of a negotiated reality, will underscore appropriate limits for all authority figures.

The jury is an institution that serves well the functions Kelman and Hamilton describe as important to the maintenance of a nonauthoritarian society. It promotes individual agency, dispersion of authority, and the recognition of multiple perspectives.[10] This cultural role should not be ignored.

A change in the model will lead to a change in the society for which it is a model. Thus, in addition to asking whether a proposed deep change in a disputing institution makes sense instrumentally, this suggests that we ask whether the signal it gives as to the proper ordering of society is acceptable. To quote Mirjan Damaška, writing on the rise of authoritarianism in Continental Europe, "People became adapted to strong central rule, regarding it as both antagonist and savior. Liberal cynics would probably prefer to say that people became insensitive to the evils of concentrated power in the way that Mithridates became immune to poison: by taking it in increasing doses."[11]

For the body politic, dispute-ways can be elixirs, or poisons.

Afterword

The Classroom and the Terror of Relativism

Colleagues who have been kind enough to read drafts of this book have occasionally raised an eyebrow of the following sort: cultural sensitivity is all well and good, but surely you do not mean to say that the only difference between the oracle consultation of the Azande and the evidentiary analysis of the modern court is that they reflect different cultural assumptions. Don't you agree, they press me, that our methods are more rational and will yield better results than theirs? (This is a variant of wondering whether the traveler returning from years abroad has "gone native.") It is clear that for my interlocutors there is only one answer. This brings me to the seminar on culture and disputing that I described in the preface. I love to teach it for many reasons, but the most important is the opportunity it gives students to confront the very same question. It prompts that liberation of mind that is the point of all serious education. Like all moments of true liberation, it combines terror and elation.

Taught to law students and graduate students in the NYU Law and Society program, it presents the themes and arguments of this book: systems of dispute resolution do not exist in nature—they are created by human beings and are culture specific; moreover, disputing procedures are one of the important institutions through which the construction of social life is in turn accomplished. There are readings from comparative law, socio-legal studies, and anthropology. We ask the students to join us as we wander back and forth across boundaries. But to describe the pedagogic process as I have just done is to risk the distancing of abstraction. It is confronting difference in the specific that makes it real.

One example comes from comparative law. Chapter 4, "American 'Exceptionalism' in Civil Litigation," conveys some sense of how differently otherwise similar societies can think about the best way to resolve disputes. Ideas about the relationship between governed and government, about fairness, and even about how truth can be established inform the rules of procedure. More fundamentally, one encounters an unexpected incommensurability of concept. It is not just that the rules are different; it is that the vocabulary of one system does not adequately explain another. Consider the word "trial." For U.S. lawyers it is the key event. It requires the continuous presentation of mostly oral evidence before a judge and a jury that then considers the information and makes findings of fact. Even if the trial is not reached because of settlement or the like, anticipation of trial colors all that comes before it. But, as I learned from the sometimes sharp reaction of respected Continental colleagues, the trial is an Anglo-Americentric concept with little relevance to those following the civil law tradition. To assume that a trial, as Americans know it, is of equal relevance to, say, an Italian lawyer, would be like assuming the relevance of the "double play" to an Italian sports fan.

There is no single event called a "trial" in Continental litigation. Evidence is instead presented to a judge during a series of meetings attended by the parties and their lawyers. When all are satisfied that what is necessary to resolve the disputed facts has been presented, no further sessions will be held. The judge will later review a written summary of the proceedings, called "the dossier," and in due course issue a decision. The English-language phrase used to describe this process is the "first instance proceeding"—"first instance" because it is the initial proceeding in the case and takes place before the lower court, as opposed to an appellate (or "second instance") court. So in order to converse intelligently across national frontiers we must accept the parochialism of the word "trial." Yet "first instance proceeding" cannot substitute for "trial" because the latter is but one type of such proceedings. The language difficulties are further complicated by a trend in some civil law countries, especially Germany, to organize the first instance proceeding so that it builds toward a "main hearing." There will still be other, prior proceedings before the court, but they will have more of a preparatory flavor. It is at the "main hearing" that the parties are expected to bring in whatever remaining proof they have and to make their legal arguments to the court. Is this a trial? It is tempting to call it that, but to do so would be to ignore its place as one, albeit the most important, of a series of events in the first instance proceeding.

There is no word that conveys both the American trial and the first instance proceeding. That is why the English language title of Kafka's book, *The Trial* (*Der Prozess* in German) is a misnomer. As fans of the book will recall, there is no "trial" in *The Trial.* Yet what English word or phrase would be a better title? Perhaps "The Legal Process." But even apart from its inelegance, it would be little better than *The Trial* in conveying the meaning of the German title, because it is so open ended.

The recognition of incommensurability of concept is valuable to lawyers who may someday engage in cross-border legal practice. It also speaks to the difficulties of translation generally, a lesson that transcends law and legal practice. To push further, our struggle with the "trial" even suggests the impossibility of labels. Thus, we could insist on "first instance procedure" to include American trials, Italian episodic proof sessions, and German "main hearings." Yet we must recognize that this solution disguises real differences, even as it encompasses similarities. The pedagogic point is to get students to see that what is familiar is not necessarily universal and is hardly "natural."

We take the point further when we move outside of modernity altogether. With as much neutrality as we can muster, we therefore introduce our students to the oracular justice of the Azande, as described in chapter 2. We choose this example precisely because of the reaction it engenders. Like the English skeptics described by Evans-Pritchard, our students are bemused, dubious, and amused. They ask the same questions: Can't the Azande see that their oracles are nonsense? Don't they see that the oracle's decision is often wrong? Isn't the whole process open to manipulation? What happens when the oracle contradicts itself?

To use these very apt queries as door openers you need first of all to locate the specific process of divination within the general context of a culture in which what we call the supernatural is an obvious, well observed fact of physical life. Then you must locate the divination process in the mind of an individual who has lived all of his life in that culture. Only then can you ask, Does this make "sense"? You turn the questions around. You ask your American students whether a judge can disagree with a jury that has heard the very same evidence, whether trials are subject to manipulation, and whether juries reach wrong conclusions. After hearing the predictable answers to all of those questions—and it helps to have some students in the class who are from civil law countries, for they usually regard the jury as only slightly less nonsensical than giving *benge* to baby chicks—you explore the underlying conundrum. Is the truth about contested past events ever knowable with certainty? We ask our students whether the jury should be purged from our legal system. Almost all say "no." Pressed, they describe what they come to see as the culture-bound assumptions that underlie that special institution: "Well, the jury is important to us and it is the best we can do within our system."

And now, at last, I come to the disquieting part of my story. Even as students grasp the notion that "our attachment to our culture is no different from their attachment to theirs," they are moved to ask, "Does that mean that our system is no better than theirs? That our window onto reality is no more reliable than theirs?" And then, turning to authority, they add, "Do not tell us only that 'ours is better for us, theirs for them,' for that is a copout. We need to know your answer, dear professor," exclaim the now uneasy students. "Lead us back across this frontier."

"No," replies the even more unnerved teacher, suspended in a web of his own imagining, "Lead me back."

Notes

NOTE TO THE PREFACE

1. Clifford Geertz, "Fact and Law in Comparative Perspective," in *Local Knowledge*, 3rd ed. New York: Basic Books, 1983, at 167, 233.

NOTES TO CHAPTER 1

1. William L. F. Felstiner et al., "Influences of Social Organization on Dispute Processing," 9 *Law and Society Review* 63 (1974).

2. A thorough survey and description of many varieties of dispute methods and institutions found in preindustrial societies is provided in Simon Roberts, *Order and Dispute*. New York: St. Martin's Press, 1979. See especially 53–79. This book also contains a useful bibliography and a thematic review of the development of studies of order and dispute in small-scale societies. See id. at 184–206.

3. See chapter 2, infra.

4. See chapter 4, infra.

5. On the role of party testimony in trials in civil law countries, see Mirjan R. Damaska, *Evidence Law Adrift*. New Haven, Conn.: Yale University Press, 1997, at 114, n. 79.

6. This does not mean that there are no criticisms or that improvements are not sought. On modern societies, see Adrian A. S. Zuckerman, "Justice in Crisis: Comparative Dimensions of Civil Procedure," in Adrian A. S. Zuckerman, *Civil Justice in Crisis: Comparative Perspectives of Civil Procedure*. Oxford: Oxford University Press, 1999, 3–52: "A sense of crisis in the administration of justice is by no means universal, but it is widespread. Most countries represented in this book are experiencing difficulties in the operation of their system of civil justice." Id. at 12.

7. Useful works on particular aspects of the relationship between society and disputing include Richard L. Abel, "A Comparative Theory of Dispute Institutions in Society," *Law and Society Review* 217 (Winter 1974); Paul Schiff Berman, "An Observation and a Strange but True 'Tale': What Might the Historical Trials of Animals Tell Us about the Transformative Potential of Law in American Culture?" 52 *Hastings Law Journal* 123–79 (2000); Mirjan R. Damaska, *The Faces of Justice and State Authority* (1986); Mirjan R. Damaska, "Rational and Irrational Proof Revis-

ited," 5 *Cardozo Journal of International and Comparative Law* 25 (1997); William L. F. Felstiner, supra note 1; Rebecca Redwood French, *The Golden Yoke* (1995); Clifford Geertz, "Fact and Law in Comparative Perspective," in *Local Knowledge* (1983); K. N. Llewellyn and E. A. Hoebel, *The Cheyenne Way: Conflict and Case Law in Primitive Jurisprudence* (1941); Laura Nader, *The Life of the Law: Anthropological Projects*. Berkeley: University of California Press, 2002; Laura Nader and Harry F. Todd, Jr., eds., *The Disputing Process: Law in Ten Societies* (1978); Katherine S. Newman, *Law and Economic Organization* (1983); Simon Roberts, *Order and Dispute*, supra note 2 (1979).

While I am indebted to all of these scholars, I build on their work and lay out my own account for the mutually constructive relationship between culture and dispute.

8. Melford E. Spiro, *Culture and Human Nature*. New Brunswick, N.J.: Transaction Publishers, 1994, at ix. Spiro makes this distinction in the context of his discussion of the ways that "cultural heritage" influences the "psyches and actions" of persons in that society. In this book I am attending to a variation of that theme in that I want to look at the effect of a particular set of practices and their influence on the society.

9. Robert Post, ed., *Law and the Order of Culture*. Berkeley: University of California Press, 1991, see "Introduction, The Relatively Autonomous Discourse of Law," at vii.

10. On the constitutive perspective, especially as contrasted with a more traditional and instrumental view of law, see Austin Sarat and Thomas R. Kearns, eds., *Law in Everyday Life*. Ann Arbor: University of Michigan Press, 1993, Sarat and Kearns, "Beyond the Great Divide: Forms of Legal Scholarship and Everyday Life," 21–61.

11. Geertz, "Fact and Law in Comparative Perspective," supra note 7, 167, 182.

12. Geertz, supra note 7 at 181.

13. For a history of the iconography of Justice in the West, see Dennis E. Curtis and Judith Resnik, "Images of Justice," 96 *Yale Law Journal* 1727–72 (1987); and Judith Resnik, "Managerial Judges," 96 *Harvard Law Review* 374–448, Appendix (1982).

14. See Laura Nader, *The Life of the Law: Anthropological Projects*, supra note 7.

15. For a useful and insightful review of this debate, see David Nelken, *Towards a Sociology of Legal Adaptation*; David Nelken and Johannes Feest, eds., *Adapting Legal Cultures*. Oxford: Hart, 2001, at 3–15; see also Brian Z. Tamanaha, *A General Jurisprudence of Law and Society*. Oxford: Oxford University Press, 2001, chapters 3–5.

16. Tamanaha, supra note 15 at 107–32. Important criticisms of the mirror thesis are found in the work of Alan Watson, see, e.g., *The Evolution of Law*. Oxford: Blackwell, 1985, and in William Ewald, "Comparative Jurisprudence (II): The Logic of Legal Transplants," 43 *American Journal of Comparative Law* 489–510 (1995).

17. Roger Cotterrell, "Law in Culture," 17 *Ratio Juris* 1, 2 (March 2004).

18. For a thorough discussion of relevant developments, see Gerhard Walter and Fridolin M. R. Walther, *International Litigation: Past Experiences and Future Perspectives.* Bern: Stampfli Verlag AG, 2000.

19. Sally Engle Merry, "Law, Culture, and Cultural Appropriation," 10 *Yale Journal of Law and the Humanities* 575, 579 (1998).

20. See, e.g., Merry, supra note 19 at 578–88.

21. Anthony G. Amsterdam and Jerome S. Bruner, *Minding the Law.* Cambridge, Mass.: Harvard University Press, 2000, at 231. The authors adopt a view of culture that combines "social-institutional" and the "interpretative-constructivist" conceptions of culture. "The former serves to mark the importance of the forms of institutionalization and legitimization that all societies require for the establishment and maintenance of canonicity; the latter highlights the ubiquitous pressure exerted by both solitary and communal *possible-world* construction on institutionalized canonicity." Id.

22. On the utility of culture as a concept despite its difficulties, see also Roger Cotterrell, "The Concept of Legal Culture," in David Nelken, ed., *Comparing Legal Cultures,* Brookfield, Vt.: Dartmouth Publishing Co., 1997, 13, 29: "In certain contexts, however, the idea of an undifferentiated aggregate of social elements, co-present in a certain time and place, may be useful and even necessary in social research. This idea is expressed conveniently in the concept of culture."

Cotterrell has also argued for a disaggregation of the concept of culture into four Weberian ideal types of community, Roger Cotterrell, "Law in Culture," 17 *Ratio Juris* 1–14 (March 2004).

23. A. L. Kroeber and Clyde Kluckhorn, *Culture: A Critical Review of Concepts and Definitions.* New York: Vintage Books, 1952, at 357.

24. Spiro, supra note 8 at viii.

25. Id. at 32.

26. Richard A. Shweder and Jonathan Haidt, "Cultural Psychology of Emotions: Ancient and New," in Richard A. Shweder, *Why Do Men Barbecue?* Cambridge, Mass.: Harvard University Press, 2003 at 136.

27. See discussion in Roberts, supra note 2 at 154–67.

28. Roberts, supra note 2 at 54. See also id. at 166.

29. Felstiner, "The Influences of Social Organization," supra note 1.

30. Roberts, supra note 2 at 86–87.

31. Id. at 94.

32. Katherine S. Newman, *Law and Economic Organization: A Comparative Study of Preindustrial Societies.* Cambridge: Cambridge University Press, 1983.

33. Id. at 53.

34. The five dimensions are

the existence of a third party or hearing body;

a social requirement to use the third party;

the authoritativeness of third-party decisions;

the centralization of decision making;

multiple levels of jurisdiction or appeal.

35. See Newman, supra note 32 at 117–21 for her methodology.

36. Id. at 214. Newman uses "materialist" as a shorthand for "the historical-materialist approach developed by . . . Karl Marx and his collaborator Friedrich Engels." Id.

37. Id. at 210.

38. A useful taxonomy of the kinds of disputes one may encounter as well as of methods of disputing is provided by Simon Roberts, see *Order and Dispute*, supra note 2 at 45–79.

39. On the cultural factors affecting the process by which disputes are generated, see William L. F. Felstiner, Richard L. Abel, and Austin Sarat, "The Emergence and Transformation of Disputes: Naming, Blaming, Claiming . . . ," 15 *Law & Society Review* 631 (1980–81).

40. See generally Pierre Bourdieu, "The Force of Law: Toward a Sociology of the Juridical Field" (Richard Terdiman, translator), 38 *Hastings Law Journal* 805–53, at 851 (1987).

41. On the difficulty of changing legal systems in the face of cultural norms, see K. Rokumoto, "Law and Culture in Transition," 49 *American Journal of Comparative Law* 545, 559 (2001).

42. See, e.g., Marc Galanter, "The Aborted Restoration of 'Indigenous' Law in India," 14 *Comparative Studies in Society and History* 53–70 (1972).

43. See John L. Comaroff and Simon Roberts, *Rules and Processes: The Cultural Logic of Dispute in an African Context*. Chicago: University of Chicago Press, 1981, for an analysis of the role of dispute processes in the creation of social norms. They argue that it is within the context of dispute processes that norms are revealed, negotiated, and changed. I agree with their claim that "the logic of dispute is ultimately situated in the encompassing system and can be comprehended only as such [and that] it is in the context of confrontation—when persons negotiate their social universe and enter discourse about it—that the character of that system is revealed." Id. at 249. My approach is different from that of Comaroff and Roberts in that I focus on the procedures used in disputing as significations that reflect and constitute cultural values other than (or in addition to) the norms actually involved in the instant dispute.

44. See Roberts, *Order and Dispute*, supra note 2 at 170–71, for examples.

45. Rules Enabling Act, 28 U.S.C. §2072 (a), 1934.

46. See *Guaranty Trust Co. v. York*, 326 U.S. 99, 109, 1945; *Byrd v. Blue Ridge Rural Electric Cooperative*, 356 U.S. 525, 1958; *Hanna v. Plummer*, 380 U.S. 460, 1965.

47. *Sibbach v. Wilson*, 312 U.S. 1, 14, 1941. Here, the Court held that a physical

examination of a party is a procedural matter, and therefore that rule making regarding physical examinations is authorized.

48. *Sibbach*, supra note 47. (The question arose because the Federal Rules of Civil Procedure allow a defendant in a civil action to demand a physical examination of a plaintiff who seeks personal injury damages from the defendant; the plaintiff objected, arguing that the rule was invalid because not a rule of "procedure.")

49. Christopher Stone, "Should Trees Have Standing? Toward Legal Rights for Natural Objects," 45 *Southern California Law Review* 450–501 (1972).

50. Id. at 457.

51. Id. at 455.

52. Hanne Petersen, "Gender and Nature in Comparative Legal Cultures," in David Nelken, ed., *Comparing Legal Cultures*, supra note 22 (argues that an increasing recognition of the connections between humanity and nature will lead to changes in legal culture and legal doctrine).

53. In his thoughtful analysis of the cultural role of the prosecution and trial of animals in the medieval world, Paul Schiff Berman suggests that these trials can also be explained in part as an attempt to validate a particular view of the relationship between nature and humanity, see Berman, supra note 7 at 159–62.

54. "Despite the wide range of organizational forms which may be found in small-scale societies, the mechanisms for maintaining continuity and handling disputes tend almost universally to be directly embedded in everyday life, unsupported by a differentiated legal system." Simon Roberts, *Order and Dispute*, supra note 2 at 27.

55. Roberts, *Order and Dispute*, supra note 2 at 28–29, 203–4.

Notes to Chapter 2

1. A map showing the general area of occupation by the Azande is provided in E. E. Evans-Pritchard, *Witchcraft, Oracles, and Magic among the Azande*. Oxford: Clarendon Press, 1937, at xxvi. Their traditional homeland is now divided among the Central African Republic, the Sudan, and the Congo (formerly Zaire). See Eva Gillies, "Introduction," in E. E. Evans Pritchard, *Witchcraft, Oracles, and Magic among the Azande* (abridged ed. 1976) at vii.

2. *Witchcraft among the Azande*. Produced and Directed by Andre Singer, Granada Television International (Filmmakers Library 1982).

3. The form of questioning is similar to that used in adultery cases as reported by Evans-Pritchard, supra note 1 at 300. One major difference, however, is that only one chick is poisoned with respect to each question in the video.

4. I am grateful to Carol Gilligan for suggesting this last possibility. The phenomenon is not unknown in the West, as suspects sometimes confess to crimes

they did not commit not because of duress alone but because some interrogation techniques suggest such an overpowering case against them that they come to distrust their own memories.

5. So described by John Pemberton III, "Divination in Sub-Saharan Africa," in Alissa LaGamma, *Art and Oracle: African Art and Rituals of Divination* (2000) at 12.

The importance of Evans-Pritchard's work on magic and witchcraft in anthropological thought is discussed in 9 *Int'l Encyclopedia of the Social Sciences* 523 (1968). See also Pemberton, id. Evans-Pritchard's analysis (but not his reporting) is critically discussed in Philip M. Peek, "Introduction," in Peek, ed., *African Divination Systems* (1991) at 7–9.

6. Evans-Pritchard's fieldwork was done during a period of twenty months spent among the Azande during the course of three visits between 1926 and 1930. The area in which Evans-Pritchard resided was at the time under Anglo-Egyptian control, and had been since 1905, Evans-Pritchard, supra note 1 at 18. Other Azande people were in areas controlled by the French and still others, by the Belgians, id. at 14.

7. Evans-Pritchard, supra note 1 at 269. See also Pemberton, supra note 5.

8. See Fred R. Myers, *Pintupi Country, Pintupi Self* (1986) at 21.

9. According to Grootaers, who did fieldwork among the Azande in the Central African Republic in 1991–92, oracular consultation was common, although the methods used in the Central African Republic at that time had changed from those described by Evans-Pritchard. Most notably, neither the *benge* "chicken poison" oracle nor the rubbing board oracle was used by the C.A.R. Azande. Both, however, were reported to be still in use by the Azande of Sudan. See Jan-Lodewijk Grootaers, *A History and Ethnography of Modernity among the Zande*. Doctoral dissertation, U. of Chicago Department of Anthropology, 1996, at 280–310, esp. 286–87.

10. *Witchcraft among the Azande*, produced and directed by Andre Singer, Granada Television International (Filmmakers Library 1982).

11. The video film includes an interview with an Azande who is a Catholic priest. He states that although the people go to religious services, they maintain their traditional supernatural beliefs as well. In this respect the Azande are not alone; divination systems are common throughout much of contemporary Africa, see Pemberton, supra note 5, and Peek, supra note 5.

12. Evans-Pritchard, supra note 1. One cannot allow Evans-Pritchard's assessment of Azande intelligence to pass without comment. Since it implies that some people, as a collectivity, may be more or less intelligent than others, one wonders on what basis he formed his judgment. It may be helpful to quote the entire section from which the quoted portion is taken.

> [N]o effort is made to assess scientifically their psychological characters, but it may be said that in the experience of the author, as well as other Englishmen who have lived among them, the Azande are so used to authority that

they are docile; that it is unusually easy for Europeans to establish contact with them; that they are hospitable, good natured, and almost always cheerful and sociable; that they adapt themselves without undue difficulty to new conditions of life and are always ready to copy the behavior of those they regard as their superiors in culture and to borrow new modes of dress, new weapons and utensils, new words, and even new ideas and habits; that they are unusually intelligent, sophisticated, and progressive, offering little opposition to foreign administration and displaying little scorn for foreigners. . . . The royal class are more proud and conservative; they are contemptuous of their subjects and detest their European conquerors . . . generally they mask behind a cold politeness their dislike of the new order of things and those who impose it. Id. at 13.

It appears that Evans-Pritchard associated intelligence with adaptability and perhaps with docility. In other passages, he notes that "[t]hey have a sound working knowledge of nature in so far as it concerns their welfare. Beyond this point it has for them no scientific interest or appeal." Id. at 80.

At several points he comments favorably on their reasoning abilities within their own metaphysics.

13. Id. at 19.
14. Id. at 337–38.
15. Id. at 338.
16. Id. at 540. See also id. at 267.
17. Id. at 78. See also id. at 541: "It is with death and its premonitions that Azande most frequently and feelingly associate witchcraft, and it is only with regard to death that witchcraft evokes violent retaliation."
18. Id. at 72 (emphasis in original).
19. This and other examples at id. at 69–72.
20. Id. at 64.
21. Id. at 65.
22. Id. at 260–61.
23. Id. at 297.
24. Id. at 299.
25. Id. at 285.
26. Id. at 298–99.
27. The process of gathering the material is described id. at 270–80.
28. Id. at 541. Evans-Pritchard devotes a chapter to Azande medicinal practices, which he calls "leechcraft." Id. at 479–510.
29. See id. at 479–510, where traditional medicine is described.
30. Id. at 26–27, 544.
31. See the description of magic and magical rites at id. at 450–78.
32. Id. at 542.
33. Id. at 542.

34. Id. at 389.
35. Id. at 544.
36. Id. at 544.
37. Id. at 544.
38. Id. at 267.
39. Id. at 267.
40. Id. at 77.
41. Id. at 267–70.
42. Id. at 342.
43. Id. at 267.
44. Id. at 323. Evans-Pritchard notes that the interested parties are present at the consultation. He also points out that because the Azande believe that *benge* works as a supernatural agent, they do not conceive that trickery by manipulation of the doses would be possible.
45. Id. at 330–35.
46. Id. at 342.
47. Evans-Pritchard, supra note 1.
48. Id. at 293.
49. Id. at 329.
50. Id. at 329. Evans-Pritchard expresses some doubt that such dismissals actually took place.
51. Id. at 290.
52. Id. at 14–15.
53. Id. at 14–16.
54.

> The relations of ruling princes to witchcraft are peculiar. Though immune from accusations they believe in witches as firmly as other people, and they constantly consult the poison oracle to find out who is bewitching them. They especially consult it about their wives. . . . When a lesser noble dies his death is attributed to a witch and is avenged the same way as deaths of commoners, but the death of a king or ruling prince is not so avenged and is generally attributed to sorcery or cats. Id. at 33.

(Cats are believed to have witchlike powers.)
55. Id. at 32.
56. Id. at 32–33.
57. Id. at 173.
58. Id. at 168. These are more formal and dignified affairs than those of the commoners, id.
59. Id. at 173. Evans-Pritchard notes that the rules may have changed in that he witnessed nobles accused of witchcraft "on rare occasions" but doubts that it would have happened in earlier times. Id. at 173–74.
60. Id. at 75.

61. Id. at 343.
62. Id. at 293.
63. Id. at 345.
64. Id. at 343.
65. Id. at 16. One of the effects of European influence was the undermining of male authority, id. at 18.
66. Id. at 427–28.
67. Id. at 284. The author qualifies this somewhat by noting that occasionally very old women of good social position have been known to operate the poison oracle, or at least to consult it. Id.
68. Id. at 353.
69. Id. at 284–85.
70. Id. at 284.
71. Id. at 269.
72. Id. at 475.
73. Gillies, supra note 1 at xx–xxi (following Evans-Pritchard, Durkheim, and Levy-Bruhl).
74. Evans-Pritchard, supra note 1 at 313.
75. Id. at 313–51. The questions are implicitly addressed throughout the book, and in some sense the book is an attempt to understand Azande beliefs in a way that makes sense to Westerners.
76. Sally Falk Moore, "Selection for Failure in a Small Social Field: Ritual, Concord, and Fraternal Strife among the Chagga Kilimanjaro, 1968–1969," reprinted in Barbara G. Myerhoff and Sally Falk Moore, eds., *Symbols and Politics in Communal Ideology.* Ithaca, N.Y.: Cornell University Press, 1975, 109, 111–12.
77. Evans-Prichard, supra note 1 at 194–95.
78. Id. at 343–44 (emphasis added). See also id. at 477: the support of "political authority" for vengeance-magic is one of the reasons people continue to believe in magical thinking.
79. King Gbudwe was killed by the British in 1905, id. at 18.
80. Id. at 268.
81. Id. at 18.
82. Id. at 18.
83. See discussion at id. at 511–39.
84. Id. at 521.
85. Id. at 445–46.
86. Id. at 19.

NOTES TO CHAPTER 3

1. Fleming James, Jr., Geoffrey C. Hazard, Jr., and John Leubsdorf, *Civil Procedure* (4th ed. 1992) at 2. See also William Twining, *Rethinking Evidence: Ex-*

ploratory Essays (1990) at 73 (describes the assumptions that underlie this system).

2. Lawrence M. Friedman, "Is There a Modern Legal Culture?" 7 *Ratio Juris* 117–31, 122 (1994).

3. Id. at 122.

4. E. E. Evans-Pritchard, *Witchcraft, Oracles, and Magic among the Azande.* Oxford: Clarendon Press, 1937, at 337–38.

5. Philip M. Peek, "Introduction," in Philip M. Peek, ed., *African Divination Systems* (1991) at 8.

6. P. H. Gulliver, "Case Studies of Law in Non-Western Societies," in Laura Nader, ed., *Law in Culture and Society.* Berkeley: University of California Press, 1969, at 11, 22. In societies in which wealth, status, or power is an accepted determinant of outcomes, these will not, of course, be problems of the kind I am now considering.

7. For example, Justice Harry Blackmun, the author of the *Roe v. Wade* opinion legalizing abortion, was the target of death threats, see Pamela S. Karlan, "Two Concepts of Judicial Independence," 72 *Southern Cal. Law Review* 535, 537 (1999). In addition to its controversial conclusion, *Roe* has been criticized for allegedly reflecting the personal views of the majority of the Supreme Court rather than the law.

8. Judicial decision making is a kind of "domination" in the Weberian sense and Weber recognized that this (and other types of) authority could be legitimated by a combination of a system of generally accepted "rational norms" and the sacredness of tradition, *Max Weber on Law in Economy and Society*, Max Rheinstein, ed. New York: Simon and Schuster, 1967, at 336. This is another way of saying that the authority must be exercised in accordance with the culture in which it is situated.

9. For an extended discussion of norm disputes in the context of another African tribal culture, see John Comoroff and Simon Roberts, *Rules and Processes* (1981). On the conflation of norms and facts in modern dispute systems, see Mirjan R. Damaska, "Rational and Irrational Proof Revisited," 5 *Cardozo Journal of International and Comparative Law* 25–39 at 25–27 (1997).

10. See my discussion of ritual and ceremony in chapter 7. On the use of ritual in this connection, see also Martin Shapiro, *Courts* (1981) at 27–28.

11. On the use of installation ceremonies to change roles and legitimate the changes, see David I. Kertzer, *Ritual, Politics, and Power* (1988), passim; Paul Kahn, *The Cultural Study of Law: Reconstructing Legal Scholarship* (1999) at 83–84 (describing the transformation effected by the judicial confirmation hearing).

12. See, e.g., N.Y. Civil Practice Law and Rules sec. 7506: "Before hearing any testimony, an arbitrator shall be sworn to hear and decide the controversy faithfully and fairly before an officer authorized to administer an oath."

13. Sally Falk Moore, "Selection for Failure in a Small Social Field: Ritual, Concord, and Fraternal Strife among the Chagga Kilimanjaro, 1968–1969," in Barbara

G. Myerhoff and Sally Falk Moore, eds., *Symbols and Politics in Communal Ideology: Cases and Questions.* Ithaca, N.Y.: Cornell University Press, 1975, 109–43, discussed infra, chapter 7.

14. Evans-Pritchard, supra note 4 at 337–38.

15. Paul Kahn, *The Cultural Study of Law: Reconstructing Legal Scholarship.* Chicago: University of Chicago Press, 1999, 39.

16. William Blackstone, 1 *Commentaries on The Laws of England* (1825 ed.) §69 at 62.

17. Max Weber on *Law in Economy and Society,* supra note 8 at 86.

18. Others have picked up Blackstone's trope. See, e.g., G. Edward White, *The American Judicial Tradition* (1976) at 8: the assumption of mechanical jurisprudence that judges merely found the law "fostered an image of judges as oracles who could discover the law's technical mysteries. . . ." According to Ronald Dworkin, however, "The courts are the capitals of law's empire and the judges are its princes but not its seers and prophets. It falls to philosophers, if they are willing, to work out law's ambitions for itself, the purer form of law within and beyond the law we have." *Law's Empire* (1986) at 407.

19. Rene Devisch, "Mediumistic Divination among the Northern Yaka of Zaire," in Philip M. Peek, ed., *African Divination Systems* (1991) at 112, 129.

20. H. Goitein, *Primitive Ordeal and Modern Law.* Littleton, Col.: Rothman, 1980, at 100. The image reproduced in the text is from a painting on a Greek vase. Gotein observes that "all can see the elements of divination and self-absorption here brought into connection with the personification of the source of the law." Id. at 100.

21. Lon Fuller, "The Forms and Limits of Adjudication," 92 *Harvard Law Review* 393 (1978).

22. Jerome Frank, *Law and the Modern Mind* (1930) at 130.

23. See generally Ronald Dworkin, *Law's Empire* (1986); Peter Fitzpatrick, *The Mythology of Modern Law* (1992).

24. White, supra note 18 at 300.

25. Kahn, supra note 15 at 79.

26. See Kahn, id. at 78–81.

27. Kahn, id. at 115.

28. Max Rheinstein, "Introduction," in *Max Weber on Law in Economy and Society,* supra note 8 at xlvi.

29. Stanley Fish, "The Law Wishes to Have a Formal Existence," in Stanley Fish, *There's No Such Thing as Free Speech.* New York: Oxford University Press, 1994, at 141, 170 (quoting Harry Schreiber, "Public Rights and Rule of Law in American Legal History," 72 *Cal. L. Rev.* 236–37 (1984)).

30. H. L. A. Hart, *The Concept of Law,* 2nd ed. Oxford: Clarendon Press, 1997, at 95–99.

31. Id. at 95, 109.

32. On the separation of lawyers' culture from society generally, see the discus-

sion in Brian Z. Tamanaha, *A General Jurisprudence of Law and Society*. Oxford: Oxford University Press, 2001, at 107–12. I do not understand that Tamanaha would reject the claim made here.

33. *Max Weber on Law in Economy and Society*, supra note 8 at 79. See discussion of the jury's history and place in American life in chapter 4, infra.

34. Rule 50, Federal Rules of Civil Procedure. See discussion in James, Hazard, and Leubsdorf, supra note 1 at 404–7.

35. Id. at 392–93.

36. See discussion in chapter 4, infra.

37. On our inflated belief in the rationality of our own systems, see Mirjan R. Damaska, "Rational and Irrational Proof Revisited," 5 *Cardozo Journal of International and Comparative Law* 25–39 (1997).

38. Mirjan R. Damaska, *Evidence Law Adrift*. New Haven, Conn.: Yale University Press, 1997, at 151.

39. Clifford Geertz, "Local Knowledge: Fact and Law in Comparative Perspective," in *Local Knowledge: Further Essays in Comparative Anthropology* (1983) at 167, 173.

40. On fact skepticism, see Jerome Frank, *Courts on Trial*. Princeton, N.J.: Princeton University Press, 1949, esp. 17–37.

41. Martin Shapiro also makes the connection between general intellectual developments and fact finding at trials. "In the seventeenth century notions of probability or relative certainty seem to develop side by side in theology, science, and law. In Western societies a trial gradually comes to be seen as an empirical investigation designed to determine the weight of the evidence on each side rather than as an attempt to discover absolute truth." Shapiro, supra note 10 at 47.

That the trier of the fact must determine which version is more probable, and that the outcome is affected by pre-set burdens (e.g., "a preponderance of the evidence") does not undermine the central point that the evidence must be evaluated for its veracity. Otherwise, the weight of the respective positions could not be established. Thus, even to determine a probability of accuracy we must consult an "oracle" of some kind.

42. Michael Palmer and Simon Roberts, *Dispute Processes*. London: Butterworths, 1998, at 1–2.

43. See Judith Resnik, "Failing Faith: Adjudicatory Procedure in Decline," 53 *U. Chicago Law Rev.* 494 (1986).

44. See generally Sandra Day O'Connor, "The Challenge of a Woman in Law," in Shimon Shetreet, ed., *Women in Law*. Cambridge, Mass.: Kluwer International, 1998, at 5–13 (describes the progressive enlargement of female participation in the American legal system).

45. Lewis A. Kornhauser and Richard L. Revesz, "Legal Education and Entry into the Legal Profession: The Role of Race, Gender, and Educational Debt," 70 *New York University Law Review* 829–964 at 849 (table 8).

46. For a critical assessment of law schools' attempts to mold women into male points of view, see Lani Guinier, "Becoming Gentlemen: Women's Experiences at One Ivy League Law School," 143 *U. Pa. L. Rev.* 1 (1994).

47. Wolf Heydebrand and Carroll Seron, *Rationalizing Justice: The Political Economy of Federal District Courts.* Albany: State University of New York Press, 1990, at 22, quoting James Willard Hurst, *The Growth of American Law* (1950) at 194.

48. Kahn, supra note 15 at 113. See also discussion and authorities cited at Paul Schiff Berman, "An Observation and a Strange but True 'Tale': What Might the Historical Trials of Animals Tell Us about the Transformative Potential of Law in American Culture?" 52 *Hastings Law Journal* 123–80, esp. 133–37 (2000).

49. Friedman, supra note 2 at 125.

50. Id.

51. Paul Kahn claims that "[t]he rule of law shapes our experience of meaning everywhere and at all times. It is not alone in shaping meaning, but it is rarely absent." Supra note 15 at 124. He connects the patriarchal nature of the traditional family with the patriarchal authority of the state.

52. Id. at 83.

NOTES TO CHAPTER 4

1. See, e.g., Mauro Cappelletti, *Social and Political Aspects of Civil Procedure: Reforms and Trends in Western and Eastern Europe*, 69 *Mich. L. Rev.* 847, 885–86 (quotes the eminent nineteenth-century Austrian proceduralist Franz Klein observing the connection of culture and procedure). See also Richard L. Abel, "A Comparative Theory of Dispute Institutions in Society," *Law and Society Review* 217 (Winter 1974); Mirjan R. Damaska, *The Faces of Justice and State Authority* (1986); Mirjan R. Damaska, "Rational and Irrational Proof Revisited," 5 *Cardozo J. Int'l and Comp. L.* 25 (1997); William L. F. Felstiner, "Influences of Social Organization on Dispute Processing," 9 *Law and Society Review* 63 (1974); Laura Nader and Harry F. Todd, Jr., eds., *The Disputing Process: Law in Ten Societies* (1978); Katherine S. Newman, *Law and Economic Organization* (1983); Simon Roberts, *Order and Dispute* (1979). Michele Taruffo, "Transcultural Dimensions of Civil Justice" 23 *Comparative Law Review* 1 (2000).

2. E.g., John D. Jackson, "Playing the Culture Card in Resisting Cross-Jurisdictional Transplants: A Comment on 'Legal Processes and National Culture,'" 5 *Cardozo J. Int'l and Comp. L.* 51, 52–53 (1997).

3. For a thorough and insightful discussion of examples of relevant developments, see Gerhard Walter and Fridolin M. R. Walther, *International Litigation: Past Experiences and Future Perspectives.* Bern: Stampfli Verlag AG, 2000. See also Taruffo, supra note 1 at 14–18 (describes efforts to harmonize procedure).

4. ALI/UNIDROIT Principles and Rules of Transnational Civil Procedure, Pro-

posed Final Draft (The American Law Institute: Philadelphia, 2004) at 15–16 (hereafter cited as the "ALI/UNIDROIT Project"). See also Geoffrey C. Hazard, Jr., and Michele Taruffo, "Transnational Rules of Civil Procedure," 30 *Cornell Int'l L.J.* 493 (1997).

5. The proposal is discussed in Linda Silberman, "Comparative Jurisdiction in the International Context: Will the Proposed Hague Judgments Be Stalled?" 52 *DePaul L. Rev.* 319 (2002) and Peter H. Pfund, "The Project on the Hague Conference on Private International Law to Prepare a Convention on Jurisdiction and Recognition/Enforcement of Judgments in Civil and Commercial Matter," 24 *Brooklyn J. Int'l L.* 7 (1998).

6. This project is described and discussed in Marcel Storme, ed., *Approximation of Judiciary Law in the European Union.* Kluwer, 1994. See also Gerhard Walter and Fridolin M. R. Walther, *International Litigation: Past Experiences and Future Perspectives.* Bern: Stampfli Verlag AG, 2000, at 33–34.

7. Oscar G. Chase, "Culture and Disputing," 7 *Tulane J. of Int'l and Comparative Law* 81 (1999); Oscar G. Chase, "Legal Processes and National Culture," 5 *Cardozo J. of Int'l and Comparative Law* 1 (1997).

8. For a concise but thorough discussion of the distinguishing characteristics of American rules see the ALI/UNIDROIT PROJECT, supra note 4 at 7–10.

9. The argument that legal culture is distinct from national culture is presented in, e.g., John D. Jackson, "Playing the Culture Card in Resisting Cross-Jurisdictional Transplants: A Comment on 'Legal Processes and National Culture,'" 5 *Cardozo J. of International and Comparative Law* 51, 53–57 (1997). On the difficulties encountered in defining and applying the concept of legal culture, see David Nelken, "Towards a Sociology of Legal Adaptation," in *Adapting Legal Cultures.* Oxford: Hart, 2001, at 11–15; Eric A. Feldman, *The Ritual of Rights in Japan: Law, Society, and Health Policy.* Cambridge: Cambridge University Press, 2000, at 148–51.

10. See, taking a similar approach to the creation of criminal justice regimes, David Garland, *The Culture of Control.* Chicago: University of Chicago Press, 2001, at 139–42.

Robert A. Kagan notes the financial incentives for the American bar to maintain the practices of adversarial legalism, but also notes that the legal elites' vision is restricted by "distinctive American traditions," *Adversarial Legalism: The American Way of Law.* Cambridge: Harvard University Press, 2001, at 152. See also id. at 243–45.

11. Id. at 15–16. See also id. at 242–50.

12. See, e.g., Geert Hofstede, *Culture's Consequences* (1980); F. Trompenaars and C. Hampden-Turner, *Riding the Wave of Culture,* 2nd ed. New York: McGraw-Hill, 1998.

13. Seymour Martin Lipset, *American Exceptionalism: A Double-Edged Sword.* New York: Norton, 1996, at 18. Even before Tocqueville, others had commented

on particular distinctive aspects of American society. Lipset mentions Burke and Crèvecouer, id. at 33–34.

14. See supra note 13.

15. See, e.g., Jerold Auerbach, *Justice without Law?* (1983) at 10 (describes America as "a society where the dominant ethic is competitive individualism"); Geert Hofstede, *Culture's Consequences* (1980) at 222; Robert N. Bellah et al., *Habits of the Heart: Individualism and Commitment in American Life* (1985) at 142; Lawrence M. Friedman, *The Republic of Choice: Law, Authority, and Culture* (1990) at 27–35.

16. See note 13, supra, and Lipset, supra note 13, passim.

17. Lawrence Rosen, "Individualism, Community, and the Law: A Review Essay," 55 *University of Chicago Law Review* 571–84, at 581 (1988).

18. See, e.g., Larry G. Gerber, "Shifting Perspectives on American Exceptionalism: Recent Literature on American Labor Relations and Labor Politics," 31 *Journal of American Studies* 253 (1997), and authorities collected at id., n. 1.

19. Sidney Verba, Review of *American Exceptionalism: A Double-Edged Sword*, 91 *American Political Science Review* 192, 193 (1997).

20. Lipset, supra note 13 at 31. See also Herbert Jacob, "Courts and Politics in the United States," in Herbert Jacob, Erhard Blankenburg, Herbert M. Kritzer, Doris Marie Provine, and Joseph Sanders, *Courts, Law, and Politics in Comparative Perspective* (1996) at 16, 28 (the "widely held beliefs [that] affect the American legal system" are individualism, rights orientation, and egalitarianism). And see Sally Engle Merry, *Getting Justice and Getting Even: Legal Consciousness among Working-Class Americans*. Chicago: University of Chicago Press, 1990, at 181–82. Merry finds a similar dynamic among the working-class Americans she studied.

21. Lipset, supra note 13 at 19.

22. De Tocqueville also recognized the mutually supporting relationship between egalitarianism and individualism, see *Democracy in America* (Anchor Books ed., 1969) at 641.

23. Lipset, supra note 13 at 20. In addition to the sources cited by Lipset in support of the claim that American culture is more individualistic than others, see authorities cited at n. 15.

24. Lipset, supra note 13 at 39.

25. Damaska, *The Faces of Justice*, supra note 1 at 233.

26. Lipset, supra note 13 at 58.

27. Id. at 22.

28. Lipset, supra note 13 at 23, quoting Mary Ann Glendon, "Rights in Twentieth-Century Constitutions," in Geoffrey R. Stone, Richard A. Epstein, and Cass R. Sunstein, eds., *The Bill of Rights in the Modern State* (1992) at 521.

29. Auerbach, *Justice without Law?* (1983) at 138.

30. Damaska, *The Faces of Justice*, supra note 1 at 11. Damaska does not claim that political organizations and goals are the only determinants of legal processes.

Significantly, he acknowledges the limits imposed by "existing inventories of moral and cultural experience, the fabric of inherited beliefs, and similar considerations." Id. at 241.

31. Lipset, supra note 13 at 43. But most English-speaking countries are more like the United States in this respect.

32. Id. at 49–50. The claim of American litigiousness is supported by statistics showing that the United States leads five other industrialized European nations, by far, in number of lawyers per population and tort costs as a percentage of GNP. See id. Table 1-1 at 50. See also id. at 227, showing similar disparities between the United States and Japan. The connection between American individualism and high court use is also asserted by Auerbach, see *Justice without Law* (1983) at 10–11, 138–40.

Marc Galanter has elsewhere challenged the claim that Americans are more litigious than other peoples, see "Reading the Landscape of Disputes: What We Know and Don't Know (and Think We Know) about Our Allegedly Contentious and Litigious Society," 31 *UCLA L. Rev.* 4 (1971).

33. Lipset, supra note 13 at 235, quoting Ronald Dore, "Elitism and Democracy," 14 *Tocqueville Review* 71 (1993) (emphasis in original).

34. Sally Engle Merry, supra note 20 at 181.

35. ALI/UNIDROIT Project, supra note 4 at 7–8.

36. See *The Faces of Justice*, supra note 1 at 4 (noting that "[t]o Anglo-Americans, . . . the two concepts are suffused with value judgments: the adversary system provides tropes of a rhetoric extolling the virtues of liberal administration of justice in contrast to an antipodal authoritarian process"). Another trenchant criticism of the terminology is found in Mauro Cappelletti and Bryant G. Garth, "Civil Procedure," 16 *International Encyclopedia of Comparative Law* ch. 1, 31–32 (1987), who emphasize, however, the fact that many common law jurists continue to use the term "inquisitorial" to refer to the civil law procedural system.

37. Damaska, *The Faces of Justice*, supra note 3.

38. See Lipset, supra note 13 at 108: "The American social structure and values foster the free market and competitive individualism." See also Herbert Jacob in *Courts, Law, and Politics*, supra note 20 at 29: "[T]he legal system in the United States reflects core values of the nation's political and legal tradition, particularly an emphasis on individual rights, a focus on constitutionalism of proposed actions, limited government, and aspirations of egalitarianism."

39. William W. Schwarzer and Alan Hirsch, "The Modern American Jury: Reflections on Veneration and Distrust," in Robert E. Litan, ed., *Verdict* (1993) at 399. See also George L. Priest, "Justifying the Civil Jury," id. at 103. Judith Resnik notes, however, that the American legal system is in the process of devaluing fact finding, whether by jury or judge, see "Finding the Factfinders" in *Verdict*, id. at 500.

40. Mirjan R. Damaska, *Evidence Law Adrift* (1997) at 28 (notes that while ju-

ries were established in France and elsewhere following the French Revolution, "the Continental love affair with the jury was one of short duration." Juries are used in criminal cases only in Belgium, Switzerland, and Denmark, id. at n. 5.

41. The Seventh Amendment provides, "In suits at common law, where the value in controversy shall exceed twenty dollars, the right of trial by jury shall be preserved and no fact tried by a jury, shall be otherwise reexamined in any Court of the United States, than according to the rules of common law."

In criminal cases, the right to a trial by an "impartial jury" is guaranteed by the Sixth Amendment to the Constitution.

42. Federal Rule Civ. Proc. 38(a).

43. The Constitution of the State of New York, Art. I, Sec. 2.

44. Damaska, *The Faces of Justice*, supra note 1 at 36, noting that lay participation in decision making was introduced into the criminal process. See also id. at 208, observing the use of lay jurors in French criminal trials after the revolution.

45. Id. at 219–20. The passage refers to the pre-twentieth-century period when "classic civil procedure" was still used in England, including the civil jury.

46. On the decline of the civil jury in the United Kingdom, see Mary Ann Glendon, Michael Wallace Gordon, and Christopher Osakwe, *Comparative Legal Traditions*, 2nd ed. (1994) at 613–27. The materials there collected indicate that the atrophy of the civil jury in the United Kingdom began during the First World War and culminated in 1965 when the Court of Appeal decided that there was no right to a jury trial except where specifically authorized by statute.

47. Benjamin Kaplan and Kevin M. Clermont, "England and the United States" in chapter 6, "Ordinary Proceedings in First Instance, Civil Procedure," 16 *International Encyclopedia of Comparative Law* 3, 29 n. 265 (1984) (reports that there is some variation among the provinces of Canada and Australia but that in general the jury is seldom used in civil cases in those countries).

48. Damaska, *Evidence Law Adrift*, supra note 40 at 39.

49. Federal Rule Civil Proc. 50(a). The judge can also set the verdict aside if it is "against the weight of the evidence," but in such a case there is a new trial before a new jury.

50. Damaska, *Evidence Law Adrift*, supra note 40 at 42.

51. See Taruffo, supra note 1 at 28 (use of jury trials reflects a cultural preference for direct rule of "the people" as opposed to the values of "professional training and efficiency").

52. Mark Curriden, "Power of 12," *ABA Journal*, 37 (August 2000).

53. Jeffrey Abramson, *We, the Jury* (1994) at 57–95. Several examples of juries' refusal to convict despite overwhelming evidence of guilt are presented.

54. Unanimity is not required in all jurisdictions. In New York, for example, a verdict of five-sixths is sufficient in civil cases, see N.Y. Civil Practice Law and Rules 4113(a).

55. Valerie P. Hans and Neil Vidmar, *Judging the Jury* (1986) at 32.

56. Jeffrey Abramson, *We, the Jury* (1994) at 23–33 and authorities cited. See also Hans and Vidmar, supra note 55 at 31–38.

57. Hans and Vidmar, supra note 55 at 32.

58. Id. at 35.

59. Id. at 255.

60. As quoted by Jeffrey Abramson, *We, the Jury* (1994) at 31.

61. As quoted by Hans and Vidmar, supra note 55 at 249.

62. Id. at 248–49.

63. Id. at 18. On the role of the jury in softening the harsh application of the contributory negligence rule in America, see Stephan Landman, "The History and Objectives of the Civil Jury System," in *Verdict*, supra note 39 at 22, 46–47.

64. See Priest, "Justifying the Civil Jury," supra note 39 at 103.

65. Jerome Frank, *Courts on Trial: Myth and Reality in American Justice*. Princeton, N.J.: Princeton University Press, 1949, at 110–25.

66. For an argument that the popular conception of the jury in America has undergone changes over the life of the country, see Jeffrey Abramson, "The Jury and Popular Culture," 50 *DePaul L. Rev.* 497 (2000).

67. Valerie P. Hans and Neil Vidmar, *Judging the Jury* (1986) at 31–46; in 1999, less than 2 percent of all civil actions brought in federal courts were resolved by a jury trial, see *New York Times*, March 2, 2001, at 1.

68. See text, supra at 56.

69. Stephen Yeazell argues that the different fates of the British and American juries reflect more pervasive differences between the two cultures, most notably different attitudes about the concentration of governmental power: "The persistence of the civil jury in the United States reflects a distrust of concentrated governmental power." Stephen C. Yeazell, "The New Jury and the Ancient Jury Conflict," *U. Chi. Law Forum* 87, 106 (1990).

70. See the surveys collected in Valerie P. Hans's "Attitudes toward the Civil Jury: A Crisis of Confidence?" In *Verdict*, supra note 39 at 248. An "ambitious national survey" conducted in 1978 found that 80 percent of the respondents rated the right of trial by jury as "extremely important" and most of the others rated it as "important." Id. at 255.

71. Under an amendment to the Federal Rules of Civil Procedure that became effective in 2002, each party must also make available to his or her adversary a list of documents and witnesses on which he or she intends to rely to prove his or her case. See Fed R. Civ. Proc. 26(a)(1).

72. John Lew, as quoted in *The Daily Deal*, May 15, 2001, at 5.

73. Damaska, *Evidence Law Adrift*, supra note 40 at 115, n. 80. See also id. at 132–33; Mauro Cappelletti and Bryant G. Garth, "Introduction: Policies, Trends, and Ideas in Civil Procedure," in 16 *International Encyclopedia of Comparative Law, Civil Procedure* 1–5 (1987) (noting that a "characteristic" of contemporary procedure in the civil law countries "is that the investigative power of the parties

and their lawyers is either extremely limited, as in Spain and Italy, or at least not as great as in common law countries." See also Damaska, *The Faces of Justice*, supra note 1 at 132–33.

The new Japanese Code of Civil Procedure (promulgated June 26, 1996), however, includes Article 163, which allows litigants to serve written requests for information on other parties. This rule, modeled on American interrogatories, is a "landmark in the history of Japanese civil procedure," Masahiko Omura, "A Comparative Analysis of Trial Preparation: Some Aspects of the New Japanese Code of Civil Procedure," in *Toward Comparative Law in the Twenty-first Century* (1998) at 723, 731.

74. See the ALI/UNIDROIT Project, supra note 4 at 7–8.

75. See discussion and authorities cited in Rudolf B. Schlesinger, Hans W. Baade, Peter E. Herzog, and Edward M. Wise, *Comparative Law*, 6th ed. (1998) at 469–75.

76. Id. at 67.

77. See discussion of the "Anglo-American" model, as distinguished from the Continental, in Damaska, *The Faces of Justice*, supra note 1 at 221.

78. See Jack I. H. Jacob, *The Fabric of English Civil Justice*. London: Stevens, 1987, 93–94; Robert Wyness Millar, *Civil Procedure of the Trial Court in Historical Perspective* (1952) at 201–28; Stephen N. Subrin, "Fishing Expeditions Allowed: The Historical Background of the 1938 Federal Discovery Rules," 39 *B.C.L. Rev.* 691 (1998).

79. Damaska, *The Faces of Justice*, supra note 1 at 133, n. 67.

80. Jacob, *The Fabric of English Civil Justice*, supra note 78 at 99. Compare Ian Grainger and Michael Fealy, *The Civil Procedure Rules in Action*, 2nd ed. London: Cavendish, 2000, at 87 (describes a broader availability of document discovery prior to the adoption of the new Civil Procedure Rules in 1999 than that implied by Jacob).

81. See Adrian A. S. Zuckerman, *Civil Procedure*. London: LexisNexis UK, 2003, at 464–65; Neil Andrews, *English Civil Procedure: Fundamentals of the New Civil Justice System*. Oxford: Oxford University Press, 2003, at 600–601; Ian Grainger and Michael Fealy, *The Civil Procedure Rules in Action*, 2nd ed. London: Cavendish, 2000, at 87–94.

82. Rule 34.8 and Comment 34.81, *The Civil Procedure Rules*, 2nd ed. London: Sweet and Maxwell, 1999, 460. See also David Greene, *The New Civil Procedure Rules*. London: Butterworths, 1999, at 316–17 ("[I]t is unlikely that the Court will go marching down the road of full deposition hearings as in the American model. In any event in the USA the taking of depositions and the deposition hearing are part of the discovery process. Rule 34.8 is not part of the discovery process within this jurisdiction.").

83. In the federal courts this may be done only if the court so orders, Rule 35, Fed. R. Civ Proc., but such orders are routinely granted. In many state courts judicial permission need not be obtained. See, e.g., N.Y. Civil Practice Law and Rules § 3121.

84. Stephen N. Subrin, "Fishing Expeditions Allowed: The Historical Background of the 1938 Federal Discovery Rules," 39 *B.C. L. Rev.* 691, 695 (1998) (argues that individualist attitudes were a source of resistance to the expansion of pretrial discovery).

85. See the ALI/UNIDROIT Project, supra note 4 at 7–10.

86. Otto G. Obermaier, quoting from "Defending Billy Ryan" by George V. Higgins (1992), in "The Lawyer's Bookshelf," *New York Law Journal*, December 1, 1992, at 2.

87. The passivity of the English judge is discussed in Konrad Zweigert and Hein Kötz, *An Introduction to Comparative Law* (1987) at 281–83. The new Civil Procedure Rules, which came into force in April 1999, grant the trial judge considerably more discretion and responsibility. According to the 1999 "White Book," a "radical" feature of the Rules is "that the *reactive judge* (for centuries past the heart of the English Common Law concept of the independent judiciary) has gone. Instead, we have a *proactive judge*, whose task is to take charge of the action at an early stage and manage its conduct in a way we have never seen before in this jurisdiction." *The Civil Procedure Rules*, 2nd ed. London: Sweet and Maxwell, 1999, at ix. See also id., Rule 32.1; Neil Andrews, "A New Civil Procedural Code for England: Party-Control 'Going, Going, Gone,'" 19 *Civil Justice Quarterly* 19, 28 (2000).

88. John H. Langbein, "The German Advantage in Civil Procedure," 52 *U. Chi. L. Rev.* 823, 863 (1985). On the power of the judge in civil law countries following the Romanist system, such as France, see Alphonse Kohl, "Romanist Legal Systems" in chapter 6, "Ordinary Proceedings in First Instance, Civil Procedure," 16 *International Encyclopedia of Comparative Law* 57, 63, 79, 99 (1984). In Germanic countries, see Hans Schima and Hans Hoyer, "Central European Countries," id. at 101, 122, 127.

89. For an excellent recent English-language description of adjudication in Germany see Peter L. Murray and Rolf Stürner, *German Civil Justice*. Durham, N.C.: Carolina Academic Press, 2004 (hereafter Murray and Stürner). I have previously discussed the role of the German judge vis-à-vis the American in Chase, "Legal Processes and National Culture," 5 *Cardozo J. of Int'l and Comparative Law* 1 (1997).

90. Benjamin Kaplan, Arthur T. von Mehren, and Rudolf Schaefer, "Phases of German Civil Procedure," 71 *Harvard Law Review* 1193 at 1224 (1958). See also Murray and Stürner, supra note 89 at 164–65.

91. Kaplan, supra note 90 at 1225. See also id. at 1472:

In Germany and the neighboring countries in Continental Europe procedural law is rather based on the idea that it will be easier to get at the truth if the judge is given a stronger role: he should be entitled, indeed bound, to question, inform, encourage, and advise the parties, lawyers and witnesses so as to get a true and complete picture from them.

Compare the discussion in Ronald J. Allen, Stefan Köck, Kurt Riecherberg, and D. Toby Rosen, "The German Advantage in Civil Procedure: A Plea for More Details and Fewer Generalities in Comparative Scholarship," 82 *NW. U. L. Rev.* 705 at 723–24 (1988), emphasizing rules that bind the judge to the parties' definition of the issues.

92. Kaplan, supra note 90 at 1233, nn. 161–62. See also Herbert L. Bernstein, "Whose Advantage After All? A Comment on the Comparison of Justice Systems," 21 *U.C. Davis L. Rev.* 587 (1988), at 593, stressing the rule that the German judge can call only those witnesses who have been nominated by the parties. See also Kaplan and Clermont, supra note 47 at 1224, 1228, noting that the judge may draw adverse inferences if the party refuses to follow the court's lead and nominate a particular witness.

93. Kaplan, supra note 90 at 1232–33. This is consistent with the previously mentioned power the court exercises over the development of the case in general.

94. Mauro Cappelletti and Bryant G. Garth, supra note 73 at 1–24. The actual control over the substance of the questions varies by country. In Italy, for example, the judge is restricted to asking questions drafted by the parties, id. at 28.

95. In some of the civil law countries, "Witnesses may be summoned and testimony ordered by the judge without a prior request from the parties." Mauro Cappelletti and Bryant G. Garth, "Chapter 1, Civil Procedure," 16 *International Encyclopedia of Comparative Law* 28 (1987). But see Damaska, *The Faces of Justice,* supra note 1 at 221, suggesting that if a Continental civil judge called a witness on his own, "such behavior would immediately provoke sharp reaction and rebuke from higher courts."

96. Kaplan, supra note 90 at 1234–35. See generally Murray and Stürner, supra note 89 at 254–59, 596–600.

97. An interesting example is provided by Allen, Köck, Riecherberg, and Rosen, supra note 91 at 728–29, where is reproduced portions of a German trial transcript. The judge's examination of the witness sounds much like an American lawyer conducting a skillful cross-examination. Allen and his coauthors contend that the judge has thus "created the testimony he wanted. . . . ," id. at 729. Compare the discussion of this trial at Langbein, "Trashing the German Advantage," 82 *NW U.L. Rev.* 963 (1988) at 771. He argues that in fact the transcript reveals "an innocuous exchange in which a judge encourages a witness to be more precise by probing the circumstances that the witness volunteers."

Regardless of which view of the questioning one takes, it is clearly quite different from the approach one expects from an American judge.

98. See, e.g., Judith Resnik, "Managerial Judges," 96 *Harvard Law Review* 374, 376–85 (1982) (discusses and criticizes this trend).

99. Adrian A. S. Zuckerman, "Justice in Crisis: Comparative Dimensions of Civil Procedure Reform," in Adrian A. S. Zuckerman, ed., *Civil Justice in Crisis.* Oxford: Oxford University Press, 1999, at 3, 47 (notes a trend toward greater control in common law countries). See also Taruffo, supra note 1 at 29.

100. In her leading article on the topic, Judith Resnik focused on the pretrial and post-trial role of the judges—there is no claim that they have taken over the interrogation of witnesses at trial, see "Managerial Judges," 96 *Harvard Law Review* 376 (1982).

101. Neil Andrews, "A New Civil Procedural Code for England: Party-Control 'Going, Going, Gone,' 19 *Civil Justice Quarterly* 19, 28 (2000).

102. Id. at 33.

103. See Murray and Stürner, supra note 89 at 611–12.

104. Taruffo, supra note 1 at 30.

105. See Joe S. Cecil and Thomas E. Willging, *Court-Appointed Experts: Defining the Role of Experts Appointed under Federal Rule of Evidence 706.* Federal Judicial Center, 1993, at 7–11 (reports on a survey of all federal district judges). See also Langbein, supra note 88 at 841; John C. Reitz, "Why We Probably Cannot Adopt the German Civil Procedure," 75 *Iowa Law Review* 987, 992 n. 2 (1992).

106. Langbein, supra note 88 at 835.

107. Id. at 835–36.

108. Damaska, *The Faces of Justice*, supra note 1.

109. Id. at 9.

110. Id. at 8–14, 240–41.

111. Id. at 66.

112. Id. at 17.

113. Id. at 47.

114. Id. at 17.

115. Id. at 19–20.

116. Id. at 20–21.

117. Id. at 22–23.

118. Id. at 56.

119. Id. at 17.

120. Id. at 23.

121. Id. at 25–26.

122. Id. at 57–65.

123. Id. at 18.

124. Damaska traces it to the eleventh-century organization of the Catholic Church, supra note 1 at 29–38.

125. Id. at 38.

126. Id. at 71–88.

127. Id. at 147.

128. Id. at 194–204.

129. Id. at 94–96.

130. Id. at 108.

131. Id. at 231–39.

132. Id. at 232.

133. Id. at 240.

134. Id. at 241.

135. See E. Allan Lind and Tom R. Tyler, *The Social Psychology of Procedural Justice* (1988) and John Thibaut and Laurens Walker, *Procedural Justice: A Psychological Analysis* (1975).

136. Lind and Tyler, supra note 135 at 239.

137. See studies described by Lind and Tyler, id. at 88, 143–44.

138. Thibaut and Walker, supra note 135 at 67–80. This experiment is also reported and discussed by Lind and Tyler, supra note 135 at 31–36. The experiment was later criticized on the ground that the models presented to the subjects did not accurately represent existing differentiations between the systems used in the various nations, see Paul G. Chevigny, "Fairness and Participation" (Review) 64 *NYU Law Review* 1211, 1214–15 (1989).

An additional study of procedural preferences comparing a sample of German university students with a similar American sample found that the Americans were far more likely to approve a full "adversary" model, but that they were also more likely than the Germans to approve an "inquisitorial" model as opposed to reliance on mediation, Stephen LaTour, Pauline Houlden, Laurens Walker, and John Thibaut, "Procedure: Transnational Perspectives and Preferences," 86 *Yale Law Journal* 258, 276, Fig. 1 (1978). The authors conclude that the participants from both countries preferred to control the presentation of evidence themselves when a third party was vested with decisional control.

139. Lind and Tyler, supra note 135 at 31.

140. Another set of studies comparing American and German students found that fairness concerns were important to both groups. Germans, however, accorded "much more importance to correctability than did the Americans." Lind and Tyler, supra note 135 at 142.

141. Id. at 203–20.

142. Id. at 233.

143. Lind and Tyler, supra note 135 at 235. See also Tom R. Tyler, *Why People Obey the Law* (1990) at 177 (adopts the view that different socialization accounts for different procedural preferences in different nations).

144. Lind and Tyler, supra note 135 at 235.

145. Id.

NOTES TO CHAPTER 5

1. "[P]erhaps the most significant twentieth–century change in the fundamentals of the legal system has been the tremendous growth of discretionary power." Kenneth Culp Davis, *Discretionary Justice: A Preliminary Inquiry*. Baton Rouge: Louisiana State University Press, 1969, 20.

2. The discretionary power of judges is acknowledged more openly in the com-

mon law countries than in those on the Continent, but the trend in most of the world's legal systems is toward greater freedom of judges to manage litigation, in other words, greater discretion, see Burkhard Hess, "Judicial Discretion," in Marcel Storme and Burkhard Hess, eds., *Discretionary Power of the Judge: Limits and Control.* Ragheno: Kluwer, 2003.

3. Charles Alan Wright and Arthur R. Miller, *Federal Practice and Procedure*, Vol. 4, 3rd ed. St. Paul, Minn.: West Group, 2002, §1029 at 155. See also P. S. Atiyah, "From Principles to Pragmatism: Changes in the Function of the Judicial Process and the Law," 65 *Iowa Law Review* 1249–72, at 1255 (1980), noting that "[r]ules of procedure and evidence tend increasingly to be subject to discretion rather than fixed rule; and even where there are rules they tend increasingly to be of a prima facie nature, rules liable to be displaced where the court feels they may work injustice."

4. Stephen N. Subrin, "How Equity Conquered Common Law: The Federal Rules of Civil Procedure in Historical Perspective," 135 *University of Pennsylvania Law Review* 909–1002, at 923, n. 76 (1987).

5. Federal Rules of Civil Procedure 16(a).

6. Federal Rules of Civil Procedure Rule 26(c), "provides the courts with broad discretion to protect a party or other person from 'annoyance, embarrassment, oppression, or undue burden or expense.'" Jack H. Friedenthal et al., *Civil Procedure*, 3rd ed. St. Paul, Minn.: West Group, 1999, at 428–29.

7. Federal Rules of Civil Procedure 60(b)(1).

8. See discussion infra at notes 28–30.

9. See discussion of the doctrine of *forum non conveniens*, infra at notes 31–33.

10. One aspect of the relationship between culture and discretion is usefully developed in M. P. Baumgartner, "The Myth of Discretion," in Keith Hawkins, ed., *The Uses of Discretion.* Oxford: Clarendon Press, 1992, at 129–62. Baumgartner describes the ways in which social and cultural factors confine discretionary decision making. She does not, however, provide a cultural account for the rise of discretion. For a bibliography of the literature on discretion, see id. at 391–416.

11. Paul Kahn, *The Cultural Study of Law: Reconstructing Legal Scholarship.* Chicago: University of Chicago Press, 1999, at 2. Kahn here adapts Geertz's general prescription to the analysis of law, see Clifford Geertz, "Thick Description: Toward an Interpretive Theory of Culture," in *The Interpretation of Cultures.* New York: Basic Books, 1973, 3–30, at 5.

12. Davis, Kenneth Culp, *Discretionary Justice: A Preliminary Inquiry.* Baton Rouge: Louisiana State University Press, 1969, at 4.

13. Various taxonomies of the general concept of discretion have been elucidated. A very useful discussion of these approaches can be found at id. at 14–15. See also Ronald Dworkin, *Taking Rights Seriously.* Cambridge, Mass.: Harvard University Press, 1977, at 31–33, distinguishing between "strong" and "weak" discretion.

14. As to the New York Court of Appeals see Rules of Practice, 22 New York Compilation of Codes, Rules, and Regulations §500.11(d)(1)(v), which directs parties seeking review of a civil judgment to show "why the questions presented merit review by this court, such as that they are novel or of public importance, or involve a conflict with prior decisions of this court, or there is a conflict among the Appellate Divisions."

15. For an early and prescient discussion of the problem, see Henry Hart and Nathan Isaacs, "The Limits of Judicial Discretion," 32 *Yale Law Journal* 339 (1922).

16. Lon L. Fuller, *The Morality of Law*. New Haven, Conn.: Yale University Press, 1964, at 106.

17. Solum lists three ways in which equity conflicts with the rule of law, i.e., by violating the principles of regularity (by treating differently cases that are similar with respect to "features that should count"); publicity (because the rules applied are not known until the case is decided); and generality (because equity requires the judge to focus on the particular fact pattern presented). All of these apply to discretion, as equity is a special case of discretionary authority. Lawrence B. Solum, "Equity and the Rule of Law," in Ian Shapiro, ed., *The Rule of Law*. New York: New York University Press, 1994, 120–47, at 125–26. See also the discussion of the incompatibility between law and discretion in Davis, supra note 1 at 28–33.

18. Davis, supra note 1 at 17. See also id. at 17–21, discussing the necessity for discretionary authority.

19. Id. at 30.

20. Id. at 34.

21. Cf. James J. Brudney et al., "Judicial Hostility towards Labor Unions? Applying the Social Background Model to a Celebrated Concern," 60 *Ohio State Law Journal* 1675–1762, 1678 (1999), noting that "[j]udges and many legal scholars recognize that appellate courts have considerable discretion in deciding particular cases, but they emphasize the importance of language, precedent and logical reasoning in cabining the exercise of such discretion."

22. As the examples given show, Davis's definition of discretion is broad: "A public officer has discretion whenever the effective limits on his power leave him free to make a choice among possible courses of action or inaction." Davis, supra note 1 at 4.

23. Steven J. Burton, "Particularism, Discretion, and the Rule of Law," in Ian Shapiro, ed., *The Rule of Law*. New York: New York University Press, 1994, 178–201, at 189.

24. Davis, supra note 1 at 34.

25. Keith Hawkins, "The Use of Legal Discretion: Perspectives from Law and Social Science," in Keith Hawkins, ed., *The Uses of Discretion*. Oxford: Clarendon Press, 1992, 11–46, at 37.

26. E.g., *Martin v. Mieth*, 35 N.Y.2d 414, 417, 1974, holding that although *forum non conveniens* is an equitable doctrine that allows a court "in its discretion" to

dismiss an action for prosecution in another forum, the issue posed by the court is whether the motion should have been denied "as a matter of law."

27. Wright and Miller, supra note 3, §1029 at 154–57.

28. Federal Rules of Evidence 102 provides, "These rules shall be construed to secure fairness in administration, elimination of unjustifiable expense and delay, and promotion of growth and development of the law of evidence to the end that the truth may be ascertained and proceedings justly determined."

29. Jack B. Weinstein and Margaret A. Berger, *Weinstein's Federal Evidence: Commentary on Rules of Evidence for the United States Courts,* 2nd ed. Newark, N.J.: Matthew Bender, 1997, at 102–11.

30. Id. at 102–11.

31. *Gulf Oil Corp. v. Gilbert,* 330 U.S. 501, 1947.

32. Id. at 508.

33. Id. at 508–9.

34. *Asahi Metal Industry Co., Ltd. v. Superior Court of California, Solano County,* 480 U.S. 102, 113, 1987.

35. Id. at 113.

36. Id. at 116.

37. *Piper Aircraft Co. v. Reyno,* 454 U.S. 235 (1981).

38. Cardozo recognized this when he described the functioning of the common law judge when deciding legal questions: "He is to exercise a discretion informed by tradition, methodized by analogy, disciplined by system, and subordinated to 'the primordial necessities of order in the social life.'" Benjamin N. Cardozo, *The Nature of the Judicial Process.* New Haven, Conn.: Yale University Press, 1921, at 141.

39. E. E. Evans-Pritchard, *Witchcraft, Oracles, and Magic among the Azande.* Oxford: Clarendon Press, 1937, at 281–312, discussing the role of supernatural beliefs among a people of Central Africa, including the use of oracles in determining disputes. See, generally, chapter 2, supra.

40. The Massim are a Melanesian people who engage in competitive food exchanges with group or individual enemies. They are described in Michael Young, *Fighting with Food* (1977).

41. Subrin, supra note 4 at 931–39. See also John Leubsdorf, "The Myth of Civil Procedure Reform," in Adrian A. S. Zuckerman, ed., *Civil Justice in Crisis: Comparative Perspectives of Civil Procedure.* Oxford: Oxford University Press, 1999, 53–67, at 58.

42. Subrin, supra note 4 at 935.

43. Id. at 934–39.

44. Id. at 939.

45. Id. at 944–45.

46. 29 A.B.A. Rep. 395 (1906).

47. Subrin, supra note 4 at 944.

48. Id. at 948–73.

49. Id. at 922, 973, 1000–1001.

50. Leubsdorf, supra note 41 at 58. In Leubsdorf's view, the main proponents of the Rules Enabling Act (which authorized the Federal Rules of Civil Procedure) were the conservative leaders of the ABA, while the leading opponent was the liberal Senator Thomas Walsh. "This line-up apparently reflects support by conservatives for federal judges, whose discretion the Federal Rules expanded, and who were then considered a bulwark against progressive legislation and tort plaintiffs." Id. at 60.

51. See Subrin, supra note 4 at 1000–1001, citing a list of political causes as well as the influence of the legal realists as reasons for reform.

52. Christine B. Harrington, "Delegalization Reform Movements: A Historical Analysis," in Richard L. Abel, ed., *The Politics of Informal Justice*. Vol. 1, *Comparative Studies*. New York: Academic Press, 1982, at 35–71.

53. Id., quoting William L. Ransom, "The Layman's Demand for Improved Judicial Machinery," 73 *Annals of the American Academy of Political and Social Science* 132, 147 (1917).

54. In this respect they were typical of their respective ages. See Grant Gilmore, *The Ages of American Law*. New Haven, Conn.: Yale University Press, 1977, at 87. The Realists and their formalist forebears both believed that law was a science, but for the Realists it became a "social science." Id. at 87.

55. Subrin, supra note 4 at 935.

56. Id. at 966.

57. Wolf Heydebrand and Carroll Seron, *Rationalizing Justice: The Political Economy of Federal District Courts*. Albany: State University of New York Press, 1990, at 13–14. For a description of how the impact of the drive for efficiency affected other legal doctrines, see William E. Nelson, *The Legalist Reformation*. Chapel Hill: University of North Carolina Press, 2001, at 362–66.

58. Heydebrand and Seron, supra note 57 at 13, internal quotations omitted.

59. Id. at 34.

60. Subrin, supra note 4 at 959.

61. Heydebrand and Seron, supra note 57 at 56, 194–96. The increasing dependence on bureaucratization has also been traced by others to the growing role of the state, see Hawkins, "The Uses of Legal Discretion," supra note 25 at 12.

62. Partly for this reason, Heydebrand and Seron argue that "the courts' capacity for legitimation is undermined by the very institution they are to legitimate: the interventionist and regulatory state." Heydebrand and Seron, supra note 55 at 22. See also id. at 200 et seq.

63. Id. at 204.

64. Judith Resnik, "Managerial Judges," 96 *Harvard Law Review* 374–448, at 391–403 (1982). See esp. id. at 395, "Since the early 1900s, judges have attempted to respond to criticism of their efficiency by experimenting with increasingly more managerial techniques." Except by implication, however, Resnik does not develop the role of discretionary authority as an enabler of those techniques.

65. Recall that in the United States, unlike some civil law countries, court filing fees are minimal and the losing party in general has no responsibility for the costs of the winner.

66. Between 1904 and 1910 the total number of civil and criminal cases filed in the federal courts dropped from 33,376 to 28,652. See Heydebrand and Seron, supra note 57 at 46, Table 2.1.

67. James Landis, *The Administrative Process* (1938) at 123. I am grateful to Richard Stewart for bringing this connection to my attention.

68. Construction of the current Supreme Court building was begun in 1932 and completed in 1935. It was one of the last federal buildings constructed in the neoclassical style, Geoffrey Blodgett, "Cass Gilbert Architect: Conservative at Bay," 72 *Journal of American History* 615–36, at 632 (1985).

69. Good illustrations are presented in A. Benjamin Handler, *The American Courthouse: Planning and Design for the Judicial Process.* Ann Arbor, Mich.: Institute of Continuing Legal Education, 1973, 229–44. On the relationship between Greek Revival architecture and post-Revolutionary iconography, see John C. McConnell, "The Houses of the Law," in Robert J. Brink, ed., *Courthouses of the Commonwealth.* Amherst: University of Massachusetts Press, 1984, 91–99.

70. Excellent examples of both genres may be found in the photographic display at www.nycourts.gov/history/Courts.htm (last visited on November 18, 2004). See also the illustrations of the "contemporary courthouses" in *The American Courthouse*, supra note 69 at 254–300. The point is developed well in Jonathan Rosenbloom, "Social Ideology as Seen through Courtroom and Courthouse Architecture," 22 *Columbia Journal of Law and the Arts* 463 (1998).

71. "Balancing has its roots in legal realism, which explicitly acknowledges the variety of political forces and interests that influence the development of law." Kahn, supra note 11 at 105.

72. Cardozo, *The Nature of the Judicial Process*, supra note 38 at 73, quoting Roscoe Pound, "Administrative Application of Legal Standards," *Proceedings of the American Bar Association* 441, 449 (1919).

73. Benjamin N. Cardozo, *The Paradoxes of Legal Science.* New York: Columbia University Press, 1928, at 61.

74. Atiyah, supra note 3 at 1251.

75. See, e.g., Roger Cotterrell, *The Sociology of Law: An Introduction*, 2nd ed. London: Butterworths, 1992, at 217–18; Gilmore, supra note 54 at 68–92.

76. Alan Hunt, *Explorations in Law and Society: Toward a Constitutive Theory of Law.* New York: Routledge, 1993, at 301: "The modern history of legal thought can be understood as a series of attempts to escape [from] the iron grip of the model of rules."

77. Gilmore, supra note 54 at 92. With a touch of his usual irony, Gilmore sums up the contribution of the Legal Realists in this passage: "The Realists had

stripped the judges of their trappings of black-robed infallibility and revealed them to be human beings whose decisions were motivated much more by irrational prejudice than by rules of law."

78. Cardozo, *The Nature of the Judicial Process*, supra note 38 at 116, 137, 166–69, 171–77.

79. Kahn, supra note 11 at 113.

80. Heydebrand and Seron, supra note 57 at 22, quoting James Willard Hurst, *The Growth of American Law: The Law Makers*. Boston: Little, Brown, 1950, at 194.

81. Lon L. Fuller, "The Forms and Limits of Adjudication," 92 *Harvard Law Review* 353–409, at 393 (1978).

82. Gilmore, supra note 54 at 68.

83. This problem was addressed in the context of law's relation to administration by Peter Fitzpatrick, *The Mythology of Modern Law*. London: Routledge, 1992, at 146–82. He argues that law and administration are in fact symbiotic.

84. One of the possible functions of ideology is denial; a society or group within it can adopt an ideology that denies strain within the society by "denying it outright or by legitimizing it in terms of higher value." Clifford Geertz, "Ideology as a Cultural System," in *The Interpretation of Cultures*. New York: Basic Books, 1973, 193–233, at 205.

85. Id. at 203.

86. Id.

87. Id. at 204–5.

88. Vernon Valentine Palmer, "From Embrace to Banishment: A Study of Judicial Equity in France," 47 *American Journal of Comparative Law*, 277–301, at 279 (1999).

89. Duncan Kennedy, *A Critique of Adjudication*. Cambridge, Mass.: Harvard University Press, 1997, 191–212.

90. Id. at 203.

91. Id. at 204.

92. Id. at 207–8.

93. Kahn, supra note 11 at 74.

94. Id. at 75.

95. Clifford Geertz, "Deep Play: Notes on the Balinese Cockfight," in *The Interpretation of Cultures*. New York: Basic Books, 1973, 412–53, at 446.

96. Id. at 446.

Notes to Chapter 6

1. For other extensive and thoughtful accounts of the ADR expansion see Richard L. Abel, "Introduction," in *The Politics of Informal Justice*, vol. 1, Richard L. Abel, ed. New York: Academic Press, 1982, at 1 and other essays in this volume. In addition, see Deborah R. Hensler, "Our Courts, Ourselves: How the Alternative

Dispute Resolution Movement Is Reshaping Our Legal System," 108 *Penn State Law Review* 165 (2003). See also authorities cited infra note 88.

2. A useful treatment of the various forms of ADR is provided in Alan S. Rau, Edward F. Sherman, and Scott R. Peppet, *Processes of Dispute Resolution: The Role of Lawyers*, 3rd ed. New York: Foundation Press, 2002. For a sociological examination see Michael Palmer and Simon Roberts, *Dispute Processes: ADR and the Primary Forms of Decision Making*. London: Butterworths, 1998.

3. Thomas J. Stiponawich, "ADR and the 'Vanishing Trial': The Growth and Impact of Alternative Dispute Resolution," 1 *Journal of Empirical Legal Studies* 843, 849 (2004). This is approximately one-seventh of the total number of dispositions by the federal courts in that year. Importantly, not all of the cases referred to ADR were resolved by those processes. An undetermined number would have been restored to the judicial docket.

4. American Arbitration Association, *Annual Report* (2003).

5. Theodore Eisenberg and Elizabeth Hill, "Arbitration and Litigation of Employment Claims: An Empirical Comparison," 58 *Dispute Resolution Journal* 44 (2003).

6. Abel, supra note 1 at 1.

7. Richard Chernick, "'ADR' Comes of Age: What Can We Expect in the Future?" 4 *Pepperdine Dispute Resolution Law Journal* 187–88 (2004).

8. Hensler, supra note 1 at 166.

9. Id. at 166–67.

10. Id. at 185.

11. James J. Alfini, *Mediation Theory and Practice*. Newark, N.J.: Lexis, 2001, 13.

12. Hensler, supra note 1 at 165–66, n. 3.

13. See Donna Sienstra and Thomas E. Willging, "Alternatives to Litigation: Do They Have a Place in the Federal District Courts?" Federal Judicial Center, 1995.

14. Rules 83.10 and 83.11, Local Rules of the United States District Courts for the Southern and Eastern Districts of New York (1997).

15. Id., Rule 83.11(a).

16. For a critical description and assessment of these cases, see Jean Sternlight, "Panacea or Corporate Tool? Debunking the Supreme Court's Preference for Binding Arbitration," 74 *Washington U. Law Quarterly* 637 (1996).

17. *Wilko v. Swann*, 346 U.S. 427 (1953).

18. *Prima Paint Corp. v. Flood and Conklin Mfg. Co.*, 388 U.S. 395 (1967).

19. *Moses H. Cone Mem. Hosp. v. Mercury Constr. Corp.*, 460 U.S. 1, 24–25 (1983).

20. 465 U.S. 1 (1984).

21. *Allied-Bruce Terminix Companies v. Dobson*, 513 U.S. 265 (1995).

22. *Rodriguez De Quijas v. Shearson/American Express, Inc.*, 490 U.S. 477.

23. Id. at 490 U.S. 481.

24. Rau, Sherman, and Peppet, supra note 2 at 789.

25. *Gilmer v. Interstate/Johnson Lane Corp.*, 500 U.S. 20 (1991).

26. See generally Sternlight, supra note 12.

27. Dispute Resolution Act of 1980, Pub. L. No. 96-190, 94 Stat. 17 (1980). Funding was appropriated for five years for these programs.

28. H.R. Rep. No. 100-889 (1988); Judicial Improvements and Access to Justice Act of 1988, Pub. L. 100-702, 102 Stat 4642 (1988).

29. Civil Justice Reform Act of 1990, Pub. L. 101-650, § 102, 104 Stat 5089.

30. Administrative Dispute Resolution Act of 1990, Pub. L. 101-552, § 2, 104 Stat 2736 (1990). Extended indefinitely in the Administrative Dispute Resolution Act of 1996, Pub. L. 104-320, 110 Stat 3870.

31. Id.

32. *Hearing on ADRA of 1995*, S. Hrg. 104-401 (1995) (statement of Peter R. Steenland, Jr., Senior Counsel, Office of Alternative Dispute Resolution, Department of Justice).

33. Id.

34. Id.

35. 28 U.S.C.A. §§651–658.

36. H.R. Rep. No. 105-487, at 2 (1998).

37. Alternative Dispute Resolution Act of 1998, Pub. L. 105-315, §2 (1998).

38. Jerold S. Auerbach, *Justice without Law*. New York and Oxford: Oxford University Press, 1983.

39. Id. at 21.

40. Id. at 23.

41. Id. at 41.

42. Id. at 32–33.

43. Id. at 95.

44. Id. at 96.

45. Id. at 98.

46. Id. at 107.

47. Id. at 108.

48. Id. at 113.

49. Paul Kahn, *The Cultural Study of Law*. Chicago: University of Chicago Press, 1999, at 13.

50. Richard A. Posner, *The Federal Courts: Challenge and Reform*. Cambridge, Mass.: Harvard University Press, 1996, at 237.

51. The source for all figures is Marc Galanter, "The Vanishing Trial: An Examination of Trials and Related Matters in Federal and State Courts," 1 *Journal of Empirical Legal Studies* 459 (2004). See also Posner, supra note 50 at 53–86 (details growth of federal caseload and workload, with the sharpest rise coming in the period around 1960).

52. New York City experienced so much delay that it led to an overhaul of its

code of procedure. For a description of the problem and its ingredients, see Oscar G. Chase, "The Paradox of Procedural Reform," 62 *St. John's U. Law Review* 453 (1988).

53. This was a major theme of the historic "Pound Conference," the National Conference on the Causes of Popular Dissatisfaction with the Administration of Justice, 70 F.R.D. 79 (1976). See, for example, the remarks of the then solicitor general of the United States, who said,

We were brought to study [the federal courts] by the observation that there is, and for some years has been, a slow crisis building in the administration of justice by the federal court system. . . .

The cause of the crisis is simply overload, an overload so serious that the integrity of the federal system is threatened, an overload so little recognized that the bleak significance of plain, not to say obtrusive, symptoms is not fully credited by the bar, and, apparently, not by Congress.

Robert H. Bork, "Dealing with the Overload in Article III Courts," 70 F.R.D. 232 (1976).

54. Posner, supra note 50 at 238. See also Judith Resnik, "Failing Faith: Adjudicatory Procedure in Decline," 53 *U. Chicago L. Rev.* 494, 538 (1986): "In sum, on both the criminal and the civil sides—and relying upon rules, cases, and informal practices—the judiciary is in the midst of devising or borrowing mechanisms to bypass adjudication."

55. Posner, supra note 50 at 126, Table 5.1.

56. See discussion in Posner, supra note 50 at 238–39.

57. For a superlative presentation of existing and original research, see Kim Dayton, "The Myth of Alternate Dispute Resolution in the Federal Courts," 76 *Iowa Law Review* 889 (1991).

58. Posner, supra note 50 at 130–31.

59. Id. at xiii.

60. For a discussion of these and other possibilities, see id. at 193–243. As Richard Abel points out, the claim that the courts were overburdened necessarily raises the subjective questions of what constitutes overcrowding, and how many cases are too many, see Abel, supra note 1 at 7.

61. Frank E. Sanders, "Varieties of Dispute Processing," 70 F.R.D. 111, 114 (1976). See also Simon H. Rifkind, "Are We Asking Too Much of Our Courts?" 70 F.R.D. 96 (1976). For a discussion of the link between the asserted litigation explosion and the hyperlexis critique, see Austin Sarat, "The Litigation Explosion, Access to Justice, and Court Reform: Examining the Critical Assumptions," 37 *Rutgers Law Review* 319 (1985).

62. See Warren E. Burger, "Agenda for 2000, A.D.: A Need for Systematic Anticipation," 70 F.R.D. 83, 95 (1976), discussed infra.

63. Laura Nader, *The Life of the Law: Anthropological Projects*. Berkeley: University of California Press, 2002, at 144.

64. Robert H. Bork, "Dealing with the Overload of Article III Courts," 70 F.R.D. 231, 233–235 (1976).

65. On this point see Resnik, supra note 54 at 512.

66. See Judith Resnik, "For Owen M. Fiss: Some Reflections on the Triumph and the Death of Adjudication," 58 *U. of Miami Law Review* 1973 (2003) (traces the "death" of adjudication in part to such a reaction).

67. Burger, supra note 62 at 95.

68. Id. at 93.

69. Id. at 93.

70. Id. at 94–95.

71. Id. at 94.

72. Sanders, supra note 61 at 111.

73. Id. at 114.

74. Id. at 130–31.

75. Id. at 121.

76. Auerbach, supra note 38 at 115–31. See also Hensler, supra note 1 at 174–75.

77. Charles A. Reich, *The Greening of America: How the Youth Revolution Is Trying to Make America Livable.* New York: Random House, 1970.

78. See id. at 225–63 for a description of the "new consciousness." For a more recent argument that ADR promotes democratic values by allowing disputants to determine how much confidentiality, confrontation, dialogue, and flexibility they want to bring to the process, see Carrie Menkel-Meadow, "Whose Dispute Is It Anyway?: A Philosophical and Democratic Defense of Settlement (In Some Cases)," 83 *Georgetown Law Journal* 2663, 2690 (1995).

79. Reich, supra note 77 at 8–9.

80. Id. at 230.

81. Id. at 228.

82. Id. at 256.

83. Id. at 226.

84. Auerbach, supra note 38 at 116.

85. Hensler, supra note 1 at 170. Auerbach sounds a similar theme, see Auerbach, supra note 38 at 116–20.

86. Hensler, supra note 1 at 171.

87. Resnik, supra note 54 at 537.

88. See Laura Nader, "The ADR Explosion: The Implications of Rhetoric in Legal Reform," *Windsor Yearbook* 269–91 (1989). See also Carrie Menkel-Meadow, "Mothers and Fathers of Invention: The Intellectual Founders of ADR," 16 *Ohio State Journal on Dispute Resolution* 1–37 (2000), summarizing the growth of ADR as an arena of academic study; Andrew W. McThenia and Thomas L. Shaffer, "For Reconciliation," 94 *Yale Law Journal* 1660–68, at 1665–67 (1985).

89. Robert A. Baruch Bush and Joseph P. Folger, *The Promise of Mediation: Re-*

sponding to Conflict through Empowerment and Recognition. San Francisco: Jossey-Bass, 1994, at 259.

90. Id. at 20.

91. Id.

92. Id.

93. Id. at 255.

94. Id. at 259.

95. See generally *The Reagan Record: An Assessment of America's Changing Domestic Priorities.* Cambridge, Mass.: Ballinger, 1984.

96. Sally Engle Merry, *Getting Justice and Getting Even: Legal Consciousness among Working-Class Americans.* Chicago: University of Chicago Press, 1990. Merry describes the process of diversion in a New England court. Issues such as neighbor-to-neighbor conflicts, domestic violence, and consumer disputes are regarded as "garbage cases" by the judges and weeded out by clerks for handling through alternative processes.

97. F. David Peat, *From Certainty to Uncertainty: The Story of Science and Ideas in the Twentieth Century.* Washington, D.C.: Joseph Henry Press, 2002.

98. David Garland, *The Culture of Control.* Chicago: University of Chicago Press, 2001, at 88. A more sanguine view of legal process is provided in Robert P. Burns, *A Theory of the Trial.* Princeton, N.J.: Princeton University Press, 1999.

99. Peat, supra note 97 at 199.

100. See text at notes 79–83.

101. Reich, *The Greening of America*, supra note 77 at 257.

102. An extended argument to this effect is made in Peter Huber, *Galileo's Revenge: Junk Science in the Courtroom.* New York: Basic Books, 1991.

103. On the relationship between the cognitive revolution and legal analysis, see Anthony G. Amsterdam and Jerome Bruner, *Minding the Law.* Cambridge, Mass.: Harvard University Press, 2000, at 9–10, 54–109.

104. Peat, supra note 97 at 213.

NOTES TO CHAPTER 7

1. There is a variety of theories about the social and mental functions of ritual. An informative survey and analysis is provided in Catherine Bell, *Ritual* (1997), see esp. 1–88. The role of ritual in the maintenance of political systems is described in David Kertzer, *Ritual, Politics, and Power* (1988). The role of ritual in the operation of criminal sanction is discussed in David Garland, *Punishment and Modern Society* (1990) at 67–81, 254–76.

2. Kertzer, supra note 1 at 9.

3. Id. at 9.

4. Id. at 185, n. 6, quoting Clifford Geertz.

5. Bell, supra note 1 at 138. The concepts are discussed by Bell at id. at 138–69. These concepts are "neither exclusive nor definitive." Id.

6. Garland, supra note 1 at 69.

7. Bell, supra note 1 at 82.

8. Kertzer, supra note 1 at 101.

9. Garland, supra note 1 at 67.

10. S. Freud, "Obsessive Acts and Religious Practices," reprinted in S. Freud, *Character and Culture* (1963) at 23–24.

11. Sally Falk Moore, "Selection for Failure in a Small Social Field: Ritual, Concord, and Fraternal Strife among the Chagga Kilimanjaro, 1968–1969," reprinted in Barbara G. Myerhoff and Sally Falk Moore, eds., *Symbols and Politics in Communal Ideology* (1975) at 109, 112.

12. Moore, supra note 11 at 112.

13. Pat Carlen, *Magistrates' Justice* (1976) at 111. Eventually the defendant pleads guilty in a manner that the court can accept and the proceeding continues.

14. Moore, supra note 11 at 109.

15. Id. at 111–12 (her italics).

16. Id. at 114.

17. Arnold van Gennep, *The Rites of Passage*. Chicago: University of Chicago Press, 1960.

18. Victor W. Turner, *The Ritual Process*. Chicago: Aldine, 1969.

19. Id. at 94–95.

20. Van Gennep recognized that the passage to occupational specialization and advancement to a higher class are among the life passages marked by rites in many societies. See supra note 17 at 2–3.

21. Turner, supra note 18 at 170.

22. Id. at 201.

23. Paul Kahn, *The Cultural Study of Law: Reconstructing Legal Scholarship*. Chicago: University of Chicago Press, 1999, at 79. Kahn maintains that this depersonalization is crucial to our belief in law as an autonomous world, see id. at 79–80.

24. On judicial robes and their significance, see Jerome Frank, *Courts on Trial: Myth and Reality in American Justice*. Princeton, N.J.: Princeton University Press, 1949, chapter 18, "The Cult of the Robe," 254–61; Kahn, supra note 23 at 101.

25. D. Graham Burnett, *A Trial by Jury*. New York: Vintage Books, 2001.

26. See discussion in Dennis Curtis and Judith Resnik, "Images of Justice," 96 *Yale L. J.* 1727 (1987).

27. Kahn, supra note 23 at 79.

28. Kahn, supra note 23 at 113.

29. 531 U.S. 98, 121 S.Ct. 525 (2000).

30. Kahn, supra note 23 at 81, 83.

31. Garland, supra note 1 at 255.

32. Id. Italics in original.

33. Id. at 67.

34. Clifford Geertz, "Centers, Kings, and Charisma: Reflections on the Symbolics of Power," in *Local Knowledge*. New York: Basic Books, 1983, at 121–46.

NOTES TO CHAPTER 8

1. Melford E. Spiro, *Culture and Human Nature*. New Brunswick, N.J.: Transaction Publishers, 1994, at ix. See discussion in chapter 1, supra.

2. Spiro, supra note 1 at 32.

3. Id. at ix. See discussion, supra at 2–3.

4. See, e.g., V. Lee Hamilton and Joseph Sanders, *Everyday Justice*. New Haven, Conn.: Yale University Press, 1992, at 48–71, who compare socialization in the United States and Japan, arguing that the Japanese promote "contextualism" and the Americans promote individualism.

5. Spiro, supra note 1 at 38 (italics in original).

6. See discussion in id. at 120–21.

7. Id. at ix.

8. Balkin provides a helpful discussion of the relationship between individual variation and social continuity. See J. M. Balkin, *Cultural Software: A Theory of Ideology*. New Haven, Conn.: Yale University Press, 1998, at 52–54.

9. Id. at 39.

10. Richard A. Shweder, *Why Do Men Barbecue?* Cambridge, Mass.: Harvard University Press, 2003, at 28.

11. Pierre Bourdieu, "The Force of Law: Toward a Sociology of the Juridical Field," 38 *Hastings Law Journal* 805, 839 (1987)(Richard Terdiman, trans.)

12. Id. at 846–847.

13. Balkin, supra note 8 at 13.

14. A full explication of Balkin's concept is unnecessary and would require more space than is available here. See generally Balkin, supra note 8 at 13–19.

15. Id. at 5. See generally Jerome Bruner, *Acts of Meaning* (1990).

16. Balkin, supra note 8 at 5 (emphasis added).

17. Id. at 85.

18. Id. at 188–258.

19. Id. at 75.

20. Id. at 78, 188–215.

21. Id. at 90.

22. Judith Resnik, "Tiers," 57 *S.Cal. L. Rev.* 837 (1984).

23. The argument that governmental acts have symbolic power has been developed elsewhere, see Joel Feinberg, "The Expressive Function of Punishment," 49 *Monist* 397 (1965); Elizabeth S. Anderson and Richard H. Pildes, "Expressive The-

ories of Law: A General Restatement," 148 *University of Pennsylvania L. Rev.* 1503 (2000). My position differs from those of these "expressivists" in that I focus on the processes rather than the result of the government's acts.

24. Hamilton and Sanders, supra note 4 at 32. The relationship between Japanese culture and legal institutions has attracted much scholarly discussion, some of which minimizes the role of culture. A good discussion of the main themes and sources is found in Eric A. Feldman, *The Ritual of Rights in Japan: Law, Society, and Health Policy*. Cambridge: Cambridge University Press, 2000, at 141–62. Feldman argues for an integrated approach and decries the "false dichotomy between structure and culture," 160.

25. Homer, *The Iliad, Book 18*. (W. H. D. Rouse trans.) New York: Signet, 1999, at 225–26.

26. Franz Kafka, *The Trial*. (Breon Mitchell trans.) New York: Shocken Books, 1988, at 29.

27. For a discussion of the attraction of legal proceedings as manifested in modern entertainment media, see Richard K. Sherwin, *When Law Goes Pop: The Vanishing Line between Law and Popular Culture*. Chicago: University of Chicago Press, 2000.

28. On the dramatic quality of rituals in political life see David I. Kertzer, *Ritual, Politics, and Power*. New Haven, Conn.: Yale University Press, 1988, at 10–11. Interestingly, the dramatic techniques through which fictionalized accounts of law are presented have been appropriated by lawyers seeking to persuade juries of the validity of their client's story.

29. David Garland, *Punishment and Modern Society: A Study in Social Theory*. Chicago: University of Chicago Press, 1990, at 265.

30. *Olmstead v. United States*, 277 U.S. 438, 485 (1928) (Brandeis, J., dissenting). The question addressed by the Court was whether wiretapping evidence was admissible in a criminal prosecution when the tapping was unlawful. The majority upheld the admission of the evidence.

31. Sally Falk Moore, "Selection for Failure in a Small Social Field: Ritual, Concord, and Fraternal Strife among the Chagga Kilimanjaro, 1968–1969," reprinted in Barbara G. Myerhoff and Sally Falk Moore, eds., *Symbols and Politics in Communal Ideology* (1975) at 109, 115.

32. "It would be a terrible mistake to forget that a typical law suit, whether civil or criminal, is only in part an objective search for historical truth. It is also, and no less importantly, a ritual." Lawrence H. Tribe, "Trial by Mathematics: Precision and Ritual in the Legal Process," 84 *Harvard L. R.* 1329, 1376–77 (1971). See also Kertzer, supra note 28 at 131–32 (discusses the ritual nature of judicial proceedings and its importance for the social role of courts in many societies: "Indeed, judicial procedures, from the simplest societies to modern nation-states, are highly ritualized. Rites of the law court are not all that different from rites of the royal court. In both cases, the image of sacrality, of legitimacy, is fostered through rit-

ual, while aggressive behavior is sharply contained and lines of authority bolstered." Id. at 132. The ritualistic nature of the judicial process and its consequent power is also discussed at Garland, supra note 29 at 68–69 and in Lawrence Friedman, "Law, Lawyers, and Popular Culture," 98 *Yale Law Journal* 1579 at 1594 (1989).

33. Kertzer, supra note 28 at 9. See also Lawrence Rosen, "Individualism, Community, and the Law: A Review Essay," 55 *University of Chicago Law Review* 571–84, 581 (1988) ("Whatever we may think of the merits of these [myths and rituals associated with the legal and political process], one can no more dismiss them because of doubts as to their ultimate truth value than one can dismiss people's religious beliefs for their irrational elements.")

34. Barbara Myerhoff, *Number Our Days* (1978) at 86 (Touchstone Edition 1980).

35. Clifford Geertz, "Local Knowledge, Fact, and Law in Comparative Perspective," in Clifford Geertz, *Local Knowledge: Further Essays in Interpretive Anthropology*. New York: Basic Books, 2000, 167–234, 180.

36. David Garland, who discusses the constitutive functions of penalty in culture in chapter 11 of *Punishment and Modern Society*, supra note 29 faced the same problem. I can do no better than adopt his approach, noting that "my theoretical arguments will outrun the available data. . . . To the extent that this calls for excuse or apology—and if it does then so does much of modern social theory—my defence plea is one of necessity. . . ." Id. at 251.

37. See supra, chapter 4.

38. See supra, at 55–58.

39. R. C. van Caenegem, "Chapter 2: History of European Civil Procedure" 16 *International Encyclopedia of Comparative Law* 2–25 (1987). On the emergence of the jury in place of magical decision making, see also Max Weber, *On Law in Economy and Society*. Cambridge, Mass.: Harvard University Press, 1976, at 79 and authorities cited at id., n. 36.

40. van Caenegem, supra note 39 at 2–25.

41. Hamilton and Sanders, supra note 4 at 21 (emphasis in original).

42. Id. note 4 at 33.

43. Id.

44. Id. at 37.

45. See my discussion of this point in chapter 4, supra.

46. See generally J. O. Haley, "The Politics of Informal Justice: The Japanese Experience, 1922–1942," in R. Abel, ed., *The Politics of Informal Justice*, Vol. 2. New York: Academic Press, 1982, at 125–47.

47. See developments described by Hamilton and Sanders, supra note 4 at 33–35.

48. See Hamilton and Sanders, supra note 4 at 155–56 (solidarity of relationships found to explain difference in preferred sanctions for wrongdoers, with the

Japanese sample preferring relation-restoring sanctions while American subject preferred isolation as a sanction.) See also id. at 134 (greater sensitivity of Japanese subjects to "role" in assessing responsibility found consistent with "the more tightly woven web of hierarchical and solidary relationships that characterizes Japanese social life.")

49. Hamilton and Sanders, supra note 4 at 196.

50. R. Abel, "A Comparative Theory of Dispute Institutions in Society," *Law and Society Review*, 217–347, see esp. Fig. 6, at 301 and accompanying text (1973).

51. Id. at 302–3.

52. Id.

53. Id. at 335, n. 364. See also Bruner, *Acts of Meaning*, supra note 15 at 23–24, noting the same dynamic and lamenting "the invasive bureaucratization of life in our times, with its resultant erosion of selfhood and compassion."

54. Abel, supra note 50 at 296. See discussion at id. at 295–96.

55. Balkin, supra note 8 at 245–48. The context is Balkin's exploration of how certain modes of human thought produce "ideological" effects. Balkin's "theory of ideology is a theory of cultural software and its effects." Id. at 3.

56. Id. at 247.

57. Robert A. Baruch Bush and Jospeh P. Folger, *The Promise of Mediation: Responding to Conflict through Empowerment and Recognition*. San Francisco: Jossey-Bass, 1994, at 259.

58. Id. at 20.

59. Id. at 255.

60. Sally Engle Merry, "The Social Organization of Mediation in Nonindustrial Societies: Implications for Informal Community Justice in America," in Richard L. Abel, ed., *The Politics of Informal Justice*. Vol. 2, *Comparative Studies*. New York: Academic Press, 1982, 17–45, at 33. See also Jerold S. Auerbach, *Justice without Law?* New York: Oxford University Press, 1983.

61. Trina Grillo, "The Mediation Alternative: Process Dangers for Women," 100 *Yale Law Journal* 1545–1610, at 1581 (1991). On the dangers of ADR generally, see Laura Nader, *The Life of the Law* (2002). Carrie Menkel-Meadow, on the other hand, presents nuanced arguments in favor of ADR in particular situations and for particular kinds of disputes. See Menkel-Meadow, "Whose Dispute Is It Anyway?: A Philosophical and Democratic Defense of Settlement (In Some Cases), 83 *Georgetown Law Journal* 2663 (1995) and Menkel-Meadow, "Pursuing Settlement in an Adversary Culture: A Tale of Innovation Co-opted, or 'The Law of ADR,'" 19 *Florida State University Law Review* 1 (1991).

62. See Penelope E. Bryan, "Killing Us Softly: Divorce Mediation and the Politics of Power," 40 *Buffalo Law Review* 441–523 (1992). But see Kenneth Kressel and Dean G. Pruitt, "Conclusion: A Research Perspective on the Mediation of Social Conflict," in *Mediation Research: The Process and Effectiveness of Third-Party Intervention*. San Francisco: Jossey-Bass, 1989, at 399, finding "no evidence that

women are more dissatisfied with mediation than men or feel forced into unfair agreements by it."

63. Mark H. Lazerson, "In the Halls of Justice, the Only Justice Is in the Halls," in Richard L. Abel, ed., *The Politics of Informal Justice*. Vol. 1, *The American Experience*. New York: Academic Press, 1982, 119–63, at 159, noting that a "legal system that encourages conciliation between landlord and tenants—two parties with vastly unequal resources—by curtailing the procedural rights of the weaker can only succeed in amplifying that inequality."

64. Richard L. Abel, "Introduction," in Richard L. Abel, ed., *The Politics of Informal Justice*. Vol. 1, *The American Experience*. New York: Academic Press, 1982, 1–13, at 9.

65. Jonathan G. Shailor, *Empowerment in Dispute Mediation: A Critical Analysis of Communication*. Westport, Conn.: Praeger, 1994, at 11.

NOTES TO CHAPTER 9

1. Max Weber, *On Law in Economy and Society*, ed. Max Rheinstein. New York: Simon and Schuster, 1967, at 67.

2. Id. at 68–69.

3. On the utility of comparative law as enriched by cultural analysis, see Roger Cotterrell, "Law in Culture," 17 *Ratio Juris* 1–2 (March 2004).

4. This example is not entirely hypothetical. Rising costs for medical malpractice insurance have been attributed by some commentators to the profligacy of the civil jury. A proposed solution would eliminate the role of jurors in such cases and allow a panel of medical experts to decide them, see proposals described in "An End to Nuisance," *The Economist*, August 2, 2003, at 33.

5. Herbert C. Kelman and V. Lee Hamilton, *Crimes of Obedience: Toward a Social Psychology of Authority and Responsibility*. New Haven, Conn.: Yale University Press, 1989, at 322–23.

6. Kelman and Hamilton, supra note 5.

7. Other supportive studies are referenced at id. at 334.

8. Id. at 323 (emphasis in original).

9. Id. at 328 (emphasis in original).

10. More generally, a notable feature of the formal American dispute process is that it does promote multiple perspectives through the devices discussed in chapter 4, such as adversary control of the process. See generally Judith Resnik, "Managerial Judges," 96 *Harvard Law Review* 374–448 (1982).

11. Mirjan R. Damaška, *Structures of Authority and Comparative Criminal Procedure*, 84 *Yale L. J.* 480, 540 (1975).

Bibliography

Abel, Richard L. "A Comparative Theory of Dispute Institutions in Society." *Law and Society Review* 8 (1974): 217–347.

———. "Introduction." In *The Politics of Informal Justice*. Vol. 2, *Comparative Studies*, edited by Richard L. Abel, 1–13. New York: Academic Press, 1982.

Abramson, Jeffrey. "The Jury and Popular Culture." *DePaul Law Review* 50 (2000): 497–523.

———. *We, the Jury: The Jury System and the Ideal of Democracy*. New York: Basic Books, 1994.

Alfini, James J., Sharon B. Press, Jean R. Sternlight, and Joseph B. Stulberg. *Mediation Theory and Practice*. Newark, N.J.: Lexis, 2001.

Allen, Ronald J., Stefan Köck, Kurt Riecherberg, and D. Toby Rosen. "The German Advantage in Civil Procedure: A Plea for More Details and Fewer Generalities in Comparative Scholarship." *Northwestern University Law Review* 82 (1988): 705–62.

Amsterdam, Anthony G., and Jerome S. Bruner. *Minding the Law*. Cambridge, Mass.: Harvard University Press, 2000.

Andrews, Neil. *English Civil Procedure: Fundamentals of the New Civil Justice System*. Oxford: Oxford University Press, 2003.

———. "A New Civil Procedural Code for England: Party-Control 'Going, Going, Gone.'" *Civil Justice Quarterly* 19 (2000): 19–38.

Asahi Metal Industry Co., Ltd. v. Superior Court of California, Solano County, 480 U.S. 102 (1987).

Atiyah, P. S. "From Principles to Pragmatism: Changes in the Function of the Judicial Process and the Law." *Iowa Law Review* 65 (1980): 1249–72.

Auerbach, Jerold S. *Justice without Law?* New York: Oxford University Press, 1983.

Balkin, J. M. *Cultural Software: A Theory of Ideology*. New Haven, Conn.: Yale University Press, 1998.

Baumgartner, M. P. "The Myth of Discretion." In *The Uses of Discretion*, edited by Keith Hawkins, 129–62. Oxford: Clarendon Press, 1992.

Bellah, Robert N., Richard Madsen, William M. Sullivan, Ann Swidler, and Steven M. Tipton. *Habits of the Heart: Individualism and Commitment in American Life*. Berkeley: University of California Press, 1985.

Berman, Paul Schiff. "An Observation and a Strange but True 'Tale': What Might the Historical Trials of Animals Tell Us about the Transformative Potential of Law in American Culture?" *Hastings Law Journal* 52 (2000): 123–80.

Blackstone, William. *Commentaries on the Laws of England.* Vol. 1. New York: W. E. Dean, 1836.

Blodgett, Geoffrey. "Cass Gilbert, Architect: Conservative at Bay." *Journal of American History* 72 (1985): 615–36.

Bork, Robert H. "Dealing with the Overload in Article III Courts." *Federal Rules Decisions* 70 (1976): 231–39.

Brudney, James J., Sara Schiavoni, and Deborah J. Merritt. "Judicial Hostility towards Labor Unions? Applying the Social Background Model to a Celebrated Concern." *Ohio State Law Journal* 60 (1999): 1675–1762.

Bruner, Jerome. *Acts of Meaning.* Cambridge, Mass.: Harvard University Press, 1990.

Bryan, Penelope E. "Killing Us Softly: Divorce Mediation and the Politics of Power." *Buffalo Law Review* 40 (1992): 441–523.

Burger, Warren E. "Agenda for 2000, A.D.: A Need for Systematic Anticipation." *Federal Rules Decisions* 70 (1976): 83–96.

Burnett, D. Graham. *A Trial by Jury.* New York: Vintage Books, 2001.

Burns, Robert P. *A Theory of the Trial.* Princeton, N.J.: Princeton University Press, 1999.

Burton, Steven J. "Particularism, Discretion, and the Rule of Law." In *The Rule of Law,* edited by Ian Shapiro, 178–201. New York: New York University Press, 1994.

Cappelletti, Mauro. "Social and Political Aspects of Civil Procedure: Reforms and Trends in Western and Eastern Europe." *Michigan Law Review* 69 (1971): 847–86.

Cappelletti, Mauro, and Bryant G. Garth. "Chapter 1: Introduction—Policies, Trends and Ideas in Civil Procedure." In *International Encyclopedia of Comparative Law.* Vol. 16, Civil Procedure, edited by Mauro Cappelletti. Tübingen: Mohr, 1987.

Cardozo, Benjamin N. *The Nature of the Judicial Process.* New Haven, Conn.: Yale University Press, 1921.

———. *The Paradoxes of Legal Science.* New York: Columbia University Press, 1928.

Carlen, Pat. *Magistrates' Justice.* London: Robertson, 1976.

Chase, Oscar G. "Culture and Disputing." *Tulane Journal of International and Comparative Law* 7 (1999): 81–90.

———. "Legal Processes and National Culture." *Cardozo Journal of International and Comparative Law* 5 (1997): 1–24.

———. "The Paradox of Procedural Reform." *St. John's Law Review* 62 (1988): 453–474.

The Civil Procedure Rules, 1999. 2nd ed. London: Sweet and Maxwell, 1999.

Comaroff, John L., and Simon Roberts. *Rules and Processes: The Cultural Logic of Dispute in an African Context.* Chicago: University of Chicago Press, 1981.

Cotterrell, Roger. "The Concept of Legal Culture." In *Comparing Legal Cultures,* edited by David Nelken, 13–31. Brookfield, Vt.: Dartmouth Publishing Co., 1997.

———. "Law in Culture." *Ratio Juris* 17, no. 1 (March 2004): 1–14.

———. *The Sociology of Law: An Introduction.* 2nd ed. London: Butterworths, 1992.

Curriden, Mark. "Power of 12." *American Bar Association Journal* 87 (2001): 36–41.

Curtis, Dennis E., and Judith Resnik. "Images of Justice." *Yale Law Journal* 96 (1987): 1727–72.

Damaška, Mirjan R. *Evidence Law Adrift.* New Haven, Conn.: Yale University Press, 1997.

———. *The Faces of Justice and State Authority: A Comparative Approach to the Legal Process.* New Haven, Conn.: Yale University Press, 1986.

———. "Rational and Irrational Proof Revisited." *Cardozo Journal of International and Comparative Law* 5 (1997): 25–39.

———. "Structures of Authority and Comparative Criminal Procedure." *Yale Law Journal* 84 (1975): 480–544.

Davis, Kenneth Culp. *Discretionary Justice: A Preliminary Inquiry.* Baton Rouge: Louisiana State University Press, 1969.

Dayton, Kim. "The Myth of Alternate Dispute Resolution in the Federal Courts." *Iowa Law Review* 76 (1991): 889–957.

Delikat, Michael, and Morris M. Kleiner. "An Empirical Study of Dispute Resolution Mechanisms." *Dispute Resolution Journal* 58, no. 4 (November 2003–January 2004): 56–58.

Devisch, René. "Mediumistic Divination among the Northern Yaka of Zaire: Etiology and Ways of Knowing." In *African Divination Systems: Ways of Knowing,* edited by Philip M. Peek, 112–32. Bloomington: Indiana University Press, 1991.

De Waal, Frans. *Peacemaking among Primates.* Cambridge, Mass.: Harvard University Press, 1989.

Dore, Ronald. "Elitism and Democracy." *Tocqueville Review* 14, no. 2 (1993): 64–72.

Dworkin, Ronald. *Law's Empire.* Cambridge, Mass.: Harvard University Press, 1986.

———. *Taking Rights Seriously.* Cambridge, Mass.: Harvard University Press, 1977.

Eisenberg, Theodore, and Elizabeth Hill. "Arbitration and Litigation of Employment Claims: An Empirical Comparison." *Dispute Resolution Journal* 58, no. 4 (November 2003–January 2004): 44–53.

Evans-Pritchard, E. E. *Witchcraft, Oracles, and Magic among the Azande.* Oxford: Clarendon Press, 1937.

Federal Rules of Civil Procedure. Section 16(a).

———. Section 26.

———. Section 35(a).

———. Section 38(a).

———. Section 50.

———. Section 60(b)(1).

Federal Rules of Evidence. Section 102.

Feldman, Eric A. *The Ritual of Rights in Japan: Law, Society, and Health Policy,* Cambridge: Cambridge University Press, 2000.

Felstiner, William L. F. "Influences of Social Organization on Dispute Processing." *Law and Society Review* 9 (1974): 63–94.

Felstiner, William L. F., Richard L. Abel, and Austin Sarat. "The Emergence and Transformation of Disputes: Naming, Blaming, Claiming . . ." *Law & Society Review* 15 (1980–81): 631–54.

Fish, Stanley. "The Law Wishes to Have a Formal Existence." In *There's No Such Thing as Free Speech, and It's a Good Thing Too,* 141–79. New York: Oxford University Press, 1994.

Fitzpatrick, Peter. *The Mythology of Modern Law.* London: Routledge, 1992.

Frank, Jerome. *Courts on Trial: Myth and Reality in American Justice.* Princeton, N.J.: Princeton University Press, 1949.

———. *Law and the Modern Mind.* New York: Coward-McCann, 1930.

French, Rebecca Redwood. *The Golden Yoke: The Legal Cosmology of Buddhist Tibet.* Ithaca, N.Y.: Cornell University Press, 1995.

Freud, Sigmund. "Obsessive Acts and Religious Practices." In *Character and Culture,* 17–26. New York: Collier, 1963.

Friedenthal, Jack H., Mary Kay Kane, and Arthur R. Miller. *Civil Procedure.* 3rd ed. St. Paul, Minn.: West Group, 1999.

Friedman, Lawrence M. "Is There a Modern Legal Culture?" *Ratio Juris* 7 (1994): 117–31.

———. "Law, Lawyers, and Popular Culture." *Yale Law Journal* 98 (1989): 1579–1606.

———. *The Republic of Choice: Law, Authority, and Culture.* Cambridge, Mass.: Harvard University Press, 1990.

Fuller, Lon L. "The Forms and Limits of Adjudication." *Harvard Law Review* 92 (1978): 353–409.

———. *The Morality of Law.* New Haven, Conn.: Yale University Press, 1964.

Galanter, Marc. "The Aborted Restoration of 'Indigenous' Law in India." *Comparative Studies in Society and History* 14 (1972): 53–70.

———. "Reading the Landscape of Disputes: What We Know and Don't Know (and Think We Know) about Our Allegedly Contentious and Litigious Society." *UCLA Law Review* 31 (1983): 4–71.

———. "The Vanishing Trial: An Examination of Trials and Related Matters in Federal and State Courts." *Journal of Empirical Legal Studies* 1 (2004): 459–570.

Garland, David. *The Culture of Control: Crime and Social Order in Contemporary Society*. Chicago: University of Chicago Press, 2001.

———. *Punishment and Modern Society: A Study in Social Theory*. Chicago: University of Chicago Press, 1990.

Geertz, Clifford. "Centers, Kings, and Charisma: Reflections on the Symbolics of Power." In *Local Knowledge: Further Essays in Interpretive Anthropology*, 121–46. New York: Basic Books, 2000.

———. "Common Sense as a Cultural System." In *Local Knowledge: Further Essays in Interpretive Anthropology*, 73–93. New York: Basic Books, 1983.

———. "Deep Play: Notes on the Balinese Cockfight." In *The Interpretation of Cultures*, 412–53. New York: Basic Books, 1973.

———. "Fact and Law in Comparative Perspective." In *Local Knowledge: Further Essays in Interpretive Anthropology*, 167–234. New York: Basic Books, 1983.

———. "Ideology as a Cultural System." In *The Interpretation of Cultures*, 193–233. New York: Basic Books, 1973.

———. "Thick Description: Toward an Interpretive Theory of Cultures." In *The Interpretation of Culture*, 3–30. New York: Basic Books, 1973.

Gerber, Larry G. "Shifting Perspectives on American Exceptionalism: Recent Literature on American Labor Relations and Labor Politics." *Journal of American Studies* 31 (1997): 253–74.

Gilmore, Grant. *The Ages of American Law*. New Haven, Conn.: Yale University Press, 1977.

Glendon, Mary Ann. "Rights in Twentieth-Century Constitutions." In *The Bill of Rights in the Modern State*, edited by Geoffrey R. Stone, Richard A. Epstein, and Cass R. Sunstein, 521. Chicago: University of Chicago Press, 1992.

Glendon, Mary Ann, Michael W. Gordon, and Christopher Osakwe. *Comparative Legal Traditions: Text, Materials, and Cases on the Civil and Common Law Traditions, with Special Reference to French, German, English, and European Law*. 2nd ed. St. Paul: West Group, 1994.

Goitein, H. *Primitive Ordeal and Modern Law*. Littleton, Col.: Rothman, 1980.

Grainger, Ian, and Michael Fealy. *The Civil Procedure Rules in Action*. 2nd ed. London: Cavendish, 2000.

Greene, David. *The New Civil Procedure Rules*. London: Butterworths, 1999.

Grillo, Trina. "The Mediation Alternative: Process Dangers for Women." *Yale Law Journal* 100 (1991): 1545–1610.

Grootaers, Jan-Lodewijk. *A History and Ethnography of Modernity among the Zande*. Ph.D. diss., University of Chicago, 1996.

Gulf Oil Corp. v. Gilbert, 330 U.S. 501. (1947).

Gulliver, P. H. "Case Studies of Law in Non-Western Societies." In *Law in Culture and Society*, edited by Laura Nader, 11–23. Chicago: Aldine Publishing, 1969.

Hamilton, V. Lee, and Joseph Sanders. *Everyday Justice: Responsibility and the Individual in Japan and the United States*. New Haven, Conn.: Yale University Press, 1992.

Hans, Valerie P. "Attitudes toward the Civil Jury: A Crisis of Confidence?" In *Verdict: Assessing the Civil Jury System*, edited by Robert E. Litan, 248–81. Washington: Brookings Institution, 1993.

Hans, Valerie P., and Neil Vidmar. *Judging the Jury*. New York: Plenum Press, 1986.

Hart, H. L. A. *The Concept of Law*. 2nd ed. Oxford: Clarendon Press, 1997.

Hawkins, Keith. "The Use of Legal Discretion: Perspectives from Law and Social Science." In *The Uses of Discretion*, 11–46. Oxford: Clarendon Press, 1992.

Hazard, Geoffrey C., Jr., and Michele Taruffo. "Transnational Rules of Civil Procedure: Rules and Commentary." *Cornell International Law Journal* 30 (1997): 493–539.

Hensler, Deborah R. "Our Courts, Ourselves: How the Alternative Dispute Resolution Movement Is Reshaping Our Legal System." *Penn State Law Review* 108 (2003): 165–97.

Hess, Burkhard. "Judicial Discretion." In *Discretionary Power of the Judge: Limits and Control*, edited by Marcel Storme and Burkhard Hess. Ragheno: Kluwer, 2003.

Heydebrand, Wolf, and Carroll Seron. *Rationalizing Justice: The Political Economy of Federal District Courts*. Albany: State University of New York Press, 1990.

Hofstede, Geert H. *Culture's Consequences: International Differences in Work-Related Values*. Beverly Hills, Cal.: Sage, 1980.

Hunt, Alan. *Explorations in Law and Society: Toward a Constitutive Theory of Law*. New York: Routledge, 1993.

Hurst, James Willard. *The Growth of American Law: The Law Makers*. Boston: Little, Brown, 1950.

Jackson, John D. "Playing the Culture Card in Resisting Cross-Jurisdictional Transplants: A Comment on 'Legal Processes and National Culture.'" *Cardozo Journal of International and Comparative Law* 5 (1997): 51–67.

Jacob, Herbert. "Courts and Politics in the United States." In *Courts, Law, and Politics in Comparative Perspective*, edited by Herbert Jacob, Erhard Blankenburg, Herbert M. Kritzer, Doris Marie Provine, and Joseph Sanders, 16–80. New Haven, Conn.: Yale University Press, 1996.

Jacob, Jack I. H. *The Fabric of English Civil Justice*. London: Stevens, 1987.

James, Fleming, Jr., Geoffrey C. Hazard, Jr., and John Leubsdorf. *Civil Procedure*. 4th ed. Boston: Little, Brown, 1992.

Kafka, Franz. *The Trial*. New York: Shocken Books, 1988.

Kagan, Robert A. *Adversarial Legalism: The American Way of Law.* Cambridge, Mass.: Harvard University Press, 2001.

Kahn, Paul. *The Cultural Study of Law: Reconstructing Legal Scholarship.* Chicago: University of Chicago Press, 1999.

Kaplan, Benjamin, and Kevin M. Clermont. "England and the United States." In "Chapter 6: Ordinary Proceedings in First Instance." In *International Encyclopedia of Comparative Law.* Vol. 16, *Civil Procedure,* edited by Mauro Cappelletti, 3–56. Tübingen: Mohr, 1987.

Kaplan, Benjamin, Arthur T. von Mehren, and Rudolf Schaefer. "Phases of German Civil Procedure I." *Harvard Law Review* 71 (1958): 1193–1268.

Karlan, Pamela S. "Two Concepts of Judicial Independence." *Southern California Law Review* 72 (1999): 535–58.

Kelman, Herbert C., and V. Lee Hamilton. *Crimes of Obedience: Toward a Social Psychology of Authority and Responsibility.* New Haven, Conn.: Yale University Press, 1989.

Kennedy, Duncan. *A Critique of Adjudication.* Cambridge, Mass.: Harvard University Press, 1997.

Kertzer, David I. *Ritual, Politics, and Power.* New Haven, Conn.: Yale University Press, 1988.

Kohl, Alphonse. "Romanist Legal Systems." In "Chapter 6: Ordinary Proceedings in First Instance." In *International Encyclopedia of Comparative Law.* Vol. 16, *Civil Procedure,* edited by Mauro Cappelletti, 57–100. Tübingen: Mohr, 1987.

Kressel, Kenneth, and Dean G. Pruitt. "Conclusion: A Research Perspective on the Mediation of Social Conflict." In *Mediation Research: The Process and Effectiveness of Third-Party Intervention.* San Francisco: Jossey-Bass, 1989.

Kroeber, A. L., and Clyde Kluckhorn. *Culture: A Critical Review of Concepts and Definitions.* New York: Vintage Books, 1952.

Landman, Stephan. "The History and Objectives of the Civil Jury System." In *Verdict: Assessing the Civil Jury System,* edited by Robert E. Litan, 22–60. Washington: Brookings Institution, 1993.

Langbein, John H. "The German Advantage in Civil Procedure." *University of Chicago Law Review* 52 (1985): 823–66.

———. "Trashing the German Advantage." *Northwestern University Law Review* 82 (1988): 763–84.

Lazerson, Mark H. "In the Halls of Justice, the Only Justice Is in the Halls." In *The Politics of Informal Justice.* Vol. 1, *The American Experience,* edited by Richard L. Abel, 119–63. New York: Academic Press, 1982.

Leubsdorf, John. "The Myth of Civil Procedure Reform." In *Civil Justice in Crisis: Comparative Perspectives of Civil Procedure,* edited by Adrian A. S. Zuckerman, 53–67. Oxford: Oxford University Press, 1999.

Lipset, Seymour Martin. *American Exceptionalism: A Double-Edged Sword.* New York: Norton, 1996.

Martin v. Mieth, 35 N.Y. 2d 414 (1974).

Menkel-Meadow, Carrie. "Mothers and Fathers of Invention: The Intellectual Founders of ADR." *Ohio State Journal on Dispute Resolution* 16 (2000): 1–37.

———. "Pursuing Settlement in an Adversary Culture: A Tale of Innovation Co-opted or, 'The Law of ADR.'" *Florida State University Law Review* 19 (1991): 1–47.

———. "Whose Dispute Is It Anyway?: A Philosophical and Democratic Defense of Settlement (In Some Cases)." *Georgetown Law Journal* 83 (1995): 2663–97.

Merry, Sally Engle. *Getting Justice and Getting Even: Legal Consciousness among Working-Class Americans.* Chicago: University of Chicago Press, 1990.

———. "Law, Culture, and Cultural Appropriation." *Yale Journal of Law and the Humanities* 10 (1998): 575–603.

———. "The Social Organization of Mediation in Nonindustrial Societies: Implications for Informal Community Justice in America." In *The Politics of Informal Justice.* Vol. 2, *Comparative Studies*, edited by Richard L. Abel, 17–45. New York: Academic Press, 1982.

Meyer, Linda Ross. "Burns v. Received View." *Law and Social Inquiry* 28, 533–38 (Spring 2003).

Millar, Robert Wyness. *Civil Procedure of the Trial Court in Historical Perspective.* New York: Law Center of New York University for the National Conference of Judicial Councils, 1952.

Moore, Sally Falk. "Selection for Failure in a Small Social Field: Ritual, Concord, and Fraternal Strife among the Chagga Kilimanjaro, 1968–1969." In *Symbols and Politics in Communal Ideology: Cases and Questions*, edited by Barbara G. Myerhoff and Sally Falk Moore, 109–143. Ithaca, N.Y.: Cornell University Press, 1975.

Murray, Peter L., and Rolf Stürner. *German Civil Justice.* Durham, N.C.: Carolina Academic Press, 2004.

Myerhoff, Barbara G. *Number Our Days.* New York: Simon and Schuster, 1978.

Myers, Fred R. *Pintupi Country, Pintupi Self: Sentiment, Place, and Politics among Western Desert Aborigines.* Washington: Smithsonian Institution Press, 1986.

Nader, Laura. *The Life of the Law: Anthropological Projects.* Berkeley: University of California Press, 2002.

Nader, Laura, and Harry F. Todd, Jr., eds. *The Disputing Process: Law in Ten Societies.* New York: Columbia University Press, 1978.

Nelken, David. "Towards a Sociology of Legal Adaptation." In *Adapting Legal Cultures*, edited by David Nelken and Johannes Feest, 7–54. Oxford: Hart (2001).

———. *Comparing Legal Cultures.* Brookfield, Vt.: Dartmouth Publishing Co., 1997.

Nelson, William E. *The Legalist Reformation.* Chapel Hill: University of North Carolina Press, 2001.

Newman, Katherine S. *Law and Economic Organization: A Comparative Study of Preindustrial Societies.* Cambridge: Cambridge University Press, 1983.

New York Civil Practice Law and Rules. Section 3121(a).

————. Section 4113(a).

————. Section 7506.

New York Compilation of Codes, Rules and Regulations 22. Section 500.11(d)(1)(v).

New York Constitution. Article I. Section 2.

New York Times, March 2, 2001, p. 1.

Olmstead v. United States, 277 U.S. 438 (1928).

Omura, Masahiko. "A Comparative Analysis of Trial Preparation: Some Aspects of the New Japanese Code of Civil Procedure." In *Toward Comparative Law in the Twenty-first Century,* 723–35. Tokyo: Chuo University Press, 1998.

Palmer, Vernon Valentine. "From Embrace to Banishment: A Study of Judicial Equity in France." *American Journal of Comparative Law* 47 (1999): 277–301.

Peat, F. David. *From Certainty to Uncertainty: The Story of Science and Ideas in the Twentieth Century.* Washington, D.C.: Joseph Henry Press, 2002.

Peek, Philip M., ed. "Introduction: The Study of Divination, Present and Past." In *African Divination Systems: Ways of Knowing,* 1–22. Bloomington: Indiana University Press, 1991.

Pemberton, John, III. "Divination in Sub-Saharan Africa." In *Art and Oracle: African Art and Rituals of Divination,* by Alissa LaGamma, 10–21. New York: Metropolitan Museum of Art, 2000.

Petersen, Hanne. "Gender and Nature in Comparative Legal Cultures." In *Comparing Legal Cultures,* edited by David Nelken, 135–54. Brookfield, Vt.: Dartmouth Publishing Co., 1997.

Pfund, Peter H. "The Project of the Hague Conference on Private International Law to Prepare a Convention on Jurisdiction and the Recognition/Enforcement of Judgments in Civil and Commercial Matters." *Brooklyn Journal of International Law* 24 (1998): 7–15.

Posner, Richard A. *The Federal Courts: Challenge and Reform.* Cambridge, Mass.: Harvard University Press, 1996.

Post, Robert, ed. "Introduction: The Relatively Autonomous Discourse of Law." In *Law and the Order of Culture,* vii. Berkeley: University of California Press, 1991.

Priest, George L. "Justifying the Civil Jury." In *Verdict: Assessing the Civil Jury System,* edited by Robert E. Litan, 103–36. Washington: Brookings Institution, 1993.

Reitz, John C. "Why We Probably Cannot Adopt the German Advantage in Civil Procedure." *Iowa Law Review* 75 (1990): 987–1009.

Resnik, Judith. "Failing Faith: Adjudicatory Procedure in Decline." *U. Chicago Law Review* 53 (1986): 494–556.

———. "Finding the Factfinders." In *Verdict: Assessing the Civil Jury System*, edited by Robert E. Litan, 500–530. Washington: Brookings Institution, 1993.

———. "For Owen M. Fiss: Some Reflections on the Triumph and the Death of Adjudication." *U. of Miami Law Review* 58 (2003): 173–200.

———. "Managerial Judges." *Harvard Law Review* 96 (1982): 374–448.

———. "Tiers." *Southern California Law Review* 57 (1984): 837–1030.

Rheinstein, Max. Introduction to *On Law in Economy and Society*, by Max Weber. Cambridge, Mass.: Harvard University Press, 1954.

Rifkind, Simon H. "Are We Asking Too Much of Our Courts?" *Federal Rules Decisions* 70 (1976): 96–111.

Roberts, Simon. *Order and Dispute: An Introduction to Legal Anthropology*. New York: St. Martin's Press, 1979.

Roe v. Wade, 93 S.Ct. 705 (1973).

Rosen, Lawrence. "Individualism, Community, and the Law: A Review Essay." *University of Chicago Law Review* 55 (1988): 571–84.

Rouse, W. H. D., trans. *The Iliad, Book 18*. New York: Signet, 1999.

Saks, Michael S. "Court-Appointed Experts: Defining the Role of Experts Appointed under Federal Rule of Evidence 706." *Jurimetrics Journal* 35 (1995): 233–42.

Sanders, Frank E. "Varieties of Dispute Processing." *Federal Rules Decisions* 70 (1976): 111–34.

Sarat, Austin. "The Litigation Explosion, Access to Justice, and Court Reform: Examining the Critical Assumptions." *Rutgers Law Review* 37 (1985): 319–36.

Sarat, Austin, and Thomas R. Kearns, eds. "Beyond the Great Divide: Forms of Legal Scholarship and Everyday Life." In *Law in Everyday Life*, 21–61. Ann Arbor: University of Michigan Press, 1993.

Schima, Hans, and Hans Hoyer. "Central European Countries." In "Chapter 6: Ordinary Proceedings in First Instance." In *International Encyclopedia of Comparative Law*. Vol. 16, *Civil Procedure*, edited by Mauro Cappelletti, 101–40. Tübingen: Mohr, 1987.

Schreiber, Harry N. "Public Rights and the Rule of Law in American Legal History." *California Law Review* 72 (1984): 217–51.

Schwarzer, William W., and Alan Hirsch. "The Modern American Jury: Reflections on Veneration and Distrust." In *Verdict: Assessing the Civil Jury System*, edited by Robert E. Litan, 399–413. Washington: Brookings Institution, 1993.

Shailor, Jonathan G. *Empowerment in Dispute Mediation: A Critical Analysis of Communication*. Westport, Conn.: Praeger, 1994.

Shapiro, Martin. *Courts: A Comparative and Political Analysis*. Chicago: University of Chicago Press, 1981.

Sherwin, Richard K. *When Law Goes Pop: The Vanishing Line between Law and Popular Culture*. Chicago: University of Chicago Press, 2000.

Shweder, Richard A. *Why Do Men Barbecue?* Cambridge, Mass.: Harvard University Press, 2003.

Sibbach v. Wilson & Co., 312 U.S. 1 (1941).

Silberman, Linda. "Comparative Jurisdiction in the International Context: Will the Proposed Hague Judgments Convention Be Stalled?" 52 *DePaul Law Review* (2002): 319–49.

Singer, Andre, director. *Witchcraft among the Azande.* New York: Filmakers Library, 1982.

Solum, Lawrence B. "Equity and the Rule of Law." In *The Rule of Law*, edited by Ian Shapiro, 120–47. New York: New York University Press, 1994.

Stiponawich, Thomas J. "ADR and the 'Vanishing Trial': The Growth and Impact of Alternative Dispute Resolution." *Journal of Empirical Legal Studies* 1 (2004): 843–912.

Stone, Christopher. "Should Trees Have Standing? Toward Legal Rights for Natural Objects." *Southern California Law Review* 45 (1972): 450–501.

Subrin, Stephen N. "Fishing Expeditions Allowed: The Historical Background of the 1938 Federal Discovery Rules." *Boston College Law Review* 39 (1998): 691–745.

———. "How Equity Conquered Common Law: The Federal Rules of Civil Procedure in Historical Perspective." *University of Pennsylvania Law Review* 135 (1987): 909–1002.

Tamanaha, Brian Z. *A General Jurisprudence of Law and Society.* Oxford: Oxford University Press, 2001.

Taruffo, Michele. "Transcultural Dimensions of Civil Justice." *Comparative Law Review* 23 (2000): 1.

Tocqueville, Alexis. *Democracy in America.* New York: HarperPerennial, 1966.

Transnational Rules of Civil Procedure: Proposed Final Draft. Philadelphia: American Law Institute, 2004.

Tribe, Laurence H. "Trial by Mathematics: Precision and Ritual in the Legal Process." *Harvard Law Review* 84 (1971): 1329–93.

Trompenaars, F., and C. Hampden-Turner. *Riding the Wave of Culture.* 2nd ed. New York: McGraw-Hill, 1998.

Turner, Victor W. *The Ritual Process: Structure and Anti-Structure.* Chicago: Aldine Publishing, 1969.

Twining, William. *Rethinking Evidence: Exploratory Essays.* New York: Oxford, 1990.

U.S. Constitution, Seventh Amendment.

Van Gennep, Arnold. *The Rites of Passage.* Chicago: University of Chicago Press, 1960.

Verba, Sidney. Review of *American Exceptionalism: A Double-Edged Sword. American Political Science Review* 91 (1997): 192–93.

Walter, Gerhard, and Fridolin M. R. Walther. *International Litigation: Past Experiences and Future Perspectives.* Bern: Stampfli Verlag AG, 2000.

Watson, Alan. *Society and Legal Change.* 2nd ed. Philadelphia: Temple University Press, 2001.

Weber, Max. *On Law in Economy and Society.* Cambridge, Mass.: Harvard University Press, 1954.

Weinstein, Jack B., and Margaret A. Berger. *Weinstein's Federal Evidence: Commentary on Rules of Evidence for the United States Courts.* 2nd ed. Newark, N.J.: Bender, 1997.

White, G. Edward. *The American Judicial Tradition: Profiles of Leading American Judges.* New York: Oxford University Press, 1976.

Wright, Charles Alan, and Arthur R. Miller. *Federal Practice and Procedure.* Vol. 4. 3rd ed. St. Paul, Minn.: West Group, 2002.

Yalman, Nur. "Magic." In *International Encyclopedia of the Social Sciences*, edited by David L. Sills, 9: 521–27. New York: Macmillan, 1968.

Yeazell, Stephen C. "The New Jury and the Ancient Jury Conflict." *University of Chicago Legal Forum* (1990): 87–117.

Zuckerman, Adrian A. S. *Civil Procedure.* London: LexisNexis UK, 2003.

———, ed. "Justice in Crisis: Comparative Dimensions of Civil Procedure." In *Civil Justice in Crisis: Comparative Perspectives of Civil Procedure* 3–52. Oxford : Oxford University Press, 1999.

Zweigert, Konrad, and Hein Kötz. *An Introduction to Comparative Law.* Vol. 1, *The Framework.* 2nd ed. Oxford: Clarendon Press, 1987.

Index

Abel, Richard, 96, 134
Action and belief, 126, 131
Activist *vs.* reactive states, 68–69
Administrative Dispute Resolution Act (1990), 100
Administrative Procedures Act, 107
Adoption, 107
ADR (Alternative Dispute Resolution), 94–113; case-diversion efforts, 103–104, 178n96; democratic values, 177n78; forms, 94–95; "garbage cases," 178n96; housing courts, 136; in Japan, 133–134; landlord-tenant proceedings, 136; magnification of inequalities, 136; medical malpractice suits, 184n4; modern dispute resolution systems, 42–43; National Conference on the Causes of Popular Dissatisfaction with the Administration of Justice (Pound Conference), 107–108, 111, 176n53; reflexivity, 113, 135; statistics about, 95, 174n3; suspicion of government, 52–53, 94. *See also* Arbitration; Mediation
Age Discrimination in Employment Act, 99
Aigeus, King, 36
Alternative Dispute Resolution. *See* ADR (Alternative Dispute Resolution)
Alternative Dispute Resolution Act (1988), 100

American Arbitration Association (AAA), 95–96, 102
American exceptionalism in civil litigation, 47–71; adversarial nature of the legal system, 49, 54–55, 68, 133, 158n10; civil juries, 40, 55–58, 162n69; court filing fees, 172n65; litigiousness, 50, 52, 103–109, 160n32, 172n66; "managerial judging," 63, 166n100, 171n64; pretrial discovery/investigation, 58–62, 166n100; rule of law, 87–92
Amsterdam, Anthony G., 6
Andrews, Neil, 64
Antistatism, 54, 56, 58, 61, 64
Appellate courts, 76, 142, 169n21
Arbitration: business interests, 95, 101, 102; in colonial America, 101; commercial arbitration, 102; court-annexed programs, 104; diversion of litigation, 107; employment agreements, 99; enforceability of, 102; franchise agreements, 98; home-improvement contracts, 99; inequality in bargaining power, 99; judicial supervision of, 111; med-arb, 95; mediation, 101–102; number of federal cases, 95–96; securities fraud, 98; Supreme Court, 98–99; within trade groups, 101; violation of federal anti-discrimination statutes, 99

Arbitration clauses, 99

Architecture, 85, 119–120, 172n68

Asahi Metal Industry Co., Ltd. v. Superior Court of California, Solano County, 78–79, 86

Atiyah, P. S., 86

Attorneys, 62–63, 121

Auerbach, Jerold, 52, 100–101

Authoritarianism, 139–140

Authority: Azande society, 150n12; culture, 154n8; dispersion of, 140; fragmentation and decentralization in U.S., 51, 64; hierarchical *vs.* coordinate authority models, 67–68, 69; male authority in Azande society, 153n65; in modern dispute resolution systems, 46; political authority, 45; rule of law, 45; suspicion in U.S., 66

Azande society, 15–29; authority, 150n12; *benge* oracle (*see Benge* oracle); British colonial rule, 10, 19, 28–29, 132, 153n65; in Central African Republic, 150n9; death, 151n17, 152n54; dispute practices, 13, 21; Evans-Pritchard and, x, 17–18, 20–21, 23, 25, 27–28, 31–32; gender, 24–25, 28, 132; intelligence, 17, 150n12; legitimization of verdicts, 33; magic, 20, 24, 25, 28, 66; male authority, 153n65; metaphysical world, 22, 25–26, 132; oracles in, 4, 16, 17, 22, 23, 25–26, 28, 29, 130; ritual, x, 4, 19; royal class, 150n12, 152n54; social distinctions, 4; supernatural forces, 16–20, 25, 152n44; suspension of disbelief, 42; witchcraft, ix–x, 18–20, 23, 24, 25, 28, 151n17, 152n54; women, 24–25, 28, 44, 132

Balkin, J. M., 127–128, 135

Bargaining power, 99

Belief, 126, 128–129, 131

Bell, Catherine, 115

Benge oracle: Azande descriptions of, 35; British opposition to, 28; Central African Republic Azande, 150n9; cheating, 21, 26; confirmation of the verdict, 19; conflicting verdicts, 26; English view of, 25–26; importance to Azande, 18; incorrect verdicts, 21; magic, 19–20; modern dispute resolution systems compared to, 31–32, 34, 38, 42, 44; mysticism, 38; procedure, ix, 1, 15–16, 18–20; right to appeal, 21–22; ritual, 19; students' reactions to, 141, 143; supernatural forces, 152n44; testing of, 21, 36; trickery by manipulation, 152n44; vengeance, 19–20, 23, 25, 28; Western view of, 25–26, 38, 141, 143; witchcraft, ix–x, 18, 152n54; women's exclusion from, 24–25, 132. *See also* Azande society

Benin diviners, 4

Berman, Paul Schiff, 149n53

Bill of Rights, 52, 55

Blackmun, Harry, 154n7

Blackstone, William, 35, 36

Bork, Robert H., 106, 176n53

Bourdieu, Pierre, 10, 48, 127

Brandeis, Louis, 131

Brown v. Board of Education, 124

Bruner, Jerome S., 6, 183n53

Burger, Warren Earl, 98, 107

Bush, Robert Baruch, 110, 135–136

Bush v. Gore, 120

Business interests: arbitration, 95, 99, 101, 102; economic deregulation, 111; mediation, 95

Camaroff, John L., 148n43

Capitalism, 52

Cardozo, Benjamin, 86, 170n38

Categorization, 113

Chagga tribe, 117

Chernick, Richard, 96

Child custody, 107
"Civil" (meaning of), 53–54
Civil juries, 40, 55–58, 162n69
Civil Justice Reform Act (1990), 99–100
Civil law systems: as an inquisitorial systems, 54; common law systems compared to, 53–54; compulsory production of evidence, 59–60; convergence with common law systems, 63–64; first instance proceedings, 59, 142–143; judges in, 54, 63, 64; second instance proceedings, 142; "trial" in, 142; trials (concentrated), 59; witnesses in, 63
Claims of low monetary value, 107
Clark, Charles, 83
Class structure, 22–23
Cognitive processes, 134–135
Common law systems, 53–54, 55, 63–64
Communitarianism, 95, 109
Community justice movement, 110
Comparative law, 5, 141–142
Competitive individualism, 54–55, 60–62
Compulsory production of evidence, 59–60
Conciliation. *See* Mediation
Confessions, 112
Conflicting verdicts, 26
Conservatism, 123
Contextualization, 3
Coordinate authority model, 67–68, 69
Cotterrell, Roger, 147n22
Counterculturalism, 109–111
Court-annexed programs, 96, 97–98, 104, 108
Court filing fees, 172n65
Courthouse architecture, 85, 120, 172n68
Courtrooms, 122, 130
Courts, loss of access to, 108
Critical Legal Studies, 45
Cultural bricolage, 128, 130, 132–133
Cultural heritage, 146n8

Cultural mental units, 128
"Cultural software," 127–128
Culture: ADR, 95; authority, 154n8; construction and maintenance of, 125–129; cultural bricolage, 128, 130, 132–133; cultural heritage, 146n8; cultural mental units, 128; "cultural software," 127–128; definition, 6–7, 125; dispute resolution systems, ix–x, xiii, 6–8, 10–11, 32, 42, 48–53, 67, 114, 123, 125–137, 138; explanatory power, 7–9; history, 127; human memory, 128; internalization, 125–126; "interpretative-constructivist" conception, 147n21; judicial discretion, 92–93; law, 4; modern dispute resolution systems, 10, 31, 34–35, 47, 69; national boundaries, 50; need for the concept, 6; procedural values, 69–71; process and, 10; professional elites, 10; public institutional practices, 128–129; reflexivity, 114, 125–126, 138; small-scale societies, 7; social change, 138–139; "social-institutional" conception, 147n21; socialization, 125–126; structural relationships, 134; as a window into reality, 144
Custom, 39, 115

Damaska, Mirjan R., 41, 66–69, 140, 159n30
Davis, Kenneth Culp, 74–75, 80
Death sentences, 112
Decision making, 67–68, 69
Defendants, fairness to, 78–80
DeLorean, John, 58
Democracies, 30
Depositions, 59
Discretion, 81, 88, 91–92. *See also* Judicial discretion
Dispersal, 8

Dispute, definition of, 9–11

Dispute Resolution Act (1980), 99

Dispute resolution systems: American compared to Japanese, 129, 133–134, 182n48; among Benin, 4; attraction of, 130; authority relations, 130–131; *benge* oracle (*see Benge* oracle); boundary between procedure and process, 11; cheating, 21, 26; cognitive processes, 134–135; conflicting verdicts, 26; conservative bent, 123; contextualization, 3; cultural bricolage, 130; culture, ix–x, xiii, 6–8, 10–11, 32, 42, 48–53, 67, 114, 123, 125–137, 138; decision maker in, 32; dispersal, 8; dyadic systems, 1; economic life, 8–9; as elixirs, 140; exemplary function, 130–131; functional understanding of, 4; holiday dinner compared to, 122–123; incorrect verdicts, 21; interpretive approach to, 3–4; intragroup disputing, 9; Japanese compared to American, 129, 133–134, 182n48; law, 3, 5, 12–13; legitimization of, 32–34; maintenance of social practices and norms, 129–137; maintenance of social structure, 17, 22–25, 27; meaning of, 3; metaphysics, xiv, 22, 123; modern societies (*see* Modern dispute resolution systems); morality, xiv; neutral judges in, 32; norms, 11–13, 129–137, 148n43; official *vs.* unofficial means, 9–10; oracles in, 1–2; personal preferences for, 70–71; personal relations, xiv; as poisons, 140; power of, 4, 122–124; precapitalist societies, 8; preindustrial societies, 8, 147n34; professional dispute-process elites, 10; reflexivity, xiv, 2, 5, 7, 29, 48, 114, 125–126, 138; research questions about, 1–2; right to appeal, 21–22; ritual in (*see* Ritual); significance of, 129; small-scale societies, 11, 30; social conventions, 2–3; standing in, 12; in sub-Saharan Africa, 134; supernatural forces, 8; symbol borrowing by, 122; symbolic understanding of, 4; transformation from a dispute to a ruling, 117–118; triadic systems, 1, 33, 119; variety of, 1, 2, 11; violent disputing, 7–8; warfare, 9. *See also* ADR (Alternative Dispute Resolution)

Dissenting opinions, 37–38

Divination, 4, 26, 36

Doctors, negligence of, 107

Document discovery, 59

Due Process Clause, 78

Dworkin, Ronald, 155n18

Dyadic disputing, 1

Early neutral evaluation, 95

Economic deregulation, 111

Economic development, 43

Economic life, 8

Efficiency as an ideal: ADR, 111; judges, 171n64; judicial discretion, 73, 81, 82–86, 88, 92

Egalitarianism: American exceptionalism in civil litigation, 54, 58, 60–61, 67, 69; coordinate authority model, 67; counterculturalism, 109; expert testimony, 66; individualism, 81; judges' role in U.S., 65; juries, 56; pretrial discovery/investigation, 60–61; United States, 50, 52, 54, 61, 69

Eisenberg, Theodore, 96

Emotion, 116

Employment agreements, 99

England: civil juries in, 55; compulsory production of evidence, 60; development of juries, 132–133; English Civil Procedure Rules, 64; judges in, 62, 64, 164n87

Equity, 169n17

European Union, 48

Evans-Pritchard, E. E.: Azande society, x, 17–18, 20–21, 23, 25, 27–28, 31–32, 150n6, 150n12, 152n44, 152n54; readers' response to, 25–26, 143; *Witchcraft, Oracles, and Magic among the Azande,* 17

Evidence: admissibility of, 72–73, 181n30; attorneys and, 62–63; *benge* oracle compared to, 40–41; compulsory production of, 59–60; judicial discretion, 168n3; legitimacy of, 35; modern dispute resolution systems, 34, 39–43; oracles, 34, 39–43, 156n41; power of, 35; truth, 156n41; wiretapping evidence, 181n30

Evidentiary fact finding, 41, 112

Experts in civil litigation, 65–66

Eyewitness testimony, 42, 112

Fact finding, 41, 112, 156n41

Fairness, 70–71, 78–80, 167n140, 169n26

Federal Arbitration Act (FAA, 1925), 98–99, 111

Federal Rules of Civil Procedure, 55, 72, 76, 82–83

Federal Rules of Evidence, 65, 76, 170n28

Feldman, Eric A., 181n24

Field, David Dudley, 82, 83

Field Code, 82, 83

Fingerprinting, 112

First instance proceedings, 59, 142–143

Flexibility as an ideal, 73, 81, 82–86

Folger, Joseph, 110, 135–136

Forbidden acts, 116

Formalism, 82–86

Forum non conveniens ("inconvenient forum"), 77–80, 169n26

Fourteenth Amendment, 77, 78, 80

Frank, Jerome, 36, 42, 58

Frankfurter, Felix, ix

Freud, Anna, 116

Freud, Sigmund, 116

Fuller, Lon L., 36, 74, 88

Galanter, Marc, 160n32

Garland, David, 112, 116

Gbudwe (king of the Azande), 21–22, 29

Geertz, Clifford, xiii, 3, 88, 91, 115

Gender in Azande society, 24–25, 28, 132

Germany, 62–63, 142, 164n91, 165n92, 165n97

Gilmore, Grant, 88

Gilmore v. Interstate/Johnson Lane Corp., 99

Glendon, Mary Ann, 52

Globalization, 5, 47–48

Government, 45, 66–69, 99–100, 106

"Grand discriminant" between American and Continental legal cultures, 62, 63

Greene, David, 163n82

Gulf Oil Corp. v. Gilbert, 77–78

Habit, 115

Hague Convention on the Enforcement of Judgments, 47–48

Hamilton, Andrew, 57

Hamilton, V. Lee, 129, 133–134, 139–140

Harrington, Christine, 83

Hart, H. L. A., 39

Hawkins, Keith, 75

Henry II (King of England), 132

Hensler, Deborah, 96–97

Heydebrand, Wolf, 83–84

Hierarchical *vs.* coordinate ideal, 67–68

Hill, Elizabeth, 96

History, 127

Holiday dinners, 122–123

Holmes, Oliver Wendell, 43

Home-improvement contracts, 99

Homer, 129

Hospitals, negligence of, 107

Housing courts, 136

How-do-you-describe-water-to-a-fish problem, 31–32
Humanization of large-scale institutions, 94
"Hyperlexis critique," 105–109

"Inconvenient forum" *(forum non conveniens)*, 77–80, 169n26
Incorrect verdicts, 21
Individualism: American exceptionalism in civil litigation, 54, 58, 61–62, 67, 69; coordinate authority model, 67; counterculturalism, 109; discretion, 92; egalitarianism, 81; judges' role in U.S., 65; juries, 56–57; mediation, 136; pretrial discovery/investigation, 61–62; rule of law, 102; United States, 50, 52, 54, 69
Informal processes, 31, 134, 136
Institutions and values, 134
Interrogation of witnesses, 63
Interrogatories, 59
Intragroup disputing, 9
Involuntary medical examinations, 11, 149n48
Italy, attorneys in, 63

Jacob, Herbert, 160n38
Jacob, Jack, 60
Japan: ADR, 133–134; Code of Civil Procedure, 162n73; United States compared to, 129, 133–134, 182n48
Jefferson, Thomas, 57, 132
Judges: American exceptionalism in civil litigation, 52, 62–65, 105; Cardozo on, 170n38; in civil law systems, 54, 63, 64; in common law systems, 64; conservation of judicial time, 104; costume worn by, 119, 130; depersonalization of, 33–34, 119–120; divination and, 36; efficiency, 171n64; in England, 62, 64, 164n87; in Germany,

62–63, 164n91, 165n92, 165n97; interpretation of texts, 90; judgments as a matter of law, 40, 56; legal realist movement, 172n77; "managerial judging," 63, 166n100, 171n64; neutrality of, 32; norms, 38; oaths taken by, 130; outcomes of cases, 87; personification of state authority, 119; policy preferences, 36–37; pretrial discovery/investigation, 166n100; right results to, 87; rite of passage of, 118; ritualistic behavior, 119–121; role in growth of ADR, 97–99, 105; task of, 43–44; transformation from one state to another, 120–121; in United States, 52, 62–65. *See also* Judicial discretion
Judgments as a matter of law, 40, 56
Judicial discretion, 72–93; appellate courts, 76, 169n21; denial of ideological bias, 88–92, 173n84; equity, 169n17; evidence, 168n3; *forum non conveniens* ("inconvenient forum"), 77–80, 169n26; rule of law, 74–81, 86–92, 169n17; worldwide trends, 167n2
Judicial Improvements and Access to Justice Act (1988), 99
Juries: ability to judge facts, 58; antistatism, 56; civil juries, 40, 55–58, 162n69; in colonial America, 101, 132–133; construction of American persona, 132; cultural bricolage, 132–133; development of Anglo-American law, 132; egalitarianism, 56; individualism, 56–57; nonauthoritarianism, 140; oaths taken by, 40, 130; oracles, 39–40; personal empowerment, 139; populism, 56; power of, 4, 56; reverence for, 57–58; right to a jury, 55; ritualistic behavior, 121–122; in societies transitioning from totali-

tarianism, 5; understanding of, 4; in
    United States, 55–58; verdicts of, 40
Jury nullification, 56
Juryless trials, 139, 143–144
Justice, rationalization of, 83

Kafka, Franz, 130, 142–143
Kagan, Robert A., 49
Kahn, Paul, 45, 91
Kaplan, Benjamin, 164n91
Kelman, Herbert C., 139–140
Kennedy, Duncan, 89
Kertzer, David, 114–115
Kluckhohn, Clyde, 6
Kroeber, A. L., 6

Laissez-faire attitudes: American excep-
    tionalism in civil litigation, 58, 61, 69;
    counterculturalism, 109; going to
    court, 53; judges' role in U.S., 65; pre-
    trial discovery/investigation, 61; rule
    of law, 102; United States, 50, 69
Landis, James, 84
Landlord-tenant proceedings, 136
Langbein, John, 62, 65
Law: balancing factors in, 76–80, 86–87;
    chief uses of, 36; codes of dress, 38;
    conception of the self, 45; culture, 4;
    custom, 39; discretionary authority,
    81, 88; dispute resolution systems, 3,
    5, 12–13; economic development, 43;
    globalization, 5, 47–48; harmoniza-
    tion between legal systems, 5, 47–48;
    judicial discretion, 76–81, 91–92; lan-
    guage of, 37, 38, 116–117, 120; legiti-
    macy of, 35; mirror theory of, 4–5, 29;
    modern dispute resolution systems,
    34, 43–46; modern law defined, 39;
    normalcy, 127; norms, 38–39; oracles,
    13, 34–38; physical space, 38; power
    of, 35; pragmatism *vs.* principle in, 86;
    procedure in, x; rational consistency,

38; ritual, 37; the sacred, 38; social
    order, 10; social relations, 90; testing
    of, 36; truth of, 35
Lazerson, Mark H., 184n63
Legal culture, 48–49
Legal education, 90
Legal realist movement, 87–90, 172n77
Legal systems: adversarial *vs.* inquisitor-
    ial, 70, 133, 167n138; complexity of, 8;
    "grand discriminant" between Ameri-
    can and Continental legal cultures, 62,
    63; mirroring society, 39
Legitimacy/legitimization: of dispute
    processes, 116; of evidence, 35; of for-
    bidden acts, 116; of government, 45;
    of law, 35; of modern resolution sys-
    tems, 32–34, 39; ritual and, 114–118,
    122; of verdicts, 33
Leubsdorf, John, 171n50
Levi-Straus, Claude, 128
Liberty, 50, 54, 69
Lind, E. Allan, 70, 71
Lipset, Seymour, 50–52, 61, 64
Litigiousness: "hyperlexis critique,"
    105–109; United States, 50, 52,
    103–109, 160n32, 172n66
Local knowledge, xiii

Magic, 19–20, 24, 25, 28, 66
"Managerial judging," 63, 166n100,
    171n64
Marriage ceremonies, 128–129
Massim people, 81, 170n40
Med-arb, 95
Mediation: arbitration, 101–102; business
    interests, 95; in colonial America, 101;
    communitarianism, 95; community
    justice movement, 110; constructive
    power, 135–136; court-annexed pro-
    grams, 97–98, 104, 108; expansion of,
    96–97; focus on interests rather than
    rights, 113, 136; individualism, 136;

Mediation (*Continued*) in Japan, 133; med-arb, 95; peripheral status, 102; *Promise of Mediation* (Bush and Folger), 110; relational society, 110–111, 135–136; self-actualization, 95

Medical malpractice suits, 184n4

Menkel-Meadow, Carrie, 183n61

Metaphor, 135

Metaphysics: Azande society, 22, 25–26, 132; common sense, 126; dispute resolution systems, xiv, 22, 123; modern dispute resolution systems, 46

Mithridates, 140

Modern dispute resolution systems, 30–46; culture, 10, 31, 34–35, 47, 69; in democracies, 10; evidentiary fact finding, 41, 112; eyewitness testimony, 42, 112; pillars of, 34, 132; processes and norms, 11; shared features, 30, 54

Moore, Sally Falk, 116, 117

Morality, xiv

Nader, Laura, 4, 106

National Conference on the Causes of Popular Dissatisfaction with the Administration of Justice (Pound Conference), 107–108, 111, 176n53

Negotiation, 95

Neighborhood justice centers, 96

Newman, Katherine S., 8–9

Ngbu, 21

Nonauthoritarianism, 140

Norms: *Brown v. Board of Education*, 124; dispute resolution systems, 11–13, 129–137, 148n43; judges, 38; law, 38–39; law-like norms in small-scale societies, 11, 149n54; modern dispute resolution systems, 39, 46; *Roe v. Wade*, 124, 154n7

Oracles: in Azande society, 4, 16, 17, 22, 23, 25–26, 28, 29, 130; *benge* oracle

(*see Benge* oracle); to British colonialists, 28; at Delphi, 36, *37*, 38; in dispute resolution systems, 1–2; evidence as, 34, 39–43, 156n41; juries, 39–40; law, 13, 34–38; in modern dispute resolution systems, 34–35; termite oracle, 24

Palmer, Vernon, 89

Particularism, 74

Peat, F. David, 112, 113

Personal jurisdiction, 77, 78–79

Personal relations, xiv

Persuasion, 116

Piper Aircraft Co. v. Reyno, 80

Pluralism, 66, 112

Populism: American exceptionalism in civil litigation, 54, 56, 67, 69; coordinate authority model, 67; counterculturalism, 109; expert testimony, 66; juries, 56; pretrial discovery/investigation, 61; United States, 50, 54, 56, 69

Posner, Richard, 103, 104–105

Postmodernism, 112–113

Pound, Roscoe, 82, 84, 107

Pound Conference (National Conference on the Causes of Popular Dissatisfaction with the Administration of Justice), 107–108, 111, 176n53

Precapitalist societies, 8

Preindustrial societies, 8, 147n34

Pretrial discovery/investigation, 58–62, 166n100

Privatization as an ideal, 94, 111–112

Procedural fairness, 70–71, 167n140

Procedural reform, 138

Procedural systems, categorization of, 66–69

Procedure, social psychology of, 69–71

Professional dispute-process elites, 10

Professionalism, 118

Rationalization of justice, 83
Reactive *vs.* activist states, 68–69
Reagan administration, 111
Reality, 66, 94, 112–113, 144
Reflexivity: ADR, 113, 135; Azande society, 29; culture, 114, 125–126, 138; dispute resolution systems, xiv, 2, 5, 7, 29, 48, 114, 125–126, 138; globalization, 48; modern dispute resolution systems, 39
Reich, Charles, 109, 112
Relativism, 112–113
Resnik, Judith, 84, 129
Resolution by agreement, 42
Resolution by settlement, 42
Rights-asserting litigants, 106, 111
Rights-based legal discourse, 52
Ritual, 114–124; Azande society, x, 4, 19; belief, 131; *benge* oracle, 19; constructive process, 131; insistence on exact words, 116–117; judicial proceedings, 181n32; language, 37, 38, 116–117, 120; law, 37; modern dispute resolution systems, 32; repetition, 131; witnesses, 122
Roberts, Simon, 7–8, 12
Roe v. Wade, 124, 154n7
Roosevelt, Franklin Delano, 102
Rule of law: American exceptionalism in civil litigation, 87–92; contingency, 91; discretion, 88; equity, 169n17; "hyperlexis critique," 106; individualism, 102; judicial discretion, 74–81, 86–92, 169n17; laissez-faire attitudes, 102; legal realist movement, 87–90; loss of faith in, 86–92; meaning and, 157n51; modern dispute resolution systems, 45; political authority, 45; United States, 45
Rules Enabling Act (1934), 82–83

Sander, Frank, 107–108, 111
Sanders, Joseph, 129, 133–134

Self-actualization, 95
Seron, Carroll, 83–84
Seventh Amendment, 55, 161n41
Shapiro, Martin, 156n41
Skepticism about objective reality, 66, 94, 112–113
Small-scale societies, 7–8, 10–11, 30, 134, 149n54. *See also* Azande society
Social change, 123–124, 138–139
Social justice, 90
Social order, 10
Social progress through individual improvement, 94, 110–111
Social psychology of procedure, 69–71
Social sentiments, 123
Social stratification, 44
Social structure, maintenance of, 17, 22–25, 27
Social transformations from one state to another, 117–118, 120–121, 122
Socialization, 3, 71, 125–126
Solum, Lawrence B., 169n17
Southland Corp. v. Keating, 98–99
Speedy Trial Act (1974), 103
Spiro, Melford, 2, 125, 146n8
Standing, 11–12
Stone, Christopher, 11–12
Sub-Saharan Africa, 134
Summary jury trials, 95
Supernatural forces, 8, 16–20, 25, 152n44
Suspension of disbelief, 42

Tamanaha, Brian Z., 4–5
Taruffo, Michele, 64–65
Technocratic rationalization, 83–84
Themis, 36, *37*
"Thinking like lawyers," 90
Tocqueville, Alexis de, 50, 57–58, 132
Triadic disputing, 1, 33, 119
"Trial" (meaning of), 142–143
Trial, The (Kafka), 142–143

Trials: American exceptionalism in civil litigation, 59; attraction of, 130; concentrated trials, 59; fact finding, 156n41; in Homer, 129–130; juryless trials, 139, 143–144; in Kafka, 130; pretrial discovery/investigation, 58–62; ritual in American, 119–122; summary jury trials, 95
Tribe, Lawrence H., 181n32
Truth and evidence, 156n41
Truth-finding process, 41–42
Turner, Victor, 117
Tyler, Tom R., 70, 71

United States: American ideology, 51; antistatism, 54, 56, 64; assimilation of immigrants, 50; authoritarianism in, 139–140; capitalism, 52; ceremonial practices in formal dispute processing, 114–124; common law system in, 53–54; competitive individualism, 54–55; economic and social regulation, 51–52; egalitarianism, 50, 52, 61, 69, 109; elusiveness of truth, 66; fragmentation and decentralization of authority, 51, 64; individualism, 50, 52, 54, 69, 109; Japan compared to, 129, 133–134, 182n48; juries in, 55–58; laissez-faire attitudes, 50, 53, 69, 109; legal education, 90; liberty, 50, 54, 69; litigiousness, 50, 52, 103–109, 160n32, 172n66; median time to disposition of cases, 104; pluralism, 66, 112; populism, 50, 54, 56, 69, 109; privatization as an ideal, 94, 111–112; rights-asserting individuals, 52, 111; rule of law, 45; skepticism about objective reality, 66; suspicion of authority/orthodoxy, 66; suspicion of government, 52–53, 162n69; technocratic rationalization, 83–84; women in law schools, 44–45. *See also*

American exceptionalism in civil litigation
United States Constitution: Bill of Rights, 52, 55; Due Process Claus, 78; Fourteenth Amendment, 77, 78, 80; Seventh Amendment, 55, 161n41; unique features, 51–52
United States Supreme Court: arbitration, 98–99; boundary between procedure and process, 11; courthouse, 172n68; employment agreements, 99; Federal Arbitration Act (FAA, 1925), 98–99, 111; franchise agreements, 98; home-improvement contracts, 99; judicial discretion, 75; norm changes, 124; securities fraud, 98; women on, 44

Values and institutions, 134
Van Gennep, Arnold, 117
Verdicts: acceptability of, 117; belief, 131; conflicting verdicts, 26; incorrect verdicts, 21; judgment as a matter of law, 40, 56; of juries, 40; legitimization of, 33; skepticism about objective reality, 66
Violent disputing, 7–8

Warfare, 9
Weber, Max, 35, 138–139
Webs of signification, 3
Wigmore, John Henry, 42
Wilko v. Swann, 98, 99
Witchcraft: Azande society, ix–x, 18–20, 23, 24, 25, 28, 151n17, 152n54; *benge* oracle, ix–x, 18
Witnesses, 63, 121, 130
Women, 24–25, 28, 44–45, 132

Yeazell, Stephen, 162n69

Zenger, John Peter, 57
Zuckerman, Adrian A. S., 145n6

About the Author

Oscar G. Chase is the Russell D. Niles Professor of Law at NYU School of Law and is Co-director of the Institute of Judicial Administration. He is a vice-president of the International Association of Procedural Law and is a member of the editorial board of the multi-volume treatise, New York Civil Practice. He has written on comparative procedure, law and culture, and American civil procedure. His books include *Civil Litigation in New York* and *The CPLR Manual* (Rev. Ed.). He has litigated successfully in many courts, including the Supreme Court of the United States.